ESTRELLA D SOLIDUM

THE POLITICS
OF
ASEAN

An Introduction to
Southeast Asian
Regionalism

EASTERN UNIVERSITIES PRESS
by Marshall Cavendish

© 2003 Times Media Private Limited

First published 2003
by Times Media Private Limited
(Academic Publishing) under the imprint
Eastern Universities Press
by Marshall Cavendish

Times Centre, 1 New Industrial Road,
Singapore 536196
Fax: (65) 6284 9772
E-mail: tap@tpl.com.sg
Online Book Store:
http://www.timesacademic.com

Printed by Vine Graphic Pte Ltd, Singapore
on non-acidic paper

National Library Board (Singapore)
Cataloguing in Publication Data
Solidum, Estrella D.
The Politics of ASEAN: An Introduction to Southeast Asian Regionalism / Estrella D. Solidum. – Singapore: Eastern Universities Press, 2003.

p. cm.
ISBN: 981-210-249-3

1. ASEAN.
2. Regionalism – Asia, Southeastern.
I. Title.

DS520.A873
341.2473 — dc21
SLS2003028738

London • New York • Beijing • Shanghai
• Bangkok • Kuala Lumpur • Singapore

Table of Contents

About the Author

Estrella D. Solidum, a Ph.D. in Political Science, is a professor of Political Science. She taught mainly at the University of the Philippines, Diliman, Quezon City. She was a Visiting Professor at the Virginia Military Institute and East Carolina University, US, a visitor at the German Democratic Republic, and taught at the Chulalongkorn University in Thailand, Free University Berlin and Trier University in Germany, Griffith University in Australia, and Moscow State University. She was a member of the Board of Academics of the National Defense College of the Philippines where she was also a lecturer, and taught at the Command and General Staff College and the Airforce Training School.

Dr. Solidum has published internationally books and articles on ASEAN, security, and international relations. She also attended numerous international conferences and conducted researches in Southeast Asia, China, Northeast Asia, the United States, Mexico, Libya, Belgium, England, Sweden, and Germany.

She was given by the University of the Philippines a Most Outstanding Faculty Award, the Maria Lanzar Carpio Professorial Chair in International Relations, and a Scholar in Residence Award. She was also a recipient of awards from the Rockefeller Foundation, Japan Foundation, DAAD and Friedrich Ebert Stiftung, the Asian Scholar in Residence (US) and the Institute of Southeast Asian Studies (Singapore).

Dr. Solidum is a member of the international honour societies Phi Kappa Phi and Pi Gamma Mu of the National Research Council of the Philippines, a member of the Board of Trustees of the Philippines Council for Foreign Relations, and a member of the Philippine Political Science Association.

Preface

My fascination with the Association of Southeast Asian Nations (ASEAN) started with my friendships with people from Thailand, Indonesia, then Malaya, and Vietnam in my younger years. Those friends had shown me interesting ways of looking at situations, quite different from how I saw them, and as they expressed their perceptions we would really enjoy the humorous side of the differences or similarities that abounded. Although the formation of ASEAN was many decades away from my college student years, my memories of my Asian friends were always fresh. Somehow I believed that I would, someday, know more about their countries and their peoples and tell stories to my local friends about them.

This was eventually validated by my choice of dissertation topic for my Ph.D studies. In spite of my statements made separately to Indonesian Foreign Minister Adam Malik and to Prince Norodom Sihanouk of Cambodia during meetings, that I would study the phenomenon of neutralism in their states and in Burma, I readily shifted to the study of ASEAN which had just been established and which I saw as the wave of the future in Southeast Asia.

Since my return to the Philippines, I have found myself travelling to the states of Southeast Asia every year and exchanging ideas on ASEAN with scholars, foreign ministers, foreign service officers, students, and business and social leaders who were equally interested in it. I learned more of ASEAN and its peoples as I participated in conferences. Every moment was a delightful learning situation.

Meanwhile ASEAN has grown in terms of principles, projects, goals, and relations, from intra-ASEAN relations to relations with Dialogue Partners and international organisations; from declarations of peace, prosperity, and security as goals to actual projects and processes for functional, economic, political, and security (not military) cooperation with states in the Asia Pacific region and in Europe, Africa, and the Middle East.

Therefore, it is time that people in the region and outside it know more about ASEAN.

The need to study ASEAN and its member states has been stated in several documents since 1967. The need to promote knowledge of ASEAN is matched by the urgency to intensify awareness of its efforts to create a strong ASEAN community supported by the peoples' growing sense of regional identity; the need to develop the capability of ASEAN to seize all initiatives in the Asia-Pacific region and in international affairs for promoting peace, progress, security; and the need to preserve the members' national identities in accordance with the ideals and aspirations of their peoples.

Cooperation is the fundamental requirement of a community such as ASEAN to achieve its stated goals. In ASEAN, peoples of diverse backgrounds – although manifesting patterns of similarities in language, culture, and values – have learned to discard old habits of turning away from each other and to welcome one another in mutual understanding, tolerance, and accommodation for closer cooperation.

ASEAN officials have agreed that ASEAN studies should be taught at all levels of education. ASEAN founders stated in their Declaration of 1967 that Southeast Asian studies should be promoted. The ASEAN Concord of the First Heads of State/Government Meeting (Summit) in 1976 provided that member states shall vigorously develop the awareness of regional identity and exert all efforts to create a strong ASEAN community. The ASEAN Sub-Committee on Education's (ASCOE) flagship project has been promoting ASEAN awareness in primary and secondary schools through the integration of ASEAN studies in school curricula. ASCOE aims to produce a source book on ASEAN studies to help develop an ASEAN Studies curriculum. A suggested framework for ASEAN cooperation is a programme of action on culture and information. The programme includes the study of ASEAN, its member states and their national languages as part of the curriculum of schools and other institutions of learning. The target for learning includes people who play leadership roles in all sectors, including the academic, and as well as the disadvantaged. Education is the means for the learning process.

The Fourth ASEAN Summit in Singapore (1992) called for the expansion of ASEAN Studies in the schools and university curricula and the promotion of ASEAN awareness at the secondary and tertiary levels of education. Student exchange programmes have also been introduced in ASEAN.

The Hanoi Plan of Action as adopted by the Sixth ASEAN Summit in 1998 issued a directive to move forward the process of transforming the ASEAN University Network (AUN) into the ASEAN University.

With my desire to see ASEAN successfully build a strong community, I have prepared this book to help students, teachers, foreign scholars, and other interested members of society to increase their understanding of ASEAN.

While preparing this modest volume, I have tried to make each chapter stand on its own so that the reader will not have to go through the documents from different chapters. I have endeavoured to provide historical backgrounds, definitions of concepts, and philosophical and documentary underpinnings for each chapter. I have also used data on ASEAN external relations, organisational structure and processes, and economic cooperation directly from the texts of ASEAN website pages and the Annual Report 1998-1999 to preserve accuracy. Whenever possible, I have added ideas of scholars as they are found in *The ASEAN Reader*, which showcases 94 articles out of thousands of published articles on ASEAN, and was published by the Institute of Southeast Asian Studies in Singapore in 1992. I have also used material from other scholars and officials of ASEAN, whose ideas are timeless and are still valid for reference. These ideas represent as many sides as possible on every point. The purpose is to stimulate readers' thoughts so that in due time, they may also contribute to the exchange of ideas for achieving ASEAN's objectives.

This book begins by reviewing the region when it comprised various settlements, going all the way up to modern times when the region was called Southeast Asia. Then the book presents the genesis of ASEAN and its early experiences with the concept of cooperation.

This book also includes the latest profile and a brief history of each member state to contribute to the readers' knowledge of the countries in ASEAN and the nature of cooperation in the region.

At the end of the book, I have reproduced four important documents that are often invoked in ASEAN relations. These are the ASEAN Declaration (1967), the Kuala Lumpur Declaration on the Zone of Peace, Freedom, and Neutrality (1971), the Treaty of Amity and Cooperation in Southeast Asia (1976), and the ASEAN Vision 2020 (1997).

In preparing this book, I received valuable assistance from the officials of the Philippine Department of Foreign Affairs' ASEAN and Asia Pacific Affairs (ASPAC) Offices' who were always responsive to my queries and needs. ASEAN member states' embassies in Manila were also cooperative in many ways.

To all of them, I would like to give my heartfelt thanks.

Let us all give our salute to ASEAN and its partners.

The Lord constantly provided me with His wisdom, strength, courage, and joy while I worked on this volume. I exalt His name.

E.D. Solidum
Quezon City, Philippines
August 2003

CHAPTER 1

From Settlement to Southeast Asia to Regionalism

PRE-COLONIAL POLITICAL UNITS IN SOUTHEAST ASIA

The concept of "Southeast Asia" begins with a patchwork of continuous settlements where inhabitants lived from about 2000 B.C. to the development of early political systems which were known to people of more developed states such as India and China. Historians urge caution when looking at how isolated settlements in forests and river deltas developed into more coherent organisations. Scholars such as O.W. Wolters[1] have identified no less than 300 settlements with artifacts from the seventh and eighth centuries A.D. in Thailand and many Khmer centres in the same period in present-day Cambodia with modern names of villages identifiable in early written records. To use care in looking at reasons for the growth of the pre-historic settlements, Wolters says that "every center was a center in its own right as far as the inhabitants were concerned and it was surrounded by its own group of neighbors".[2]

Wolters has suggested that extensive contact among the scattered settlements could not have been due to language communication although major language families have been identified by linguists. The Austroasiatic family of languages in early times was found in settlements from Burma to northern Vietnam and southern China as the Mon-Khmer language with mixtures of Thai and Burman languages. However, it was very possible that the major language families were represented by many local and isolated speech variations.[3]

Wolters therefore identified other cultural features for developing relationships in this vast geographical area. One factor is social organisation, which contained several features. Anthropologists refer to "cognatic kinship" which defined descent to be reckoned equally through males and females, both of whom are able to enjoy equal inheritance rights.[4] This feature of equality of the sexes is found throughout Southeast Asia, such as in the unisex gods in Javanese iconography. Cognative kinship also degraded the importance of claims to status based on lineage. Instead, kinship ties were the mode of social relations, disregarding generational lines, and emphasising personal accomplishments and superior attributes and personal loyalty.

In his study, Wolters says that pre-historians of Southeast Asia deny the development of statehood in the earliest known settlements where there were no fixed boundaries, no rules of succession, and no bureaucratic structures. Indian and Chinese chronologists saw a "state of Funan" whose rulers had built temples according to the Indian view of a true state with a "strategy of monumental self-validation" and according "to Indian strategies of temple-founding, inscription-raising and support for brahmanic royal cults". Thus, with an "acquired" Indian influence, Funan "moved" from settlement to state.

Likewise, the Western idea of "incipient state formation" followed "fairly extensive trade relations", wet rice culture, iron technology, probable increasing population density, and political centralisation in alluvial plains. In other words, economic development would be accompanied by the appearance of more complex political systems.

Wolters and other historians deny this theory of "passage to statehood" due to the use of criteria found in theories with economic bias and from Chinese conventions that were transferred to Southeast Asia where people had no knowledge of such practices. In fact, there is no evidence in the area to prove that religions and social behaviour could affect activities to create changes that would delineate proto-history from pre-history. Up to historical times when rulers could exercise political influence, services, as in pre-history, were seen in terms of reward, honour or posts of responsibility, altogether valued by recipients who believed that they had participated in the donor's "spiritual authority". In Vietnam, according to Chinese statistics, households increased rather than the population numbers, showing kinship characteristics.

Wolters, in his study, cited many scholars who wrote to illustrate the various terms for "soul-stuff," a complex system of personal relations, rather than the concept of state, personal loyalties, and titles to refer to home territories.[5] But he made his point clear that scholarship has not yet really shown the continuities in the passage from pre-history to historical times.

Altogether, Wolters expressed his desire to see more investigation on the passage of Southeast Asia from settlements to political systems in terms of continuities rather than discontinuities. However, he offered his study to provide the "appropriate background" to later tendencies in Southeast Asian intra-regional relations.

SOUTHEAST ASIA AS A CONCEPT

It was the Europeans who first perceived a region of the geographical area which is today known as South-east Asia, South-East Asia or Southeast Asia. Donald G. McCloud states that before the colonial period, some writers from China, Arabia, Egypt, Rome, and Greece had identified the area due to the "role played by Southeast Asian states in the international trading systems".[6] Having seen earlier in pre-colonial times that some states had already acquired identity with states external to the region, he shows how these came to be.

China, as the Middle Kingdom, viewed the world as "barbarians" according to distance and direction of the compass. Thus, the region of the Southern seas was called Nanyang. In the third century B.C., China referred to the islands in the southern seas and the ocean-going peoples as *k'un lun*.[7] Later, China separated the identity of Burma, Laos, and Annam (now central Vietnam) from the rest of Southeast Asia as seen in China's relationships with them.[8]

Japan referred to Southeast Asia as *Nan yo* .[9] The early Arabic term was *qumr* to refer to Southeast Asia; later, *Zabog* was used.

By the seventh century A.D., Arab navigators went to Southeast Asia regularly to look for spices and medicines. [10] The Greeks and the Romans also had gone to the region by the end of the second century A.D.[11]

The Southeast Asians travelled as far as Madagascar frequently, giving the idea to early navigators that it was part of Southeast Asia. Scholars who wrote on the Malay culture included Madagascar in the Malay region. As regular traders using the sea routes, Southeast Asians became part of the world trading system providing the connections through the Middle East.

3

This participation in the world trading system contributed to the growth of Southeast Asian states as well as to the flourishing trade which the Europeans wanted to control, necessitating therefore the control of Southeast Asia.

For 300 years, Europeans took control of Southeast Asia. Britain controlled Burma through India, and the Brunei Kingdom through the British trading companies. Later, Sir Stamford Raffles saw the marshes of Singapore to someday be the world's best port. Raffles went to Singapore to make his vision a reality for Britain. The British also federated the states in the Malay Peninsula. The Dutch went to the islands in the east and controlled them as Dutch East Indies which provided its trade in spices and other products that were becoming fashionably in demand in Europe. Spain arrived in the Philippines and subdued the people by the cross and the sword until the people revolted against Spanish rule. France was the last to land in Southeast Asia and this was done with the help of Spain. France controlled Vietnam, Laos and Cambodia as French Indo-China. Thailand, in those days known as Siam, remained uncolonised but it lost its kingdom of Ayuthya to Burma and some territories in the east to France but by skillful diplomacy regained its territories from what are now known as Cambodia and Laos.

Ethnocentric Europeans saw their respective colonies as "the Southeast Asia", content that they had colonies that enriched their respective kingdoms.

Not knowing the languages of Southeast Asia, Europeans believed that they had also brought civilisation to the "East" only to learn through archeological finds that each state had developed its own social, economic, and political systems based, as have been discussed earlier, on family organisation, equality of sexes, native language families, loyalty, leadership, and worship. These civilisations were enriched by the influences brought on by trade with China, India, Arabia, Madagascar, and the Pacific islands.

Islamic culture came in through Arab traders, navigators, missionaries, and scholars. Buddhism came with Indian and Chinese missionaries and Confucianism from China. These are all evidenced by the existing buildings of temples and palaces in Angkor and Cambodia, Balinese temples of Borobudur and Prambanan in Indonesia, irrigation and water systems in Cambodia, temples and palaces in Burma, Vietnam, and Laos, and the great palaces and temples in Thailand. All these cultures were syncretised with local cultures. In the Philippines, the rice terraces of the mountain provinces were discovered to be "lowland rice cultivation" up in the mountains, thanks to the native engineering skills of the mountain tribes.

Each state and its local political units had their own peculiar political and social organisations such as the datu-council system in the Philippines, the *mushawarah* process in Indonesia and Malaya for decision-making, kingship rule in Thailand, Burma, Laos, and Cambodia, and emperor rule in Vietnam. Interstate wars brought out superior cultures and relegated to near oblivion the weaker ones. However, at various times, these latter ones also became active again. Today, this is called ethnicity. Economic features such as wet rice culture; coconut harvesting as a way of life, spices, fish and fowl as foods; trading without cash and without face-to-face exchanges; boats as transportation; betel nut as a socio-economic product; and flowers as socio-religious instruments, were common to all Southeast Asian states.

All economic, social, and political intra-state exchanges were ongoing before the colonial powers arrived in Southeast Asia. But colonisation also brought in new territorial boundaries which cut across ethnic groups resulting in redistribution of peoples and development of new areas.

The 20th century formal use of the concept "Southeast Asia" has an interesting history because its beginnings were almost always in terms of theatres of war for the Second World War.

Before the Second World War, the Institute of Pacific Relations in the United States made studies on the social, economic, and political problems of Southeast Asia. In 1940, William L. Holland arranged the series of reports which appeared in 1941 and 1942 with "Southeast Asia" in their titles.[12]

K.M. Panikkar, an Indian writer on sea power who later became a diplomat, used the term Southeast Asia instead of Further India to acknowledge the rising tide of nationalism in Southeast Asia and avoid embarrassment to Prime Minister Nehru of India.

The forerunner of the concept of "Southeast Asia" was the identification of the region in military and political terms by President Franklin D. Roosevelt and Prime Minister Winston Churchill with the creation of the "Supreme Allied Command in Southeast Asia", in August 1943. The subjects of the discussions were its geographical extent, command arrangements and

5

relationships, and associated matters. Should French Indochina be in the Command? Should Thailand be in the China Theatre of War? Finally, the "Southeast Asia Command" was established, embracing Burma, Thailand, Malaya, Singapore, and Sumatra. French Indo-China remained in the China Theatre of General Chiang Kai-shek. The rest of Southeast Asia fell under the Southwest Pacific Area of General Douglas MacArthur.

Admiral Lord Louis Mountbatten, Supreme Allied Commander of the South East Asia Command (SEAC), explained years later that he and his colleagues did not know what to call the area that was being overrun by the Japanese, as the "ABDACOM" (American, British, Dutch, Australian Command) had collapsed. In the course of their discussion, the geographical area was referred to as "South-East Asia".

In August 1945, SEAC's boundaries were changed by the British and the Americans. The new boundaries included all of Southeast Asia except the Philippines, northern Indochina, and Timor. Historian R. Fifield said that they had military implications for the war as well as political implications for peace.

The Pentagon Papers of 1971 showed that since 1941, American officials in Washington D.C. saw Southeast Asia as more than a collection of colonial territories. Even by May 1945, US policy was not sure how to handle Indochina because of the view that it should not be returned to France and because of the European dependencies in Southeast Asia that were handled by the Office of European Affairs. On 25 May 1945, the US State Department arranged its jurisdictions appropriately and made the Division of Southeast Asian Affairs.

British contribution to the concept of Southeast Asia was based on the careful study of two things: first, the factor of waging war against the Japanese, and the other, the economic and political problems brought about by administering occupied territories. In addition, the problems of territories outside of Burma, Malaya, and British Borneo would have to be studied carefully. Altogether, scholars remember Mountbatten's use of "Southeast Asia" for his South East Asia Command.

Fifield points out that the perceptions of Southeast Asia as a region in military and political terms during the Second World War derived from the Japanese conquest of the entire area, destroying the colonial partition of Southeast Asia by Western powers and necessitating a unified allied approach for the defeat of the Japanese.[13] Therewith the South East Asia Command (SEAC) under Mountbatten was created.

6

THE CONCEPT OF AND EXPERIENCES IN INTERNATIONAL ORGANISATIONS

International organisation as a concept was a product of the history of international cooperation among states and people which began in the ancient empires in the Near East as people travelled and traded. Occasionally, wars arose and the destructive ones were perceived to be the result of irrational behaviour. During those times, plans were made for different ways of organising the world.[14] Organisations of states were mostly originally for peace and conflict resolution.

Writings on the earliest conceptions of world peace through world organisations are those on the then existing Delian Amphictyony, the Achaean League, the Assyrian Government of Dependencies, Federal Communities in the Greece of the Cities, Internationalism in Ancient Greece, the Greek Commonwealth of Fifth Century Athens, and Alexander the Great on the Unity of Mankind.

In China, Confucius wrote on the Grand Commonwealth of Nations. There were also other concepts of unity in ancient China.

During the Middle Ages, the histories of the Holy Roman Empire and the medieval Catholic Church led to many works on the peace negotiations of the Avignon Popes, medieval diplomacy, medieval world unity, international law for world peace and a society of nations as written in the 13th century.

Commercial leagues led to the idea of functionalism for world cooperation. The Hanseatic League was a trading group. After the Hansa's decline, the idea of regionalism arose. Internationalism such as international cooperation, international law, international pursuit of peace and supranational world government find their roots in the ancient and medieval times.

After the decline of the influence of the Papacy and the Holy Roman Empire, the nation-state came to existence in Europe but this was soon followed by inter-state wars. Many proposals to remedy these conditions of war were made by philosophers, scholars, political leaders, and even by slaves.

However, political thought on world government and world peace antedated the rise of modern states. Aristotle (384-322 B.C.) had written on a Commonwealth of Nations. Confucius from China (sixth century B.C.) wrote of a Grand Commonwealth of Nations. Thomas Aquinas (1225-1274) had the idea of a world state. Dante Alighieri (1265-1321) wrote *De Monarchia*. Pierre Dubois (1250-1312) was known as a "medieval pacifist" although he sounded modern in his time. Hugo Grotius (1583-1645), the Father of International Law, wrote on the Law of War and Peace and of international society.

Immanuel Kant (1724-1804) advocated a universal and perpetual peace through world government and his moral and political writings inspired the creation of the League of Nations after the First World War and the ideology of the United Nations Charter in 1945, after the Second World War.

From the memoirs of the Duke of Sully, Prime Minister to King Henry the Great (Henry IV) of England, were ideas of this King for a Grand Design for a League of Nations or a Commonwealth of Nations.

The Abbe de Saint-Pierre (1658-1743) wrote on a project for perpetual peace through a society of nations. Jean Jacques Rousseau wrote "Project for Perpetual Peace", advocating a strong central system of government for Europe. Similarly, John Locke (1632-1704) wrote on war and peace.

In modern China, K'ang Yu-wei, (1858-1927) wrote his One World Philosophy.

There are many books on philosophic proposals for international organisations. Some of them are: 1) John E. Harley, *From Achaean League to United Nations: Summary of Proposals and Efforts for International Cooperation and Peace*,[15] 2) Sylvester Hemleben, *Plans for World Peace Through Six Centuries*,[16] 3) Emile M. Guerry, *Popes and World Government*,[17] 4) Oscar Jaszi, *World Organization for Durable Peace*,[18] and 5) Frank M. Russell, "The Growth of the Idea of World Organization" in *Contemporary World Politics*.[19]

Quincy Wright wrote *Empires and World Government Before 1918*.[20]

In the 19th century, the Napoleonic Wars were concluded by the Congress of Vienna which met to make a Treaty of Peace. Motivated by Tsar Alexander I's idea of a Holy Alliance, the Congress of Vienna established a directorate of great powers to keep harmony and peace by dictating policy to the small powers.

In modern times, the First World War (1914-1918) ended and the League of Nations was created to prevent wars in the future. Simultaneously, there were many peace proposals and peace movements such as those started by Andrew Carnegie in his Endorsement for Peace, the Quakers' Peace Movement, Alfred Nobel's prizes for peace endeavours, the World Peace Foundation, and others. Twentieth century thought included Bertrand Russell's advocacy of total surrender of sovereignty by nations to one strong world government. John Strachey proposed a kind of condominium of two superpowers, America and Russia.

Private organisations also worked for peace. Among them were the International Committee of the Red Cross, Inter-Parliamentary Union and Chambers of Commerce.

Violations of the provisions of the League of Nations (January 10, 1920) led to the Sino-Japanese War of 1933 (undeclared war). In Europe, the inability of defeated Germany to pay war reparations to the victorious Allied Powers led to the election of Hitler, with the help of his ideology of the superiority of the Aryan race. He created employment through road-building and industrial projects. He also implemented a policy to eliminate the Jewish race. Hitler then went on to conquer the neighbouring states of Poland, France, Austria-Hungary, Czechoslovakia, and others. All these continuous wars led to the alignment of threatened countries – Britain, France, the United States, and China against the Fascist Powers of Germany, Italy, and later Japan. The Allies were joined by the Soviet Union, which ordered communist parties all over the world to make a "united front" with all anti-fascist groups hoping to capture power in coalition with those states' political parties at the end of the Second World War. This was how the countries of Eastern Europe came to be ruled by communist parties. The end of communist party rule came with the collapse of the Berlin Wall separating East and West Germany and with the collapse of the Soviet Union after the *perestroika* and *glasnost* reforms in the Soviet Union Communist Party under President Mikhail Gorbachev in 1991.

Going back to the victory of the Allied Powers (American, British, China, Dutch or ABCD) in 1945, it is important to acknowledge the preparations for a durable peace in the world.

The United Nations was set up by a Charter on June 26, 1945 by Representatives of Governments, expressing the determination of the members "to save succeeding generations from the scourge of war, to reaffirm faith in fundamental human rights, equality of rights of men and women and of nations large and small, and to unite the strength to maintain international peace and security". The UN structure and specialised agencies are engaged in peace-building, peace-keeping, and peacemaking to achieve UN objectives.

Some philosophical underpinnings strengthen the role of regional arrangements. It seems that the philosophers' dream of a universal and perpetual peace cannot be achieved by a world government or the United Nations. It is more rational to look at universal peace starting from small areas of peace, such as regional arrangements, that would end up in world peace.

Confucius said that the Universal or Grand Commonwealth based on morality may be achieved by ever-growing circles or ripples of peace like small waves of water when a stone or object is thrown into a body of water. The ever-growing circles of water, from ripples, represent growing areas of peace in a Commonwealth of Nations until the widest possible area of peace is attained.

Professor Joseph Nye of Harvard University wrote a book entitled *Peace by Parts* whose title is self-explanatory.

A paper titled "Towards a Divisible and Graduated Peace" showed the growth of divisible peace into universal peace.[21] This is to approach peace from the bottom of the ladder of international relations rather than from the top. Peace-building and conflict resolution or peacemaking by the associated states themselves can lead to decisions that are legitimate because they will be more in accordance with their prevailing cultures or values and should be more acceptable to the people than decisions by outside agents of peace. Moreover, regional decisions can exclude extraneous interests. Regional associations for international peace are the core of this paradigm.

The UN Charter has also provided for regional arrangements.[22] In Chapter VIII, Article 52 provides that:

1. Regional arrangements or agencies may deal with such matters relating to the maintenance of international peace and security as are appropriate for regional action as long as these are consistent with the purposes and principles of the UN.
2. Such regional arrangements shall make every effort to achieve pacific settlement of local disputes before referring them to the Security Council.
3. The Security Council shall encourage the development of pacific settlement of local disputes through such regional arrangements.

Article 53 provides that:

1. The Security Council shall, where appropriate, utilise such regional arrangements or agencies for enforcement action under its authority. But no enforcement action shall be taken by regional arrangements or regional agencies without the authorisation of the Security council.

Article 54 says that the Security Council shall at all times be kept fully informed of activities undertaken or in contemplation under regional arrangements or regional agencies.

The various regional arrangements in Southeast Asia find legitimacy and validity of their existence in the above Articles of the UN Charter. There have been many such regional arrangements and agencies in Southeast Asia since 1945. A study of their structures and activities leads one to understand the concept of regionalism.

The tendency of states and people towards regionalism in Southeast Asia has been spurred by the motivation of group survival in all its aspects, from the need to manage difficult problems for sheer survival, the increase in the quality of life, the establishment of harmonious relations with neighbouring states through cooperation, the achievement of regional peace and security, and in accordance with UN purposes, to maintain international peace and security.

Definition of Concepts

1. "Regionalism" is the thought or theory that underlies the behaviour of states to group themselves together or to be identified by an outsider to behave as such, for some common good.
2. "Region" is an analytic concept created by the selection of features relevant to the interest of the student or to the problem at hand. "Region" applies not only to the area under consideration but also to the number and kind of phenomena which will be included. The region is homogeneous only in terms of the applied criteria. Homogeneity implies similarity rather than identity because units are hardly ever identical.[23]
3. A "regional association" is an arrangement wherein several states group themselves together to engage in mutual cooperation for the attainment of some common good. Although not strictly a geographic entity, a region is composed of countries which are drawn together due to similarity of interests: What holds them

11

together is the political will to cooperate in a rational way rather than to engage in destructive competition. The structure of a regional association varies from flexibility and preservation of the members' sovereignty to the transfer of some aspects of sovereignty to a central structure[24] or a supranational body, and from accommodation of heterogeneous value systems to legalistic prescriptions of behaviour or code of conduct.

4. "Peace" is a situation or condition where the parts of a unit or a social organisation are in harmonious relationships over a reasonable period of time.[25] There are different kinds of peace, St. Augustine had said in his book *The City of God*. All societies aim at peace. There is peace of the dungeon when prisoners have food and bed, the peace of conspirators when they hide in a den or safe house after their criminal operations, and the peace of the family when the members give prompt obedience to the father. The peace of the body consists in the duly proportioned arrangements of its parts as when the nobler part controls the baser parts. Peace of the rational soul is harmony of knowledge and action. Peace of all things is tranquillity in the order of the universe. Peace between man and man is well-ordered concord.

But there is also the communist peace, when there is no more capitalist country standing. American peace is absence of war but this is fallacious because there are other conditions that are not "peace" if there is no war. A definition cannot be made by stating what is absent but by stating the conditions that are present by which the thing being defined, is. Hitler's peace was the rule by the "superior Aryan race". Every advocate of peace has his own implicit order of things.

5. "Cooperation" is the act of working together by certain units toward a common end. There are some ways by which cooperation is done in increasing degrees; these are listening, responding positively, and acting together toward a common end.[26] Without a common end, units acting together are only acting with each toward each unit's own reward. This is called interaction, it is not cooperation.

DEVELOPMENT OF REGIONAL ORGANISATIONS IN ASIA[27]

a. The Asian Relations Conference (28 March – 2 April 1947, New Delhi)

Representatives of 18 Asian and African countries met in New Delhi in 1947 under the sponsorship of the Indian Council of World Affairs to offer the first expressions on the idea of regional cooperation that had been in the minds of various Asian leaders for some time. Many other states were invited.

Among the Asian states present were Afghanistan, Bhutan, Burma, Ceylon, China, Egypt, India, Indonesia, Korea, Malaya, Nepal, Mongolia, Iran, the Philippines, Thailand, Tibet, Turkey, Vietnam, Azerbaijan, Kazakhstan, Kirghizstan, Tajikistan, Uzbekistan, Australia, and New Zealand, and included Palestinian Arabs and Jews. Indian Prime Minister Nehru stressed the need for Asian unity and regional cooperation. He explained that this conference would not have leaders nor followers, neither was it a Pan Asia movement directed against Europe or America. The ideal was One World.

During the conference, China and India's competition for leadership became pronounced while the smaller Asian nations expressed fear of these two powerful neighbours. A Burmese delegate was supposed to have said, "It was terrible to be ruled by a Western power, but it is even more so to be ruled by an Asian power".

The success of the conference lay in its having been held and in having the problems of regional cooperation exposed. The conference agreed to promote Asian studies, greater cooperation, freedom for colonial areas, lifting the status of women in Asia, inter-Asian communication, and economic progress. Other topics discussed were national freedom movements, racial problems and interracial migration, labour problems, and cultural affairs.

b. New Delhi Conference (20 January 1949)

The second attempt towards Asian cooperation was initiated by India on 20 January 1949 to consider the Dutch invasion of Indonesia on 18 December 1948. This conference was an official meeting of Asian governments. The participating countries agreed, among others, "to consult among themselves to explore ways and means of promoting consultation and cooperation within the framework of the United Nations".

The New Delhi Conference (NDC) acted to see how it could help the United Nations Security Council bring about a peaceful solution to the conflict. The NDC asked that Indonesia be given complete authority over its entire area by 1 January 1950.

c.   Asia-Pacific Union (4 July 1949)

This was the first attempt by the Philippines to create an organisation for cooperation among states in Asia. President Elpidio Quirino had in mind the preservation of the sovereignty of states in Asia and the Pacific and identified communism as the biggest threat to sovereignty. The Asia-Pacific Union would act as a potential third force in international affairs. Preferring not to be involved in the Cold War, most Asian states did not want to participate in the proposed Union. For India and the United States, both believed that the time was not ripe for an Asian pact.

d.   Baguio Conference (26-30 May 1950)

Undaunted by the failure of the Asia-Pacific Union, President Quirino organised the Baguio Conference of 1950, the first gathering of fully independent states of Southeast Asia and the Western Pacific on a governmental level. China and North Korea were not invited because the presence of these two would break the anti-communist nature of the conference.

Discussions in the meetings revealed many similarities in vision among the delegates. Ceylon's delegate Senenayake said that even as Asians strengthened their spiritual foundation, they should also seek benefits from materialism to ameliorate the social and economic conditions of the people.

e.   Southeast Asia Treaty Organization (SEATO, September 1954)

SEATO was established in 1954 by eight countries, three of which were Asian states, namely the Philippines, Thailand, and Pakistan. The other countries were the US, Britain, France, Australia, and New Zealand.

Conceived as a military organisation similar to NATO and designed to prevent communism from taking over the Southeast Asian states, it was a response to the Geneva Agreements of 1954 which gave temporary cessation of military hostilities in Vietnam, Laos, and Cambodia. Although the military conflicts were temporarily ceased, the established governments were slowly overtaken by communist activities through coalition governments, guerilla warfare, or subversion. The famous domino theory, although not a theory per se, but rather a speculative wisdom, stated that if the US did not maintain a military presence in the region, all the Southeast Asian states would fall like dominoes to the communists, especially if the states were neutralist such as Indonesia under President Sukarno, Cambodia under Prince Norodom Sihanouk, and Burma under U Nu.

Although the organisation was to help Laos, Cambodia, and Vietnam, called the "Protocol States" fight communism militarily, SEATO failed to help these states because the Western partners feared retaliation from China and the Soviet Union. Thus, SEATO was called a paper tiger. Pakistan opted out because it could not get military arms with which to fight India, an idea which was not within the purview of SEATO. SEATO's weak points were soon losing the trust of Thailand and the Philippines.

Meanwhile, political events changed the strategic landscape in Southeast Asia. Under the Paris Agreements of 1973, the US withdrew militarily from Vietnam, Laos, and Cambodia. In 1975 the communist parties took power to rule in each of those three states. At the same time neutralism had grown stronger as Asian and African states maintained a policy of distancing from the bipolarism of the Cold War. ASEAN states focused on real issues of economic, social, and political development and of establishing relations with China and the new socialist states of Vietnam, Laos and Cambodia. Thailand and the Philippines agreed to end SEATO in 1977.

f. Asian-African Conference (Bandung Conference, 18-24 April 1955)

The Asian-African Conference was proposed by the Prime Ministers of Burma, Ceylon, India, Indonesia, and Pakistan. Twenty-five countries were invited to be represented at the ministerial level, by Prime Ministers or Foreign Ministers.

The objectives included, to: 1) promote goodwill and cooperation among the nations of Asia and Africa and to advance their mutual and common interests; 2) consider social, economic, and cultural problems; 3) consider special problems like national sovereignty, racialism, and colonialism; and 4) promote world peace and cooperation. However, the more dominant view was that it was a response to SEATO.

The Bandung Conference laid out its principles, namely: 1) mutual respect for each other's territorial integrity and sovereignty; 2) mutual non-aggression; 3) mutual non-interference in each other's internal affairs; 4) equality; 5) mutual benefits; 6) peaceful coexistence; 7) disarmament and prohibition of nuclear weapons; and 8) respect for human rights.

The Bandung Conference took a position of being the third force in the Cold War, not siding with any bloc (non-alignment) and yet able to act on international issues without the influence of other countries.

In subsequent years, after the end of the Cold War in the 1990s, the Non-Aligned Movement (NAM) evolved from this Bandung Conference and the new objectives were for economic development.

g. Association of Southeast Asia (ASA, 31 July 1961)

The first purely Southeast Asian states' organisation on a government level, the Association of Southeast Asia (ASA) was established by the Prime Minister of Malaya, the Foreign Minister of Thailand, and the President of the Philippines in 1961. Three plans for ASA, namely the Rahman Plan, the Khoman Plan, and the Garcia Plan, spelt out the desires of the three leaders to uphold the ideals of peace, freedom, social justice, and economic well-being through active cooperation. Malaya wanted to include as many states in Southeast Asia as possible but most of the states begged off due to lack of sympathy for a formal organisation, suspicion of a Western hand in the plan, and the preference for bilateral cooperation.

The final agreement on ASA was very conducive to regional cooperation. The projects were very practical and useful for the mutual development of knowledge and understanding. These projects included promotion of Southeast Asian studies, exchange of youth and women leaders, an ASA airline, waiver of visa requirements for certain categories, an ASA coach service from Singapore to Bangkok, cooperation on shipping, tourism and trade, and common positions in international bodies. All these projects were ongoing until the MAPHILINDO (see next section for details) conflict put them in suspension, then later were to be taken over by ASEAN in 1967.

Much goodwill was generated by the wide areas of practical cooperation. This goodwill enabled the states to place their problems at a very low key, to show sincerity by giving and taking of their material and spiritual resources, to provide self-restraint and mutual consultation, to strengthen the faith and determination of members to continue regional cooperation, to use Asian solutions for Asian problems, and to preserve sovereignty, good neighbourliness, and minimum administrative machinery.

ASA refused to identify threats to the member states thereby paving the way for greater cooperation in the social, cultural, and economic fields. Long-existing mutual suspicions among the members were reduced and provocations from its neighbours were avoided.

ASA cooperation was temporarily suspended when the problem of the creation of Malaysia was challenged by Indonesia and the Philippines in 1963. However, ASA's projects were adopted by ASEAN in 1967 resulting in a shorter preparation time for ASEAN cooperation.

h. MAPHILINDO (5 August 1963)

The British-sponsored Federation of Malaysia in 1961 composed of Malaya, Singapore, North Borneo (Sabah), Brunei, and Sarawak was opposed by President Sukarno of Indonesia and President Diosdado Macapagal of the Philippines, while Brunei decided not to join Malaysia.

Sukarno perceived that the concept of Malaysia was neo-colonialist because the British would still be responsible for security in Southeast Asia. The Philippines opposed the Malaysia Plan because it incorporated Sabah which was claimed to be Philippine territory. Indonesia sent armed men to Sarawak and Singapore as part of Indonesian *Konfrontasi* i.e., the para-military confrontation of Indonesia towards the Malaysia Plan. In a meeting of the three Heads of Government they agreed to resolve their differences in the MAPHILINDO which was to be created.

The proposal for the formation of a Greater Malayan Confederation of States called MAPHILINDO was made by President Macapagal in July 1962. It would bring together 40 million Malay people, a unity forged by the Malays themselves, in reaction to the British Plan for Malaysia. This was the long-term goal. The short-term goal was the establishment of a mechanism for frequent consultations or consensus-making

17

(*mushawarah*), and the settlement of the Borneo claim based on the results of a UN-sponsored plebiscite. The principle of Asian solutions for Asian problems was also agreed on but ironically the *Konfrontasi* and the dispute over Sabah involved much foreign intervention.

MAPHILINDO was set up in 1963 by the Manila Agreements.

MAPHILINDO broke up before it could function. The disparity in the leaders' perceptions of security was brought about by the self-interests of each of them, such as Indonesia's rejection of neo-colonialism, the Philippines' claim to Sabah, and Malaysia's stake in its formation. There was also the difficulty of communication because of the "communism problems" since Indonesia had joined the People's Republic of China to eliminate NECOLIM, the Philippines became a member of SEATO to fight communism, and there was difficulty of reading correctly each other's perceptions due to "strange alliances".

By 1965, Indonesia ended Sukarno's rule but *Konfrontasi* continued. Philippine's claim to Sabah remained. *Mushawarah* never had the chance to bring about cultural, economic, and social exchanges because the political problems were sapping the goodwill and vigour of the three states.

But MAPHILINDO provided lessons for future cooperation. In the succeeding efforts to cooperate which led to ASEAN, the countries had learned that political and military matters should not be allowed during the formative years of learning cooperation, that unity comes from goodwill and trust, and that Asian solutions for Asian problems should always be used to preserve peace in the region. MAPHILINDO'S lessons and its principles of *mushawarah* and the temporariness of foreign bases in the region were adopted by ASEAN in 1967.

ENDNOTES

1   O.W. Wolters, *History, Culture, and Region in Southeast Asian Perspectives* (Singapore: Institute of Southeast Asian Political Systems) in K.S. Sandhu, Sharon Siddique, Chandran Jeshurun, Ananda Rajah, Joseph L.H. Tan and Pushpa Thambipillai. *The ASEAN Reader* (Singapore: ISEAS, 1992), p.5.

2   Wolters, "Early Southeast Asian Political Systems," ibid. p.6.

3   Ibid, p.6.

4   Ibid, p.7.

5   Ibid., pp. 8-11.

6   Donald G. McCloud, "Southeast Asia As A Regional Unit", in Sandhu, et.al., *The ASEAN Reader*, ibid., p.12.

7   Ibid, citing Keith Taylor, "Madagascar in the Ancient Malaya-Polynesian Myths" in Kenneth Hall and John K. Whitmore (eds.), *Explorations in Early Southeast Asian History: The Origins of Southeast Asian Statecraft* (Ann Arbor: Michigan Papers on Southeast Asia, 1976), p. 33.

8   Ibid, citing Wang Gungwu, "China and South-East Asia, 1402-1424" in Jerome Chien and Nicolas Tarling (eds.), *Studies in the Social History of China and South-East Asia: Studies in Memory of Victor Purcell* (Cambridge: Cambridge University Press, 1970), p. 389.

9   Ibid. footnotes 6, 9, p. 13.

10   Ibid, citing in footnote 10 G.R. Tibbetts, *Arab Navigation in the Indian Ocean Before the Coming of the Portuguese* (London: Royal Asiatic Society of Great Britain and Ireland, 1971), pp. 472-503.

11   Ibid. citing in footnote 12 Tibbetts. *A Study of Arabic Texts Containing Materials on Southeast Asia* (Leiden: 1979), p. 3.

12   Russell Fifield is one of the earliest historians and geopolitical writers of Southeast Asia's post-colonial period. The information in this part of the study is taken from "The Southeast Asia Command," an abridged version form *Southeast Asian SPECTRUM* 4, No. 1 (October 1975) pp. 42-51, as found in *The ASEAN Reader*, op.cit., pp. 20-23.

13   Fifield in *The ASEAN Reader*, p. 23.

14   Michael Haas, *International Organization, An Interdisciplinary Bibliography*, (Stanford University: Hoover Institution on War, Revolution and Peace, 1979). All succeeding information is taken from this book.

15   World Affairs Quarterly, XIII (October 1942), pp. 336-56.

16   Chicago: University of Chicago Press, 1943.

17   Baltimore: Helicon, 1964.

18   Louis Finklestein, Harold D. Lasswell and R.M. MacIver, (eds.) *Foundations of World Organization* (New York: Harper, 1950).

19   Francis Brown, Charles Hodges and Joseph S. Roucek (eds.) (New York: Wiley, 1939).

20   *Current History*, New Series XXXIX (August 1960).

21   Estrella D. Solidum, "Towards a Divisible and Graduated Peace", in Solidum, *The Small State: Security and World Peace* (Manila: Kalikasan Press, 1991).

22   For complete provisions, please read Chapter VIII: Articles 52, 53, and 54 of the United Nations Charter.

23   Roger Minshull, *Regional Geography*, (Chicago: Aldine Publishing Co., 1967), p. 122.

24   Crane Brinton, *From Many One* (Cambridge: Harvard University Press, 1948).

25   Solidum, ibid.

26   Susumo Yamakage, "ASEAN's Political Cooperation, 1967-1977: A Performance Analysis of Foreign Ministers' Meetings", Malaysia, January 1980.

27   Most of the data in this section was taken from the manuscript of Estrella D. Solidum, *Philippine Policy for Regional Cooperation*, 1947-1998.

2

Formation of ASEAN

THE BANGKOK DECLARATION OF 1967

At the end of World War II, European states and colonies in Asia tried to end their separation from one another and tried to develop contacts with the neighbouring countries. Japan's short-lived victory in and rule over Southeast Asian colonies contributed to the people's demand for freedom and independence. Japan had given "independence" within its Greater Southeast Asia Co-Prosperity Sphere to Thailand, Indonesia, Burma, and the Philippines, giving the idea to the Southeast Asian peoples that they could rule themselves and thereby quickening the spirit of nationalism.

Thailand as the only uncolonised nation in Southeast Asia tried to show the way to new relationships in the region. Thai diplomats and statesmen advocated independence for every nation and the formation of regional cooperation. But as has been shown earlier, the time in the years soon after the war was not ripe for it. Indonesia still had its war with the Dutch. Singapore and Malaya were not yet getting independence. Vietnam, Laos, and Cambodia still had to fight the French for their freedom. Burma was still to negotiate with the British for its independence.

Even as African and Asian leaders sought to bring themselves into a conference in 1947, the perceptions among them of the conditions, goals, and problems were different. Moreover, the Cold War paralysed some nations into fear of communism and having no resources to protect themselves, they re-established defence relationships with their colonial masters. The idea that they could still be responsible for the security of Southeast Asia was called by Indonesian leader Sukarno as neo-colonialism. On the other hand, some states in the region were now thinking of a third force in the bipolar world as created by the Cold War, between the democratic states led by the United States and the Marxist Socialist states led by the Soviet Union. The Third Force was not going to be a regional bloc. It was going to be a moral Third Force. The Bandung Conference of 1955 declared this. Indonesia, Burma, and Cambodia adopted a neutralist stance, the ability of every state to determine what is right and just for itself, without influence from either blocs but without cutting off relations with those states. Thus the neutralist principles were formed: cooperation for economic, social and cultural development, non-interference in domestic affairs, mutual respect for national sovereignty, disarmament and prohibition of nuclear weapons, respect for human rights, and respect for the right of self-defence "singly or collectively" in conformity with the UN Charter.

During the attempts to form regional groups, other factors created problems. Besides the Cold War, there were territorial disputes and disturbing political developments such as the "Gestapu Affair" of Indonesia in 1965 which helped to precipitate the establishment of ASEAN.

In the 1965 coup in Indonesia, President Sukarno was replaced by General Suharto who became President after several months to give due respect to Sukarno who was placed under house arrest. Indonesia needed to have a new image among its neighbours especially with Malaysia against which it had launched a *Konfrontasi*.

Indonesian Deputy Prime Minister and Foreign Minister Adam Malik went to the neighbouring states "to mend fences". While in Thailand, he met with Foreign Minister Thanat Khoman who was helping to reconcile Malaysia, Indonesia, and the Philippines which had been trying to settle the problem generated by the formation of Malaysia. Thanat proposed to Malik the idea of another organisation for regional cooperation to include more members. Malik agreed to it and after clearing it with his government, he invited to Jakarta Philippine Foreign Affairs Secretary Narciso Ramos for discussions on an expanded membership for a new regional association for cooperation. While Malik himself went to Malaysia to explore possibilities for the idea, he sent Foreign Ministry Officer Anwar Sani to the Philippines to seek assistance in persuading Thailand to "make some gracious gesture" so that Cambodia would join the proposed cooperation plan, after Malik had confirmed that Thailand had no objection to Cambodia's participation. President Suharto followed this up with a letter to Prince Norodom Sihanouk. He and his Prime Minister Son Sann declined due to their perception of intrigue.

Burma was also invited but it preferred to protect its neutrality policy which Burmese officials said would be broken if the country were to join any bloc. South Vietnam wanted to join but its enormous problems arising from its war with North Vietnam were seen as overwhelming for a newly starting association.

Three countries of the original ASEAN Five made proposals for how the new association would be. The Thai draft wanted a loose association for cooperation and good neighbourliness. Indonesia needed to see that *mushawarah* or consensus-making would be the process and that foreign military bases should be temporary in nature and would not be used against any member state. The Philippines rejected the proposal on the military bases as it was hosting the US military in Philippine bases. The Philippines also wanted a legalistic charter to formally bind the members. This idea came naturally to the Philippines due to the legacies of Spain and the US on legalism. Of course Malaysia would reject proposals from the Philippines with the Sabah conflict still simmering. Indonesia also supported Thailand's idea of a loose community of nations.

On 8 August 1967, the Bangkok Declaration announced the establishment of the Association of South-East Asian Nations (ASEAN, the acronym that Adam Malik gave to it).

Each of the five original members had a real stake in membership. Indonesia needed to project a good image to its neighbours after the recent *Konfrontasi* and "Gestapu Affair". The *Konfrontasi* was the confrontation that President Sukarno had with Malaysia which was in reality a creation of England to bring together Malaya, Singapore, Sabah, and Sarawak in 1963. England would be responsible for the security of the new Federation of Malaysia. Sukarno rejected this idea saying that Asians should be responsible for their security. This kind of set up, Sukarno said, was neocolonialism by England. Sukarno also supported the Philippine opposition to the creation of Malaysia because it had included the Philippine territory of Sabah. He sent Indonesian paramilitary troops to Malaya and Singapore. The situation continued until a coup (Gestapu Affair) by the military to prevent a communist party take-over was effected in 1965, placing Sukarno under house arrest. The military had great difficulty living under Sukarno's policy of giving the Partai Komunis Indonesia (PKI) equal participation in government, knowing that the ultimate objective of the PKI was to finally take control of the country. The military made the pre-emptive strike to immediately cut down the PKI and remove the latter's source of strength for its activities who was Sukarno himself. After this, Indonesia had to redeem its original image with Asian neighbours as it needed acceptance and legitimation by them.

Singapore was the newest state, having been expelled by Malaysia in 1965 from the Federation and needing to find strength from friends in the region. Thailand had always wanted an environment of good neighbours with which it could have mutual support. Thailand had experienced disappointment with SEATO over its failure to fulfill its promises of protection to the Protocol states. It would be best for Thailand to engage neighbours in mutual support rather than to find friendship with its Southeast Asian neighbours as it was distancing itself from the US. In 1984, Brunei Darussalam became independent and joined ASEAN.

The ASEAN Declaration referred to Southeast Asian Nations in its provisions. The original idea was to have all states in the region to be members but Burma was isolationist and Vietnam, Laos, and Cambodia had their own wars and in fact rejected ASEAN as a Western creation.

In 1973, the US military withdrew from Vietnam, Laos, and Cambodia under the Paris Peace Treaty. In 1975, the communist party in each state took control over the government. ASEAN decided to extend its hand of friendship to the three states in spite of their political and economic differences. The underlying principle was that it was better to create amity rather than enmity.

But the interstate problems grew worse. China and the Soviet Union had really been the patrons of the wars and proxy governments, because Cambodia under the Khmer Rouge and Pol Pot (of killing fields) was supported by China, while Vietnam which had control over Laos had signed a treaty with the Soviet Union making Danang and Camranh Bay Russian military bases. This arrangement undercut China's need to control access to the three states. To make this situation clear, it must be understood that China and the Soviet Union were competing fiercely for control over the communist-ruled states. This was the Sino-Soviet conflict which started in 1957. But Vietnam's great leader President Ho Chi Minh left his "Testament" instructing his people to unify the socialist (Marxist) camp of China and the Soviet Union but not to side with either of the two. Ho Chi Minh was a strategist. China was threatening on Vietnam's northern borders while the Soviet Union was the source of military and economic assistance but was far away.

When President Mikhail Gorbachev of the Soviet Union instituted *glasnost* (transparency) and *perestroika* (restructuring) in 1986, he also withdrew Soviet support from Vietnam and recognised Laos and Cambodia as separate states, in effect destroying Vietnam's "flexible hegemony"[1] over Laos and Cambodia. Gorbachev also had proposed a détente with China which the latter accepted.

As a result, Vietnam was isolated from its partners, the Soviet Union and the COMECON in East Europe. By 1990s the Marxist Socialist governments in Europe collapsed. Vietnam had lost its patrons. Vietnam worked to restore relations with its neighbours, first with each state and later with ASEAN itself. On the other hand, ASEAN had used confidence building measures on Vietnam.

ASEAN: FROM SIX TO TEN

Before Vietnam, Laos, Cambodia, and Myanmar became members of ASEAN, they were first invited as Guest or Observer in the ASEAN Ministerial Meetings (AMM).

In July 1992 (Manila), the Foreign Ministers of the Lao People's Democratic Republic and the Socialist Republic of Vietnam attended the 25th AMM as Guests. This AMM agreed that their applications for Observer status in ASEAN be approved upon the submission of their respective Instruments of Accession to the Treaty of Amity and Cooperation (TAC). In this 25th AMM, the Instruments of Accession of Laos and Vietnam to the TAC were accepted. In July 1993 Singapore, Laos and Vietnam became Observers for the first time. In 1994 (Bangkok) Laos and Vietnam attended the 27th AMM as Observers. They also participated in the First ASEAN Regional Forum (ARF). On 17 October 1994, Vietnam applied for membership in ASEAN.

On 28 July 1995 (Bandar Seri Begawan), Vietnam was admitted into ASEAN as its seventh member.

At the 28th AMM Laos attended as Observer. There the Foreign Minister of Laos announced his country's intention to join ASEAN in two years' time, that is, at the 30th AMM in Kuala Lumpur coinciding with ASEAN's 30th anniversary.

In accordance with the decision of ASEAN Heads of Government at the First Informal Summit in Jakarta on 30 November 1996, which "reaffirmed their strong commitment to the speedy realisation of an ASEAN comprising all ten Southeast Asian countries they agreed that

Cambodia, Laos, and Myanmar (CLM) be admitted as ASEAN members simultaneously...".

Before this First Informal Summit in 1996, Cambodia and Myanmar had also taken action to become members of ASEAN.[2]

Cambodia was a Guest of the Host Government during the 26th AMM (Singapore) in July 1993 and the 27th AMM (Bangkok) in July 1994. Cambodia acceded to the TAC in January 1995. At the 28th AMM in Bandar Seri Begawan, Cambodia was granted Observer status. She applied for membership in a letter by the Minister for Foreign Affairs and International Cooperation on 23 March 1996.

Myanmar was Guest of the Host Government at the 27th AMM (Bangkok) in July 1994 and of the 28th AMM (Bandar Seri Begawan) in July 1995 when she also acceded to the TAC. Myanmar became an Observer in ASEAN at the 29th AMM in Jakarta in July 1996. The Foreign Minister of Myanmar also participated in the Third ARF. In August 1996, Myanmar applied for ASEAN membership.

At the Fifth ASEAN Summit in Bangkok on 15 December 1995, the ASEAN Heads of Government held an informal meeting with the heads from Cambodia, Laos, and Myanmar (CLM countries). It was the first meeting of all leaders of Southeast Asian countries. At that momentous meeting, the Heads of Government of the ten Southeast Asia countries signed the Treaty on the Southeast Asia Nuclear Weapon-Free Zone. In their Summit Declaration, the ASEAN Heads announced that "ASEAN shall work towards the speedy realization of an ASEAN comprising all Southeast Asian countries as it enters the 21st century...".

This commitment was reiterated by the Heads of Government in Jakarta on 30 November 1996 during the First ASEAN Informal Summit. They agreed to admit Cambodia, Laos and Myanmar simultaneously. They agreed to request the relevant ASEAN bodies to continue with the necessary technical and procedural steps. The actual timing of admission could be announced in due time.

At the Special Meeting of ASEAN Foreign Ministers in Kuala Lumpur on 31 May 1997, the Secretary-General of ASEAN reported that the CLM countries had given satisfactory undertakings to fulfill all obligations and commitments under the various ASEAN agreements that they would have to accede to as new members. Based on the report, the ASEAN Foreign Ministers agreed that Cambodia, Laos, and Myanmar could be admitted in late July 1997.

Due to the political problems in Cambodia, the ASEAN Foreign Ministers held a Special Meeting in Kuala Lumpur on 10 July 1997 to assess the situation in the country. Cambodia's admission was moved to a later date.

Laos and Myanmar were admitted to ASEAN on 23 July 1997, a day before the start of the 30th AMM in Kuala Lumpur.

Cambodia was admitted to membership in ASEAN on 30 April 1999 at a special ceremony in Hanoi in accordance with the decision of the Sixth ASEAN summit.

ASEAN's goal to achieve regional cohesion was realised with the completion of ASEAN 10.[3]

MILESTONES IN THE HISTORY OF ASEAN

Many important events in ASEAN, from its founding in 1967 to 2003, have contributed to the definition of the true relationships among the member states, from five to ten members; and of ASEAN's role in realising its vision of a community of caring societies, through many directions, to include economic, political, functional, security, and external relations cooperation. Through its consensus-building approach, ASEAN has created a community of nations which are committed to achieve peace, progress, and prosperity in the region in the spirit of equality and partnership.

ORGANISATIONAL STRUCTURE[4]

ASEAN Heads of Government

The highest authority of ASEAN is the Meeting of the ASEAN Heads of Government, the ASEAN Summit. In 1992, the Fourth ASEAN Summit in Singapore decided that the ASEAN Heads of Government would meet formally every three years and informally at least once in between to lay down directions and initiatives for ASEAN activities. In 1995, the Fifth ASEAN Summit in Bangkok decided to hold annual Informal Summits between the formal ASEAN Summits which take place every three years. The first two Informal Summits have been held in Jakarta in December 1996 and in Kuala Lumpur in December 1997. The Sixth ASEAN Summit was convened in Hanoi in December 1998.

ASEAN Ministerial Meeting (AMM)

The ASEAN Foreign Ministers meet annually during the AMM. The AMM, established by the 1967 Bangkok Declaration, is responsible for the formulation of policy guidelines and coordination of ASEAN activities. At the 1977 Kuala Lumpur Summit, the ASEAN Heads of Government agreed that the AMM could include other relevant ministers as and when necessary. During an ASEAN Summit, the AMM and AEM report jointly to the ASEAN Heads of Government.

ASEAN Economic Ministers (AEM)

The AEM meets formally or informally to direct ASEAN economic cooperation. The AEM was institutionalised at the 1977 Kuala Lumpur Summit. Like the AMM, the AEM also meets annually. The AFTA Council was established by the Fourth Summit to supervise, coordinate, and review the implementation of the CEPT Scheme for AFTA. The AEM and AMM report jointly to the ASEAN Heads of Government during an ASEAN Summit.

Sectoral Ministers Meeting

Ministers for specific sectors of economic cooperation meet as and when necessary to give guidance on ASEAN cooperation. These are meetings of Ministers on Energy, Ministers on Agriculture and Forestry, Ministers on Tourism, and Ministers on Transport. The Sectoral Economic Ministers report to the AEM. The ASEAN Finance Ministers have also agreed to meet regularly. Their first meeting was held in Phuket in February 1997.

Other Non-Economic ASEAN Ministerial Meetings

Meetings of ministers in other fields of ASEAN cooperation, such as Health, Environment, Labour, Rural Development, Poverty Alleviation, Social Welfare, Education, Science and Technology, Information, Justice/Law and Transnational crimes, are held regularly. While there is coordination between meetings of other ministers and the AMM, each meeting of ministers may report directly to the Heads of Government.

Joint Ministerial Meeting (JMM)

The JMM, established by the 1987 Manila Summit, meets as and when necessary to facilitate the cross-sectoral coordination of the consultation on ASEAN activities. The JMM comprises the ASEAN Foreign Ministers and Economic Ministers under the joint chairmanship of the AMM and AEM chairmen. Such a joint meeting can be initiated either by the Foreign Ministers or the Economic Ministers. The JMM usually meets prior to the Summit.

Secretary General of ASEAN

The Secretary-General is appointed on merit by the ASEAN Heads of Government with the recommendation of the AMM. He is accorded ministerial status with the mandate to initiate, advise, coordinate and implement ASEAN activities. The Protocol Amending the Agreement on the establishment of the ASEAN Secretariat, signed in Manila on 22 July 1992, provides that the Secretary-General is responsible to the Heads of Government Meeting and to all Meetings of ASEAN Ministers when they are in session and to the chairman of the ASC. He also chairs all meetings of the ASC on behalf of the ASC chairman, except the first and the last.

ASEAN Standing Committee (ASC)

The ASC is the policy arm of coordination of ASEAN between the AMM. The ASC, which reports directly to the AMM, comprises the Chairman who is the Foreign Minister of the country hosting the AMM, the Secretary–General of ASEAN and the Directors-General of the ASEAN National Secretariats. As an advisory body to the Permanent Committees, the ASC reviews the work of Committees with a view to implementing policy guidelines set by the AMM.

Senior Officials Meeting (SOM)

The SOM was formally institutionalised as part of the ASEAN machinery at the 1987 Manila Summit. Responsible for ASEAN political cooperation, the SOM meets when necessary and reports directly to the AMM. SOM consists of heads of the Foreign Ministries of the ASEAN Member Countries.

Senior Economic Officials Meeting (SEOM)

The SEOM was also established as part of the ASEAN machinery at the Manila Summit and comprises the heads of trade, industry, finance and commerce of the ASEAN Member Countries. The Fourth ASEAN Summit agreed that the five ASEAN Economic Communities on Finance and Banking (COFAB); Industry, Minerals, and Energy (COIME); Transportation and Communications (COTAC); and Trade and Tourism (COTT) be dissolved and SEOM be tasked to handle all aspects of ASEAN economic cooperation. The SEOM meets regularly and reports directly to the AEM.

Other ASEAN Senior Officials Meeting

Other ASEAN Senior Officials Meetings comprise the ASEAN Senior Officials on the Environment (ASOEN) and ASEAN Senior Officials on Drug Matters (ASOD) as well as ASEAN Committees such as Committee on Social Development (COSD), Committee on Science and Technology (COST), ASEAN Conference on Civil Service Matters (ACCSM), and Committee on Culture and Information (COCI). These bodies report to the ASC and to the relevant meetings of Ministers.

Joint Consultative Meeting (JCM)

The JCM, set up at the 1987 Manila Summit, comprises the Secretary-General of ASEAN, SOM, SEOM, and the ASEAN Directors-General. It facilitates the intersectoral coordination of ASEAN activities at the officials level. The Secretary-General reports the results of the Meeting directly to the AMM and AEM.

ASEAN National Secretariats

Each ASEAN country has a National Secretariat in the Foreign Ministry which organises and implements ASEAN-related activities at the country level. At the head of each National Secretariat is a Director-General.

ASEAN Committees in Third Countries

ASEAN has established committees in its Dialogue Partner countries to handle ASEAN's external relations with these countries and international organisations. These committees comprise the heads of diplomatic missions of the ASEAN Member Countries in the host country. They conduct consultative meetings with their Host Governments. Presently, there are 15 ASEAN Committees in third countries, namely: Beijing, Bonn, Brussels, Canberra, Geneva, Islamabad, London, Moscow, New Delhi, Ottawa, Paris, Seoul, Tokyo, Washington, and Wellington. The Chairmen of the ASEAN Committees in Third Countries submit progress reports to the ASC on the activities of the Committees and seek guidance as needed from the ASC.

ASEAN Secretariat

The ASEAN Secretariat was established by an agreement signed by the ASEAN Foreign Ministers during the 1976 Bali Summit to enhance coordination and implementation of policies, projects, and activities of the various ASEAN bodies.

The 1992 Singapore Summit agreed to strengthen the ASEAN Secretariat so that it would effectively support the Summit's initiatives. The Protocol Amending the Agreement on the Establishment of the ASEAN Secretariat, signed at the 25th AMM in Manila in 1992, provided the Secretariat with a new structure. The Protocol vested the Secretariat with an expanded set of functions and responsibilities to initiate, coordinate, and implement ASEAN activities.

The Special Meeting of the ASEAN Foreign Ministers in Kuala Lumpur in May 1997 agreed to the creation of an additional post of Deputy Secretary-General at the ASEAN Secretariat. One Deputy Secretary will assist the Secretary-General on AFTA and Economic Cooperation while the others will assist in Functional Cooperation, ASEAN Cooperation and Dialogue Relations and Administration, Finance and Personnel. The Deputy Secretaries-General are appointed based on nominations by the governments of ASEAN member countries.

Staffing of the Secretariat has moved from national nomination to open recruitment. A total of 35 professional staff have been recruited, more than double the size of the previous professional staff of 14 before the reorganisation.

The ASEAN Secretariat adopted a mission statement which reflects the spirit and goals of the Fourth Summit, "towards strengthening and intensifying intra-ASEAN cooperation". The work of the Secretariat is guided by this mission statement in order to provide responsive support to the tasks of the various ASEAN bodies.

The Secretariat has four bureaus. The AFTA Bureau, in addition to handling the implementation and monitoring of AFTA, also handles other related issues such as the elimination of non-tariff barriers, the harmonising of tariff nomenclature, the issue of standards and conformance, and customs valuation and procedures. Apart from the meetings of the AFTA Council of Ministers, the AEM and SEOM, the bureau also fully services the meeting of the ASEAN Directors-General of Customs and the ASEAN Consultative Committee on Standards and Quality.

The Bureau of Economic Cooperation handles such matters as investment, services, finance, banking, intellectual property, food, agriculture, transportation, and energy. The bureau is also responsible for issues related to industrial cooperation and, generally, non-AFTA issues, including those involving the private sector. In addition to the AEM, the bureau services the meetings of the Ministers of Agriculture, Energy, Finance, Transport, and Communications and Tourism, as well as that of their respective officials.

The Bureau of Functional Cooperation has been actively engaged in drawing up and coordinating the implementation of the Action Plans for Science and Technology, Environment, Culture and Information, Social Development, and Drug Abuse control. In addition to this, the Bureau has also, among others, taken the initiative which resulted in the establishment of the ASEAN University Network and its Charter. The bureau services the meeting of the ministers and senior officials responsible for the respective sectors mentioned above and also services fully the five committees on functional cooperation, their sub-committees and working groups.

The Bureau for ASEAN Cooperation and Dialogue Relations is responsible for the operationalisation of the project appraisal system adopted by the ASEAN Standing Committee. Under this system, project appraisal, implementation, monitoring, and evaluation procedures have been set up and the bureau provides advisory services to the various ASEAN bodies on these procedures and in project formulation and design. The bureau also identifies funding sources and assists Member Countries by preparing papers on development cooperation policies and strategies which are used as a basis for discussion with Dialogue Partners.

COUNTRY PROFILE OF BRUNEI DARUSSALAM
(as of 29 June 1999)

POPULATION	: 315,292
POPULATION DENSITY	: 142 per sq. mile
URBAN	: 70%
ETHNIC GROUPS	: Malay 64%, Chinese 20%
PRINCIPAL LANGUAGES	: Malay (official), English, Chinese
CHIEF RELIGIONS	: Muslim (official) 63%, Buddhist 14%, Christian 8%
AREA	: 5, 765 sq. km.
LOCATION	: in Southeast Asia, on the North coast of the island of Borneo; it is surrounded on its landward side by the Malaysian state of Sarawak
CAPITAL	: Bandar Seri Begawan
TYPE	: Independent Sultanate
HEAD OF GOVERNMENT	: Sultan Sir Muda Hassanal Bolkiah Mu'izzadin Waddaulah b.July 15, 1946; in office: January 1, 1984
LOCAL DIVISIONS	: 4 districts
DEFENCE	: 6.5% of GDP
ACTIVE TROOP STRENGTH	: 5,000
INDUSTRIES	: oil and gas (more than 40% of GDP is derived from oil and gas exports)
CHIEF CROPS	: Rice, banana, cassava
CRUDE OIL RESERVES	: 1.35 bil bbls (1997)
ARABLE LAND	: 1 %
LIVESTOCK	: chickens 3.00 mil (1997)
ELECTRICITY PRODUCTION	: 1.5 bil kWh
MONETARY UNIT	: Dollar (Sept. 1998; 1.76=$1 U.S.)
GROSS DOMESTIC PRODUCT	: $4.6 bil (1995 est.)
PER CAPITA GDP	: $15,800
IMPORTS	: $2 bil; partners: Singapore 29%, UK 19% (1995 est.)

EXPORTS	: $2.7 bil. Partners: Japan 50%, UK 19% (1995 est.)
NATIONAL BUDGET	: $2.6 bil
TOURISM	: $39 mil
LIFE EXPECTANCY AT BIRTH	: 70.2 male; 73.3 female
BIRTHS	: 25 (per 1,000 popn.)
DEATHS	: 5 (per 1,000 popn.)
NATURAL INCREASE	: 1.98%
INFANT MORTALITY	: 23 (per 1,000 live births)
FREE AND COMPULSORY EDUCATION	: ages 5-17
LITERACY	: 88%
MAJOR INTERNATIONAL ORGANISATIONS	: UN and some of its specialised agencies, APEC, ASEAN, the Commonwealth
EMBASSY	: US:2600 Virginia Ave. NW, suite 300, (WS) 20037; 342-0159. ASEAN states, European states, England, Japan, others
WEBSITE	: http://www.brunet.bn

BRUNEI DARUSSALAM (ABODE OF PEACE)[5]

Brunei Darussalam is a Malay Sultanate covering a territory of 2,228 square miles or 5,765 square kilometres. It is situated on the northwest coast of the Island of Borneo and has a common border with Sarawak, one of the two eastern states of Malaysia, while having a coastline of 100 miles on the northwest coast of Borneo. Brunei Darussalam is the third largest producer of oil in Southeast Asia after Indonesia and Malaysia.

Brunei Darussalam has a long history. At about 518 A.D., envoys from China visited the country, according to early Chinese sources. It is believed that merchants and travellers from the Middle East brought Islam to Brunei as early as the 13th century. In the 15th century, Brunei had become a powerful Islamic state. In the 16th century, Brunei had political control over all Borneo and over parts of the Philippines and islands around Singapore. Brunei's trade with other countries was extensive until the 1800s when the European nations, Portugal, Spain, England, and Thailand had brought a strong presence in the area.

Due to internal problems and foreign pressures, Brunei became a British Protectorate in 1888. in 1890, Brunei lost Limbong, therewith reducing its territory to the present area of 2,226 square miles (5,765 square kilometres).

In 1906, the first British Resident from the British Government arrived. He set up a new form of government, including a State Council which lasted until 1959 when a new Constitution was promulgated, giving Brunei internal self-government, broken only by the 3½ years of Japanese Occupation. After 1959, several negotiations took place regarding the future of Brunei. In 1979, a treaty between Brunei and the United Kingdom provided for full independence on December 31, 1983. Then on January 1, 1984, Brunei regained full independence.

The present Head of State of Brunei Darussalam is His Majesty the Sultan and Yang Di-Pertuan of Brunei Darussalam, Sultan Haji Hassanal Bolkiah Mu'izzadin Waddaulah. He is also the Prime Minister, Minister of Defence, and presiding official over the Cabinet. He is assisted by five Councils—the Privy Council, the Council of Ministers (Cabinet), the Council of Succession, the Religious Council, and the Legislature.

Sultan Hassanal Bolkiah became the 29th in a line of rulers which goes back to the 15th century, when his father, Sultan Haji Oman Ali Saifuddien Sa'adul Khairi Waddien, voluntarily abdicated the throne after a reign of 17 years (1950-1967). He passed away in 1986 and is remembered as the Architect of Modern Brunei.

COUNTRY PROFILE OF THE KINGDOM OF CAMBODIA (as of 29 June 1999)

OFFICIAL NAME	: Kingdom of Cambodia
NATIONAL CAPITAL	: Phnom Penh
INDEPENDENCE / NATIONAL DAY	: 09 November
TYPE OF GOVERNMENT	: Constitutional Monarchy with separation of powers between the executive, legislative and judiciary
INCUMBENT HEAD OF STATE:	King Norodom Sihanouk
INCUMBENT HEAD OF GOVERNMENT	: Prime Minister Hun Sen
LOCATION	: Situated in the Indochinese Peninsula, Cambodia is bordered by Thailand and Laos on the north and Vietnam on the east and south. The Gulf of Siam is off the western coast. The country consists chiefly of a large alluvial plain ringed in by mountains on the east of the Mekong River. The plain is centred on Lake Tonle Sap, which is a natural storage basin of the Mekong.
SIZE OF TERRITORY	: 70,238 square miles
POPULATION	: 11.168 million
POPULATION GROWTH RATE	: 2.5% (1999)
LANGUAGES	: Khmer (Official), French
RELIGION	: Theravada Buddhism-Hinayana (90-95%); Muslim and Christians (5-10%)
GDP / P.C. (US$)	: $286
GDP GROWTH RATE (%)	: 4.50%
GNP PER CAPITA	: $270 (May 1999)
MAJOR NATURAL RESOURCES	: Timber, gem, rice, fish. The Kingdom of Cambodia, with

its rich variety of natural resources (fertile soil favourable for agriculture, good tropical forests, and minerals), and abundant labour force, offers foreign investors many possibilities for producing or processing a wide range of local products, including but not limited to wood furniture, paper, canned vegetables and fruits, precious stones and other minerals, clothes and footwear. The Mekong River and its tributaries have vast potential as a source of hydro-electric power, which, once harnessed, will supply abundant energy for industrial and commercial development and household use.

LEADING INDUSTRIES	: Agriculture, services, manufacture, ice, timber, textile and garment, rice milling, beer, soft drink production, and construction.
MAJOR EXPORTS	: Rubber, timber, maize, soya beans, and fishery products
MAJOR IMPORTS	: Fuel and petroleum products, Agriculture, materials and equipment, construction materials, machineries, and consumer goods.
MAJOR TRADING PARTNER (1996)	: Thailand, Vietnam, Singapore, Taiwan.
NATIONAL CURRENCY	: Riel
EXCHANGE RATE	: US$1.00=4,000 Riels (official rate)
FOREIGN CURRENCE RESERVES	: $0.3b (May 1999)
SIZE OF TERRITORY	: 181, 000 sq. km.

KINGDOM OF CAMBODIA[6]

Cambodia as it is today is descended from the great Khmer Empire of the 12th and 13th centuries which extended to areas of Southeast Asia now occupied by Cambodia, Laos, Thailand, and Vietnam.

The history of Cambodia is traced to an early kingdom called Funan or Kingdom of the Mountain dating to about first century A.D. Funan had vassalage over states as far as Thailand, Laos, and northern Malay Peninsula. Funan had a well developed system of authority based on the controlled distribution of water and a religion involving water spirits and sacred mountains.

Due to dynastic quarrels, Funan weakened and was overtaken by Chenla which then took control of central and upper Laos and southern Thailand. After two centuries and quarrels, Chenla split into two, then the southern part went under the Sailendra dynasty of Java. When a new ruler Jayavarman II ascended the throne of the southern part by 802, he reunited the Khmers. For about 550 years, the Khmer Empire as founded by Jayavarman II and with capital at Siem Reap, extended its borders into northern Laos, to the South China Sea, and to the Bay of Bengal. The magnificent Angkor temples and palaces and an extensive hydraulic network for the cultivation and distribution of rice were built. The greatest influence on the Khmer Empire were the Indian ideas and practices on the state and religion.

In the early 13th century, Khmer power weakened. The people had rebelled against the kings for forced labour and military campaigns; labour had been diversified to temple-building leading to the neglect of the hydraulic system. Buddhism had been preached teaching salvation of the individual by his own efforts. The Thai people began to replace Khmer authority over the Menam Basin (Chao Phraya) and along upper Mekong River. Then in 1432, the Thais sacked Angkor. Cambodia was reduced to vassalage to both Siam and Annam for 400 years.

In 1863, France offered to protect Norodom against internal and external attacks and crowned him King in 1864. In 1888, Cambodia became a *de facto* colony of France when King Norodom signed the convention under siege by Governor-General Thomson of Cochinchina.

France considered Cambodia as a buffer to Siam and England which could challenge French control over Vietnam. For this reason, France promoted law and order and less of development of human and natural resources. Education except for a few of the elite was not encouraged. Hence the Cambodians had no training for responsibility under France.[7]

Prince Sihanouk was placed on the throne by the French because he was seen to be weak and accommodating. But in reality, it was Prince Sihanouk who led the country to independence in 1953.

The Second World War revealed France's weakness before the advancing Japanese forces. Cambodians losing confidence in France started some political changes. One group favoured the return of France and a slow path to independence. Another group wanted independence from France and a republic.[8] The groups that advocated various ways to independence came mostly from the small educated elite and civil servants. King Sihanouk undertook a series of reforms to reconcile conflicting interests.

King Sihanouk led the crusade for independence. Snubbed in France, he returned to Cambodia and en route told the world his experiences. On July 3, 1953, France offered complete sovereignty and independence to Cambodia. This independence was the sword that struck the position of the Viet Minh in Cambodia on October 18, 1954.[9]

Sihanouk stepped down from the throne in March 1955 in favour of his father King Norodom Suramarit, in order to lead in the politics. His political party the Sangkum Reastr Niyum rallied most of the leaders and the people and encouraged public debate on his policies and enfranchised the women. Sihanouk himself successfully devised many strategies to bring out in open discussions all ideas that had begun to disunify the country.

Prince Sihanouk ruled Cambodia until 1970 when the dark forces in the government reared their heads as the Viet Minh-led Khmer Rouge which were communists had advanced in the country. Cambodia's neutrality was being undermined. The United States developed leaders in Cambodia as the US had abhorred neutralists, to establish a republican government. While Sihanouk was in Europe to secure guarantees from the Geneva Conference States for its security, his own Prime Minister Lon Nol staged a *coup d'etat* and replaced Sihanouk as the head of the republic. Sihanouk stayed in France and China, until in 1975, the Khmer Rouge under Pol Pot, one of the rebels in Cambodia who had been trained in China during the Cultural Revolution, began its return to Phnom Penh, bringing along Sihanouk to legitimise a new communist party-led government. Prince Sihanouk agreed to return at the risk of his life to rally the people morally and spiritually against the Khmer Rouge.

Pol Pot ruled the country and sent at least two million people to death in his campaign to produce a "new socialist man" and a "new socialist society" of the Marxist type. Sihanouk stayed out of the country while the "killing fields" spread in Cambodia.

In 1978, the Socialist Republic of Vietnam sent Hun Sen, another Cambodian communist, to take over the government from Pol Pot. Hun Sen had ruled the country since then keeping himself in the position during all the problems of Khmer Rouge attacks from the provinces where they had regrouped, and of the search for unity and self-determination. The war had been influenced by the conflict between the Soviet Union and China for influence in Southeast Asia.

ASEAN made many moves to resolve the problem. Finally, it set up in 1982 the Coalition Government of Democratic Kampuchea (CGDK) composed of three groups, the FUNCINPEC of the Sihanouk group, the Republican KPNLF group and the Khmer Rouge fighting for power in Cambodia. Indonesia set up the Jakarta Informal Meetings I and II to make the three groups engage in dialogue with the Hun Sen group. ASEAN also asked the United Nations to lend a hand in solving the problem. In 1991, the UN by the Paris Peace Agreements, set up a United Nations Transitional Authority in Cambodia (UNTAC) to pacify the country and hold elections. Cambodia has a constitutional monarchy, with elected King Norodum Sihanouk and with separation of powers for the government. The Royal government of Cambodia was accepted by ASEAN in 1999 as its tenth member.

Cambodia is a huge fertile basin for the lower Mekong River and it is where Tonle Sap, the largest lake in Southeast Asia is found. Cambodia is bounded by Thailand, Laos, Vietnam, and the Gulf of Thailand. Cambodia's 70,238 square miles has about 6,600 miles of water, 28,000 square miles of arable land which yield rice, rubber, corn, palm sugar, cotton, tobacco and others, and large forest lands with abundant supply of timber and minerals.

Cambodians comprise about 85% of the population of about 10.9 million (1999), most of whom are rice farmers, the rest being government employees and Buddhist monks. The ethnic minorities are the Chinese and the Vietnamese of about 400,000 who live around Phnom Penh and are into business. A small ethnic group is that of the Chams from Champa, who are Malays and Muslims. There are also hill tribes.

The people are about 90-95% Buddhists.

Cambodia can be very proud of its advances in education especially from 1955 to 1970. By 1999, Cambodia had brought up reconstruction in education with a growing student body and teachers. Compulsory education is up to the sixth grade. Schools were set up where the French had not attended to it.

Before 1975, the government made great progress in education, health and welfare, public works, and community development—the standard of living was sustainable. People were contented with government services.

In the year 2001, Cambodia has still to cope with many social, economic, and political problems but many countries and organisations are assisting in the country's recovery and peace.

COUNTRY PROFILE OF THE REPUBLIC OF INDONESIA

OFFICIAL NAME : Republic of Indonesia

CAPITAL : Jakarta

NATIONAL DAY : August 17

SIZE OF TERRITORY : 1,904,569 sq.km. and territorial waters four times that size

GEOGRAPHY : 17,508 islands, 6,000 are inhabited. Stretches 5,120 km. east to west and 1,760 km. north to south

TIME ZONE : Western Indonesia is GMT +7; Central Indonesia is GMT +8; and Eastern Indonesia is GMT +9

TYPE OF GOVERNMENT : Unitary, Republican and Democratic

GOVERNMENT SYSTEM : The President, who is both Chief Executive and Head of State is elected for a five-year term by the MPR. The 1945 Constitution provides for two legislative bodies, the People's Consultative Assembly (MPR) and the House of Representatives (DPR); and a Supreme Advisory Council (DPA) which advises the President; the State Audit Board; and the Supreme Court. Indonesia has 27 provinces and 242 regencies.

INCUMBENT HEAD OF STATE: President Megawati Sukarnoputri

MEMBERSHIP IN REGIONAL/
INTERNATIONAL BODIES : UN, WTO, NAM, APEC, ASEAN, IOR-ARC (Indian Ocean Rim Association for Regional Cooperation), WB,

41

OPEC,	IMF, ADB, IDB, IFC,
	IMRO (rubber), ICO
POPULATION	: 212.107 million (1998) mainly of Malay extraction and 300 ethnically distinct groups
GROWTH RATE	: 1.6% (1998)
ETHNICITY	: Majority of population is of Malay stock, although there is a rich array of some 300 distinct cultures, each with its own individual language or dialect
LANGUAGES	: Bahasa Indonesia (official), Dutch, English, and over 60 regional languages
RELIGIOUS GROUPS	: 88% Islam; 10% Christian (Protestant and Roman Catholic); 2% Hindu, Buddhist, Confucian, animist
GDP / PPP (US$)	: $755 billion (as of May 1999)
Per Capita GDP	: US$3,750 (as of May 1999)
GDP GROWTH RATE (%)	: -4.77 % (as of 2000)
CURRENT ACCOUNT DEFICIT	: -US$ 1.68 billion (Apr.–Jun. 1999)
INFLATION	: 45.4% (Feb.–Apr. 1999)
UNEMPLOYMENT RATE	: 40%
MAJOR NATURAL RESOURCES	: Oil, natural gas, tin, coal, nickel, copper, bauxite, timber, gold, and silver
LEADING INDUSTRIES	: Food and beverages, textiles, apparel, cement, construction, fertilizers, light manufacturing, wood processing, minerals and petroleum production and processing, aircraft, and tourism
MAJOR EXPORTS	: Petroleum products, natural gas, Timber, textiles
MAJOR IMPORTS	: Coconut oil

MAJOR EXPORT : Japan, USA, Singapore, South
   DESTINATIONS   Korea, Taiwan, China, and
                       Germany

MAIN IMPORT COUNTRIES : Japan, USA, Germany, Singapore,
                       South Korea, Taiwan, and
                       China

NATIONAL CURRENCY : Rupiah

EXCHANGE RATE : US$1 = Rp 8,105 (as of 31 May
                       1999)

REPUBLIC OF INDONESIA

Indonesia is an archipelago with about 17,508 islands of which 6,000 are inhabited, laid out from east to west, along the traditional trade routes of China, India, Western Asia, Europe, and North Asia. As such, Indonesia in its early history experienced great cultural contacts which produced many patterns of political organisations. Indonesia has about 1,904,569 square kilometres of land and territorial waters four times that size.

In the first three centuries A.D., Hinduism and Buddhism were brought to the islands by traders and religious groups.[10]

A clearer picture of Indonesian political organisations could be seen from the five major kingdoms in the seventh to ninth centuries, in Java and Sumatra. The Shrivijaya kingdom in South Sumatra on the Straits of Malacca and Sunda was a centre of trade for ships plying China and India and the Arab world. It was also a centre for Buddhist learning. Kingdoms of Shrivijaya type were of naval and commercial nature. Another centre of political power was Central Java where Hindu and Buddhist kingdoms of the eighth and ninth centuries built shrines and monuments such as the Borobudur. These architectural works were possible because of complex governmental organisations and the control of the labour force. Kingdoms in the inland states were of this type, subsisting on rice culture and administered by a quasi-hereditary bureaucracy.

The greatest of the old ancient empires was the Madjapahit empire of the 14th century which had great naval power and ruled over Java, Bali, Madura, Sumatra, Borneo, Celebes, and the Moluccas. Madjapahit's central and military controls later weakened and broke up into local states.

In the 16th century, Islam's political power had grown. In Indonesia where Muslims from Arab countries and India had settled, Islam was adopted by Indonesian nobles and princes first in North Sumatran trade ports. By the 1530s, many rulers in Moluccas and Madjapahit and other states became Muslims. Islam introduced a written code of law. As it penetrated Indonesian religious, cultural, and social life and became the official religion of most kingdoms, it became syncretised with local animism and Hindu beliefs.

European entry into Asia brought the Portuguese to the Moluccas for the spice trade, for the spread of Catholicism and to fight Islam. After the Portuguese, the Dutch came, primarily to trade and monopolise the spice trade. By the 18th century, the Dutch trading company had consolidated its power in Java. The Dutch introduced coffee and sugar cultivation. In its trade, the Dutch used the growing Chinese community causing the indigenous Javanese trade to decline. By 1799, the Netherlands government took over, starting "three hundred and fifty years of colonial rule".[11] In the following years after that French and British (Sir Stamford Raffles) rule were exerted. Upon return to Netherlands rule in 1816 , Indonesia came under the "Culture System" or forced cultivation by every peasant of commercial crop on two-fifths of his land for raising revenue. In Java particularly, many varieties of crops were produced—sugar, coffee, tobacco, tea, indigo, cinnamon, and cotton. The Dutch ruled through the authoritarian features of the local rule and formed the important instruments of colonial power and authority to support commercial crops production.[12] By 1909, Dutch authority was established over almost all of what was Netherlands Indonesia, including West New Guinea.

Towards the end of the 19th century there was humanitarian indignation in the Netherlands due to the declining welfare of the Indonesians. In 1901, the "Ethical Policy" was issued by which the government would play a direct and active role in providing economic welfare, public health, and educational services. Roads and railways were built, forest conservation, soil development, veterinary services, agricultural and fisheries production, and irrigation were expanded.

The Ethical Policy improved some portions of the population which were then labelled as Westernised but they really could not be considered by the resident Dutch nationals as their equals.[13]

Inevitably, there was a growing nationalism which was also anti-Dutch in Indonesia. In 1908, the first nationalist organisation Boedi

Otomo (Noble Endeavour) took a stand for educational, cultural, and economic uplift. Four years after came a political organisation Sarekat Islam (Islamic Association) with a membership of hundreds of thousands and led by the Western-educated groups. But this group had many Marxists and in 1920 they transformed themselves into the Communist Party. The government repressed this movement.

In 1927, a group of students from Bandung led by Soekarno established the Indonesian Nationalist Party (PNI) which demanded complete independence for Indonesia, using self-reliance and non-cooperation with the Dutch. Other associations came up under Hatta and Soetan Sjahrir. Nationalist activities included journalism, social welfare, and education. The leaders were arrested and exiled for these activities in 1933 and 1934. Soekarno, Hatta, and Sjahrir and others were exiled to the outermost islands and were released only with the Japanese occupation in 1942. The Japanese Occupation that lasted until 1945 provided many opportunities, though bitter, for the nationalists to organise, gain experience in public administration, military service, acquire a national language, and to prepare for independence.[14] The nationalist leaders declared independence for Indonesia in 1945 with a constitution containing the State Philosophy of Pantja Sila but fighting against the Dutch continued until 1949. In fact, in 1947 and then in 1948, the Dutch military launched full attacks on Indonesia. In 1949, the Dutch gave independence to Indonesia under international pressure.

The Federal Republic of the United States of Indonesia was proclaimed in 1949 with Soekarno as president. Soon the local states wanted a unitary state. Liberal democracy with a multi-party system made the constitution unoperational. National and local conflicts were all around and the government could hardly function. Finally by 1958, territorial integrity was restored by the government of President Soekarno who denounced liberal democracy as not appropriate for Indonesia as there was too much fighting amongst the parties. In 1959, Soekarno declared a Guided Democracy for Indonesia under the restored 1945 Constitution. The real power however was shared by Soekarno with the military and the Partai Komunis Indonesia (PKI).

Soekarno's government ended in 1965 when the military staged a pre-emptive coup to safeguard the country from falling into the hands of the communists who were then ready to capture power. Soekarno was placed under house arrest. General Suharto became President in 1965.

In 1999, Suharto was forced to resign in light of charges of scandals. Abdurrahman Wahid was elected by the MPR as President. Then Wahid was replaced by President Megawati Sukarnoputri.

Indonesia has the biggest population in Southeast Asia and the most experience in multi-party system. This is because of the pluralist society arising from ethnic loyalties, forced migrations, numerous guerilla bands, mass organisations (of villagers), diverse religious groups, and others.

New instruments for social integration were available especially in the period 1949-1958. One was education, especially Western education for the leaders who had to work for material and social progress and for spreading national awareness. Illiteracy was cut down as more secondary schools and universities were established. Education brought prestige and occupational and social mobility.

Other means for integration were the political parties and *alirans* (stream), women, youth, veterans, labour, religious, cooperative, sports, and other groups which organised the people. Unions reached down to the village levels with encouragement from the government.[15] To be with an association was to be modern or nationalist at that time. Not to be overlooked was the military by which the members pledged loyalty to a single nation. Most of all, the Pantja Sila as the state philosophy kept the organisations focused on the state.[16] In later years, government abandoned its attempts to achieve social integration on a pluralistic basis. In its place was now the expansion of the government's role.

The military has a dual role (*dwifungsi*) in Indonesia. Because the military had its origin in the Japanese Occupation, the leaders perceive the military as the chief founder of independence and must protect it by a right to help determine the direction of the policy of the state. Military officers have held high positions in the civil service and in the cabinet and it was seen that the power of the military over civilian affairs had grown.

COUNTRY PROFILE OF THE LAO PEOPLE'S DEMOCRATIC REPUBLIC

OFFICIAL NAME : Lao People's Democratic Republic
GOVERNMENT : Socialist Republic
HEAD OF STATE : President Khamtay Siphandone
HEAD OF GOVERNMENT : Prime Minister Sisavath Kheobounphanh
CAPITAL : Vientiane
NATIONAL DAY : 2 December 1975
LANGUAGES : Lao (official), French and English
MONETARY UNIT : Kip
LAND AREA : 236,800 square kilometres
POPULATION : 5.433 million (estimated)
POPULATION GROWTH : 2.9%
POPULATION DISTRIBUTION : 22% (urban) 78% (rural)
ETHNIC GROUPS : Lao 48%, Mon-Khmer tribes 25%, Thai 14%, Hmong and Yao 13% and others
ETHNICITY : The Lao population is ethnically diverse with up to 68 different ethnic groups identified inhabiting the country, with various languages, cultures and traditions which are classified into three groups: the Lao Loum, who occupy the lowlands, plains and the Mekong River Valley, and constitute about 56% of the total population; the Lao Theung, who occupy the mountain slopes, comprising about 34% of the population, and the high mountain Lao, constituting about 9% of the total population, and 1% foreigners.
RELIGIOUS GROUP : 58% Buddhist, 34% tribal

47

LIFE EXPECTANCY	:	53
ADULT LITERACY RATE	:	56.6 percent
GDP GROWTH RATE	:	5.75 percent
PER CAPITA GDP (PPP)	:	$712
PER CAPITA GNP (NOM)	:	$370
EXCHANGE RATE	:	US$1 = Kip 4,155
INFLATION	:	90.0%
EXPORTS (12 MONTHS)	:	$0.3b
CURRENCY ACCOUNT BALANCE	:	-$0.3b
RESERVES (EXCLUDING GOLD)	:	$0.1b
GDP (PPP)	:	$7.0b
MAJOR EXPORTS	:	hydropower, forest products, tin concentrates, coffee, gypsum, cardamom, rattan, clothing and textile
MAJOR IMPORTS	:	rice, foodstuffs, petroleum products, machinery and transport equipment
MAJOR TRADE PARTNERS	:	Japan, USA, Singapore, Taiwan, Australia, Germany, South Korea, China, France, and UK

Note: Figures as of May 1999.

LAO PEOPLE'S DEMOCRATIC REPUBLIC

Situated in the Indochina Peninsula, the Lao People's Democratic Republic (LPDR) extends from north to south for almost 700 miles and in width about an average of 150 to 200 miles. Being a landlocked country of about 91,000 square miles, its waterways are the rivers that flow from the mountain chain separating Laos and Vietnam westward into the Mekong River which then is the communication link between north and south Laos and is also the border of Laos with Thailand. On the north and northwest, China and Burma form its borders, and in the south, Cambodia shares the border with Laos.[17]

About one-half of the population of Laos is from the Lao branch of the Thai population (generically referring to the peoples originating in South China and now found in the northern portions of Southeast

48

Asia). The Lao Loum constitute about 56% of the population and are the plains and river-valley dwellers. They cultivate lowland rice. There are about 68 different ethnic groups and tribes who form the rest of the population (40% of the population) and live in the mountainous regions. Among these are the Meo, Yao, Kha, and Black Thai. There are small groups of Chinese, Vietnamese, and Indians. Adult literacy rate is quite low, 58% of the people are Buddhists and 34% are tribal religious groups.

The early history of Laos is traced to the 12th century kingdom of Muong Swa in the northern part now known as Luang Prabang province. From that period the Lao moved southward into Khmer territory, meeting little resistance as the Khmer Empire seated at Angkor had waned before the growing power of the Sukhothai Kingdom of Thailand. The Lao movement to the south led to the establishment of the principalities of Xieng Khouang, Vientiane, and Champassak, which in modern times for the latter two, became seats of royal Lao families also.

Around 1340, Phaya Fa Ngum overthrew his grandfather at Muong Swa and conquered the three Lao southern principalities, establishing the kingdom of Lan Xang, which at its height extended from China to the northeastern part of present Cambodia and from the Aunamese mountain range to Korat in Thailand, beyond the Mekong River.

In the 15th and 16th centuries, problems over succession to the throne, with interferences from Annam and Siam upon the death of Souligna Vongsa in 1694, led to the break up of Lan Xang into the separate kingdoms of Luang Prabang, Vientiane, and Champassak.

Due to interfamilial quarrels, the country weakened and was conquered by Siam Burma, and Annam. Then Siam became the sole suzerain over the territory of former Lang Xang and brought thousands of people to Siam but Vientiane was ruled directly by Siam.

Between 1858 and 1880, France colonised Cochinchina, Cambodia, Annam, and Tongkin. Soon France conquered Laos to protect French interests from Siamese threats and to match Great Britain's routes to China. Agreements in Europe led to a treaty of October 3, 1893 whereby Siam renounced all rights to territory in the east bank of the Mekong, one of the arbitrary lines drawn by Europeans in Southeast Asia. Laotians lived in the west bank so this was corrected in 1902 by France and Siam giving Sayaboury and Champassak back to Laos. During the Japanese Occupation from 1941 these were ceded again to Siam.

France ruled Laos as an administrative unit within the Indochinese Union but the French respected Laotian administrative units as the preceding Siamese rulers did. More than this, France either neglected the development of Laos or tried to preserve the culture from the corruption of modern civilisation.

By 1945, Japan demanded that King Sisavang Vong declare independence from France and cooperate with Japan. The king vacillated. With Japan's defeat in 1945, the four sons of the King took separate ways. Prince Phetsarath sought to put up the Lao Issara, Prince Souphannouvong joined the Viet Minh and supported the Pathet Lao to remove French control but was later known to be under Ho Chi Minh's communist movement. Prince Souvannarath led the autonomy of Laos under the French Union. In 1954, the Geneva Agreements provided for the cessation of all military actions and the establishment of a coalition government and elections for unification in 1955. Prince Souvannaphouma became prime minister of the Royal Lao Government (RLG).

From 1958 to 1973, in spite of the Geneva Accords guarantee of neutrality for Laos, all major powers interfered in the politics of the country. North Vietnam as the base of the communist Pathet Lao, Communist China, United States, France, and the Soviet Union put up development projects in Laos to influence the politics of the country. On the side, Thailand and South Vietnam pressured the US to make moves to protect their security, causing the RLG to lean on the US more and more, leading to the total breakdown of the guaranteed neutrality of Laos.

In 1973, the US negotiated for the Paris Peace Treaty when it withdrew its military from Laos, Cambodia, and Vietnam. By 1975, all the three states had communist party rule. In Laos, Prince Souphannouvong installed the Lao People's Democratic Republic (LPDR) which is the present government. In 1975, the King and Prince Souvannaphouma were made advisers to LPDR President Souphannouvong until they passed away of old age.

The Lao People's Revolutionary Party (LPRP) or the Pathet Lao was in fraternal relations with the Communist Party of Vietnam which maintained a flexible hegemony over Laos. By 1986, Mikhail Gorbachev of the Soviet Union announced his Asian Policy and recognised Laos and Cambodia as separate from Vietnam. Without anymore aid from Soviet Union, Vietnam could no longer sustain its control over Laos. This country had earlier revised its Marxist economy in 1981, even before Gorbachev had announced his *glasnost* and *perestroika* policies in 1986, to adopt capitalist market principles since the planned economy was found to be not appropriate for the country.

By 1990s, Laos was turning to ASEAN for its foreign relations. In 1992, Laos acceded to the Treaty of Amity and Cooperation in Southeast Asia (TAC) and in 1997 became a member of ASEAN.

Laos' population has increased from about two million in the 1960s to an estimated five million in 1999 although there was never any accurate census due to the country's geography which made transport difficult to reach all parts of Laos. Education, economy, government, and weak institutions render Laos vulnerable to all kinds of pressures, including the so-called modernisation, illegal drug trade, foreign investments and the accompanying cultures that will certainly break down the traditions and customs that provide the sinews to bind the people.

The main export of Laos is hydroelectric power from the Nam Ngum Dam and other Mekong River Development Projects.

COUNTRY PROFILE OF MALAYSIA

OFFICIAL NAME : Federation of Malaysia
CAPITAL : Kuala Lumpur
NATIONAL DAY : 31 July
LAND AREA : 332,370 sq. km.
LOCATION : Malaysia is located just north of the equator and right in the heart of Southeast Asia. Its northern neighbours include Thailand, Myanmar, Laos, Cambodia, and Vietnam, while in the South, there are Singapore and Indonesia, and in the east, the Philippines
FORM OF GOVERNMENT : Federated Constitutional Monarchy
HEAD OF STATE : H.M. Sultan Salahuddin Abdul Aziz Shah Alhaj Ibni Al-Marhum Sultan Hishamuddin Alam Shah Alhaj (as of 25 April 1999)
HEAD OF GOVERNMENT : H.E. Datuk Seri Dr. Mahathir bin Mohamad Prime Minister
NATIONAL LEGISLATURE : Bicameral Federal Parliament
POPULATION : 22.244 million
RELIGION : Islam (official) 53% Buddhist – 17%, Chinese Folk Religions – 12%, Hindu – 7% Christian – 6 %
LANGUAGES : Malay (official), Chinese, Tamil, English
LITERACY RATE : 78.5%
GDP : US $89.321 million
GDP PER CAPITA : US $3,956
REAL GDP GROWTH RATE : -1.8%
INFLATION : 5.4%
UNEMPLOYMENT RATE : 2.8%
CURRENCY/EXCHANGE RATE : US $1 = 3.80 Ringgit (as of 29 January 1999)

MALAYSIA

Accounts on the early history of Malaysia are not clear. The accepted beliefs say that the earliest organised political states were first known in the northern part of the Malay Peninsula. By about 900 A.D. some of these states may have come under the influence of the Sri Vijaya Empire in Palembang. At the end of the 13th century the Javanese Madjapahit and the Thai Empires had succeeded the Sri Vijayan dominance.

A clearer picture of the history emerged by the 14th century. The Melaka Empire which marked the golden age of Malay political power was converted to Islam which had by then spread to Southeast Asia. Islam is truly one of the major external influence which has greatly changed the principal features of the Malay society.

In 1511 Melaka was captured by the Portuguese which had started the European incursions. In 1641 Melaka fell to the Dutch. In late 18th century, British commercial interests from India extended to Pulau Pinang which had been acquired by the British in 1786 from the Sultan of Kedah. In 1819, the British acquired Singapore from the Sultan of Johore. In 1824, Britain exchanged Bencoolen in Sumatra for Melaka from the Dutch. In 1826 Pulau Pinang, Melaka, and Singapore became the Straits Settlements. By the beginning of the 19th century the economic invasion of the Peninsula began with the inflow of capital and of Chinese to work in the tin mines. In 1910 the introduction of the rubber industry brought the Indian migrants to Malaya. By 1874 by the Pangkor Agreement, the British instituted radical changes in the political, social, and economic fields. In 1895, several states were combined to form the Federated Malay States (FMS). In 1914 Johore formed the Unfederated Malay States with the other states.

In 1888 the British succeeded to put together the ceded territories from Brunei, and Sulu, consisting of Sarawak, Brunei, and North Borneo (Sabah) to become British protectorates.[18]

Japan occupied Malaya and the Borneo Territories from 1941 to 1945 when Japan's surrender to the Allied Powers ended the war. The Japanese Occupation period deepened the nationalist and anti-colonialist stirrings in Malaya which had started before the Second World War. The lead was assumed by the United Malays National Organisation (UMNO) from 1946 until Malaya's final independence in 1957. The Alliance Party composed of the UMNO, the Malayan

Chinese Association (MCA) and the Malayan Indian Congress (MIC) had been in the majority until, with the addition of more political parties, the National Front (Barisan Nasional) won a landslide victory in the 1974 elections.

At the height of the Communist military terrorism all over the world, Malaya experienced a communist campaign of violence and murder to paralyse the country's economy. A state of Emergency was declared. It was lifted after 12 years, in 1960.

Malaysia was established on September 16, 1963 by the collectivity of Malaya, Singapore, Sarawak, and North Borneo (Sabah) in accordance with the proposal of then Prime Minister Tunku Abdul Rahman and British officials. Indonesia objected to the concept of Malaysia which left the protection of security to Britain, calling the plan neo-colonialist. Indonesia launched a confrontation, sending armed men to Malaya.

The Philippines objected to the inclusion of Sabah in Malaysia because Sabah was claimed to be a Philippines territory that was merely on lease to the British rulers of North Borneo. The Philippines called for the formation of MAPHILINDO, a confederation of Malay states in 1963 wherein problems could be solved. While in process, Indonesia's government was replaced by one headed by General Suharto in 1965. Indonesia then sent its Foreign Minister Adam Malik to the governments of Southeast Asia to present a new image of the country. While on these trips, the concept of ASEAN was born.

Diplomatic relations between Indonesia and Malaysia were resumed on 31 August 1967. Between Malaysia and the Philippines, relations were normalised on 3 June 1966. Meanwhile, due to political problems in Malaysia, Singapore broke off and declared its independence on 19 August 1965.

Malaysia is a member of the UN, ASEAN, APEC, the Non-Aligned Movement (NAM) and the organisation of Islamic Congress (OIC), among others.

Malaysia has a population of about 21.9 million people (1998) composed of Malays who are nearly as large as the Chinese in number, and then the Indians who are much less than either of them in a land of 332,370 square kilometres. There are small groups of foreigners such as the Europeans, Japanese, and others. In 1961 Malaya had a problem of communalism during which there were breakouts between the Malays and the Chinese. The UMNO took several steps to prevent the escalation of the riots. Because the Chinese were the economically dominant group, the government undertook to redistribute social and political power and economic holdings through the Bumiputra policies to protect the Malays by giving them more opportunities to participate fully in the economy.

The official religion in Malaysia is Islam, 58% are Muslims, 17% are Buddhists, 12% are with Chinese folk religions, Hindus are 7% and Christians are 6%. The official language is Malay but English is now widely spoken.

COUNTRY PROFILE OF THE UNION OF MYANMAR (as of 29 June 1999)

OFFICIAL NAME	: Union of Myanmar
NATIONAL CAPITAL	: Yangon
INDEPENDENCE DAY	: 4 January 1948
TYPE OF GOVERNMENT	: Military Council (On 15 November 1997, the State Law and Order Restoration Council was dissolved and was replaced by the State Peace and Development Council)
INCUMBENT HEAD OF STATE/ GOVERNMENT	: Senior General Than Shwe, Chairman of the State Peace and Development Council and Prime Minister
LOCATION	: Myanmar is situated in Southeast Asia and is bordered on the north and northeast by China, on the east and southeast by Laos and Thailand, on the south by the Andaman Sea and Bay of Bengal and on the west by Bangladesh and India.
SIZE OF TERRITORY	: 678,576 square kilometres
POPULATION	: 48.8 million (May 1999)
POPULATION GROWTH RATE	: 2.1% (May 1999)
LANGUAGES	: Burmese, English
RELIGION	: Buddhism (89.4%); Christianity (4.9%) Islam (3.8%); Hinduism (0.05%); Animism (1.3%)
GDP/PPP (US$)	: $37 billion (May 1999)
GDP/P.C. (US$)	: $790 (May 1999)
GDP GROWTH RATE (%)	: 5.0% (May 1999)
GNP PER CAPITA	: $765 (May 1999)

MAJOR NATURAL RESOURCES	: Timber, metals (gold, zinc, copper) tin, antimony, precious and semi-precious stones, crude oil and natural gas
LEADING INDUSTRIES	: Agriculture, forestry, mining, gems and jewelry
MAJOR EXPORTS (1997)	: Pulses and beans, prawns, rubber, marine products, and forest products
MAJOR IMPORTS (1997)	: Machinery and transport equipment, base metals and manufactures, electrical machinery, edible oils, and cement
MAJOR TRADING PARTNERS (1996)	: Singapore, China, Thailand, Japan, India
NATIONAL CURRENCY	: Kyat
EXCHANGE RATE	: US$1.00 = Kyats 6/6.2 official rate) = K800 (free market rate as of 2003)
FOREIGN CURRENCY RESERVES	: $0.3 billion (May 1999)

UNION OF MYANMAR

The geographical profile of Myanmar provided much influence on the early history of Burma as it was then known. North-south rivers, valleys, and mountains attracted population settlements and provided communications. The lowlands and the mountains influenced the development of political subdivisions. Thus, the lowlands which were watered by the Irrawaddy and the Chindwin Rivers and protected by the mountains on three sides became the political and economic centre and this is where Burma proper is today. The mountain region did not attract much population and deterred merchants and would-be invaders and produced a culture of isolation. In any case, Indian traders came to Burma by way of the sea.[19]

The pre-colonial history of Burma was of continuous struggles among four indigenous groups: the Burmans, the Mons or Talaings, the Shans, and the Arakanese, and between the peoples of Burma and their neighbouring states.

There were three periods of political unification before the colonial period. In the 11th century, the Burmese kings established an empire that lasted for 200 years. The Pagan dynasty was the golden age and its capital city Pagan bears the Indian-influenced Burmese culture. In 1287, the armies of Kublai Khan destroyed the empire.

In the 16th century another unification occurred, now under the Toungoo Kings who brought the neighbouring territories under their rule in the area much like in the present Burma. By the 17th century this dynasty was weakened by quarrels and it collapsed.[20]

A third dynasty came up in the 18th century in the north. It conquered the Kingdom of Arakan and engaged in foreign wars, until Burma made contact with British power in India and a war of two years was ended by the Treaty of Yandabo in 1826. By 1852 that part of Burma was annexed by Britain.

On 1 January 1886 in a precipitated war the Burmese King was captured and all of Burma was then annexed by Britain.

British rule from 1826 destroyed the traditional patterns of authority in Burma. By the introduction of British law and order, Burma was changed into a commercial granary as the world's biggest rice exporter. With it came tenancy, money lending and land alienation. Western concepts of government destroyed the traditional patterns of authority by placing salaried officials who anyway could not make people obey the laws. The British brought in Indian labourers and capitalists, in the process of displacing the Burmese landowners who became mere tenants to new Indian landowners. Buddhist monks lost their authority with the abolition of the monarchy and the opening of English schools. The social order was chaotic, exploding into violent communal riots in the 1930s.[21]

British promise of self-rule to India in 1917 was interpreted disappointingly by the Burmese as applicable to their country because Burma then had become a province of India. By 1917-1918 the first widespread political protest in Burma was started by the non-political Young Men's Buddhist Association (YMBA) and was soon transformed into a political one under the General Council of Burmese Associates (GCBA). In 1920 the University students protested the educational plan for a new university.

In 1921 the British started to give self-government to Burma. After 1928, Burma was separated from India and was given a new constitution in 1937, a parliament, and a cabinet government. The British retained control over the indigenous minorities like the Shans, Chins, Kachins, and Karens. The society's division grew.

Japan's occupation of Burma during the Second World War ended British rule. Japan trained the Thirty Heroes who were supposed to lead the Burmese Independence Army against the British but on 27 March 1945 this National Army revolted against the Japanese and joined the Allied forces. During the War, Japan gave Burma its independence and a government under Dr. Ba Maw from which the Burmese gained much experience of self-rule. A resistance movement, the Anti-Fascist People's Freedom League (AFPFL) later worked for independence from Britain under one of its Thirty Heroes, Gen. Aung San who was assassinated on the eve of independence.

Burma became independent on 4 January 1948. Soon problems arose to disrupt the unions. There were three groups that took to arms for their respective goals. The communists were of two loyalties, to China and to the Soviet Union; the People's Volunteer Organisation shifted from the AFPFL to the communists, and the Karen National Defence Organisation and other tribes who rebelled against the government. Only the leadership of U Nu and a new army led the state until 1958. But more problems came. On 2 March 1962 General New Win and the army staged a coup. The New Revolutionary Council of Seventeen held all the power to institute reforms which for a long period changed the structure of the government giving it also a philosophy, "Burmese Way to Socialism" by which the country was brought to a moral life.

By year 2003, Myanmar, the new name of Burma, is still to make a constitution. The military does not want to recognise the victory of the National League for Democracy (NLD) under Aung San Suu Kyi in 1990 and has kept her in close restraint. The NLD on the other hand does not agree to the principles of the proposed new constitution, especially its principle for a dominant role of the military. The State Law and Order Restoration Council (SLORC) has become the State Peace and Development Council (SPDC) which is still in the process of making a constitution.

Myanmar has approximately 261,600 square miles (678,576 square kilometres) of rich land, good amount of rain and a lot of natural resources such as teak wood, petroleum, tin, and precious stones. Besides having been the world's largest rice exporter, Myanmar has sufficient food for its people. Other industries include textiles, chemicals, and wood products.

The north-south river systems of the Salween, Irrawaddy, and Chindwin became the backbone of the transport system on which the Burmese and later the British built lateral jungle paths and modern roads.

Myanmar's population of about 48.8 million (1999) consists of the indigenous plains and hill ethnic groups such as the Burmans, Arakanese, Karens, Shans, Mons, Kachins, and Chins, and the aliens descended from the Indians and Chinese who were brought in by the British colonisers to develop the country economically, and from some Europeans.

Buddhism is the main religion (89.4%) but there are some people who adhere to Islam, Hinduism, or Christianity.

Education is good, a high percentage is highly literate and people can read and write in English and local languages.

The quest for national unity has been a problem even before the British came. The Shans and Kayahs were given the right to secede in 1958 but the Union government tried various means to convince the ethnic leaders to surrender their powers to the state but dissatisfaction led to many rebellions. By 1999, the SPDC had working relations with at least 16 ethnic local groups. However, new problems had come up such as constitutionalism, unity, economic productivity, education, science and technology.

Whereas since 1948 Burma had adopted a policy of neutralism in world affairs, in 1997 Burma which has been renamed Myanmar became a member of ASEAN and has been participating in all its activities. In the case of ASEAN relations with Europe, a problem has arisen regarding the rejection by European states of Myanmar's policy on human rights. But it is now a member of ASEAN which acts as a whole and Myanmar should be accepted by the European states.

One foreign policy problem is Myanmar's relations with China whose people enter Myanmar along with smuggled goods. Strategically, China needs a forward base near the Indian Ocean which is the passage way to the South China Sea where the islands are being claimed by competing states. China supports Pakistan as a reserve in case of conflict with India, the latter having a standing dispute with Pakistan over territories and religion. All three states possess nuclear arms power and are never hesitant to announce its use. Myanmar's relations with India were not good for some time due to historical experiences. Since General Ne Win's rule, Burma sought neutralist positions among its neighbours to prevent disputes from escalating. On the eastern side, Myanmar needs to have good relations with Thailand which were difficult to have since the Burmese attack on Ayuthya. In later times, the Karens and other indigenous peoples from Myanmar had crossed the Salween River to Thailand when the SLORC took punitive actions against them. Thailand's policy is always to have a congenial environment so the two states have come to terms. Myanmar asserted independent policies in the United Nations. Myanmar has excellent relations with Israel which enjoys a very high reputation in that country and with other countries. Myanmar has also balanced its relations by developing better ties with India.

COUNTRY PROFILE OF THE REPUBLIC OF
THE PHILIPPINES (as of 2003)

OFFICIAL NAME : Republic of the Philippines

CAPITAL : Manila

NATIONAL DAY : June 12

SIZE OF TERRITORY : 115,600 square miles
or 300,000 sq. km.

GEOGRAPHY : 7,101 islands, Luzon Visayas and
Mindanao being the three
major groups. The islands are
located west of the continent
of Southeast Asia, astride the
China Sea and the Pacific
Ocean

TYPE OF GOVERNMENT : Republic, Presidential type, with
separation of powers of the
Executive, Legislative and
Judiciary but with checks and
balance

PRESIDENT : Gloria Macapagal Arroyo

SYSTEM OF GOVERNMENT : Under the Constitution,
sovereignty resides in the
people. There are three
branches of government with
decentralisation of power to
the local governments Officials
are directly elected except for
the bureaucracy and the
judiciary

POPULATION : 80 million, rounded off

RELIGION : 85% Christian, 12% Muslim,
3% others

LANGUAGES : Filipino and English are official
languages. There are about 70
major languages and 300
dialects

LITERACY RATE : 85%

GROWTH RATE	: 2.3%
GDP GROWTH RATE	: 3.8%
GNP PER CAPITA	: 4.5%
MAJOR INDUSTRIES	: Agriculture, fisheries, mining (gold, nickel), handicrafts, food processing, microsoft and light manufacturing, soft drinks, textiles, services
NATIONAL CURRENCY	: Peso (P53 = US$1.00)
INFLATION	: 7%

THE PHILIPPINES

The islands in the Philippine archipelago were ruled by sultans of Mindanao and datus in many places in Luzon and the Visayan islands before 1521. The Philippines as a group of islands was already known to Chinese geographers, scholars, and traders as well as to Arab and Indian traders and missionaries who came by way of the Indian Ocean. In fact the Chinese, Japanese, and Arabs had already settled in some of the islands as well as in Manila, then the existing trading port. Trading was carried out by barter. Archaeological finds show fine porcelain ware, coins, and jewellery that were acquired by the people in the Philippine islands from the trade before 1521.

In 1521 a Portuguese sailor, Ferdinand Magellan, who sailed under the Spanish flag arrived in an island in the Visayas group and this was called by Spain the discovery of the Philippines. The Spanish government sent military, administrative, and religious men to subdue the people "by sword and by the cross". Through harsh rule by the military, political officials and priests, Spain was able to conquer many parts of the Philippines, but not Mindanao where the Muslims had retained their sovereignty. The Spaniards under Legazpi arrived in Manila in 1572 and dislodged Datu Soliman from power. Spain called the islands the Philippine Islands, after King Philip of Spain.

Spain's rule was not easy. There were hundreds of revolts by the freedom-loving people who were not used to foreign rule and who did their own travel, trade, marriage, rulership and life in general in customary ways. The Filipinos were landowners but they were dispossessed by the Spaniards who also established business monopolies.

63

From the 1600s up to 1896, the Filipinos fought the Spaniards wherever possible. In the earlier centuries, the rebellions were scattered but were quite strong. By the 18th and 19th centuries, the Filipinos had started to organise themselves. While there were rich Filipinos who had gone on for college education in schools that had been established in the Philippines by Spain, such as the University of Santo Tomas which was set up in 1608, some went to Europe where they imbibed libertarian principles. Still it was not sure whether the leaders were for an armed revolution or for reforms like representation in the Spanish Cortez. But the aspirations for freedom were expressed in paintings that won awards in Europe, in newspapers, in organisations, in poetry, in dramas, in novels, and in other forms. Before 1872, even the Filipino priests were calling for secularisation of the church due to the tyrannical practices of the Spanish priests. In 1872 Spanish officials killed three Filipino priests, Fathers Gomez, Burgos, and Zamora and other youth leaders. It was only in 1890 that new leaders arose. They were those who studied in Europe, young professionals who were willing to trade their professions for martyrdom for their country's independence. There were also leaders among the poor people, who though unschooled, were not illiterate for they read the writings of the educated. There were rich people who supported the cause and there were women who became heroines in their own right during those revolutionary years.

The confluence of all the calls for independence may have produced the best from everyone, such that the period of the 1890s may be called the Golden Age of the Philippines.

Dr. Jose P. Rizal was the leading light as he had written among many others, two novels which are now classics, depicting the problems created by Spain in the Philippines as the Social Cancer. His two novels were translated into Malay and read widely in Southeast Asia by nationalist youths. His "Last Farewell" written on the eve of his death by Spanish musketry before the public has been translated into many European and Asian languages and acclaimed by all. Rizal is called the Renaissance Man by no less than Malaysian and Indonesian leaders.

Other leaders were "brains" of the Katipunan, the secret society which triggered the final revolution in 1896, "brains" of the military, "brains" of the government, etc.

The revolutionaries had nearly succeeded in freeing the most important areas of the country and had in fact set up a civil constitutional government under President Emilio Aguinaldo, when Spain and the US came to conflict or war over Cuba. To outflank Spain, the US sent its ships to Manila Bay and demanded Spain's surrender. The US officials dealt with President Aguinaldo to get assistance in exchange for independence. This promise was unfulfilled. War between the American and Filipino soldiers continued even after the Treaty of Paris by which the US bought the Philippines from Spain. The Philippine-American War which was called by the US an "insurgency" continued until the surrender of President Aguinaldo. Then the US "pacified" the country, decided to make it a colony as the "White Man's Burden," and set up a civil government.

To the credit of the US, it gave local government, education, built roads, hospitals and public health, and gave participation to Filipino leaders at the national level as in the Departments of Interior and Justice and in Congress.

By 1935 US gave self-government to the Philippines through the Commonwealth Government under President Manuel L. Quezon with a promise of independence ten years after. But the Japanese Occupation from 1941 to 1945 seemed to set back the promise. Under instructions from Quezon, President Laurel and his officials tried to protect the people form Japanese brutality by all forms of actions, thereby honing their leadership under the direst conditions. By the end of the Second World War, the US proclaimed Philippine independence on 4 July 1946 but failed to indict the Filipino leaders under Japanese Occupation as collaborators. Since then the Philippines has been ruled by constitutional processes except during the Martial Law regime under President Ferdinand E. Marcos from 1972 to 1986.

The Philippines has had an active foreign policy. It is an original member of the United Nations, attended many conferences held to set up regional cooperation in Asia, aand is now a member of ASEAN, APEC, the Non-Aligned Nations (NAM), and other organisations that promote human rights, environmental protection and other worthy causes.

The Philippines had about 80 million people in 2003. Eighty-five per cent (85%) of the population are Christians and 12 per cent Muslims, both major religions. The country has agricultural and fisheries resources, minerals such as gold and iron, and handicrafts. The people are highly skilled as technicians and as professionals. Education among the people is a passion. Filipino and English are widely spoken while Spanish is still used. Literary is at 85%.

COUNTRY PROFILE OF THE REPUBLIC OF SINGAPORE

OFFICIAL NAME	: Republic of Singapore[22]
DATE OF INDEPENDENCE	: August 9, 1965
CAPITAL	: Singapore City
LAND AREA	: 648 sq. km.
POPULATION	: 3.8 million (as of May 1999)
LANGUAGES	: English, Chinese, Malay, Tamil
TYPE OF GOVERNMENT	: Republic, with a parliamentary system of government
HEAD OF STATE	: President S. R. Nathan
HEAD OF GOVERNMENT	: Prime Minister Goh Chok Tong
GDP (PPP)	: $88 Billion (as of 31 December 1998)
GDP/PER CAPITA	: US $28,235.00 (as of May 1999)
GDP GROWTH	: 1.2% (as of May 1999)
PER CAPITA GNP (NOM)	: $31,900.00
INFLATION	: -0.6% (as of May 1999)
UNEMPLOYMENT RATE	: 2.3% (as of 31 December 1998)
EXCHANGE RATE	: Singapore $1.00 = US$1.72 (as of May 1999)

SINGAPORE

Singapore was called by various names in its early history. A Chinese account in the third century referred to Singapore as Polouchung or island at the end of a peninsula. Around 1330, a visitor from China, Wang Dayuan, called the main settlement Pancur (spring). Singapore was also called Temasek or Sea Town by the Javanese account of 1365. In the 14th century, Singapura (Lion City in Sanskrit) was commonly used.

By the end of the 14th century, the struggle between Siam and the Madjapahit Empire of Java for control of the Malay Peninsula exerted pressures on Singapore. According to the *Sajarah Melayu* (Malay Annals), Singapore was defeated in a Madjapahit attack but Iskandar Shah Parameswara, a prince of Palembang, killed the local chieftain and installed himself as the ruler. He was soon driven out by either the Siamese or Madjapahit forces and he fled to Muar in the Malay Peninsula where he founded the Malacca Sultanate of which Singapore remained an important part for some time.

By the second half of the 18th century, the British had established dominion over India and had developed expanded trade with China, therewith needing a port-of-call in the region to protect their merchant fleet and to protect itself against any attack from the Dutch in the East Indies.

On 29 January 1819, Sir Stamford Raffles arrived in Singapore. The next day he signed a preliminary treaty with Temenggong Abdur Rahman to set up a trading port there. On 6 February 1819, a formal treaty was concluded between Sultan Hussein of Johore and the Temenggong. As a trading port, Singapore prospered and by 1823 its trade was better than Penang's. In 1924, Singapore formally became a British possession by two new treaties – one with the Dutch and another with the Sultan and the Temenggong.

In 1826, Singapore together with Malacca and Penang became the Straits Settlements under the control of the British. On 11 April 1867, the Straits Settlement became a Crown Colony under the Colonial Office in London.

With the coming of the steamships and the opening of the Suez Canal by mid 1860s, Singapore became a major port of call between Europe and East Asia. Then rubber became a prime produce and rubber planting was extensively done. Singapore became the world's best sorting and exporting centre of rubber. Singapore rapidly became prosperous by 1873, ending only with the Japanese Occupation from 15 February 1942 to the end of the war, in August 1945.

After the Second World War, Singapore became by itself a Crown Colony, while Penang and Malacca became parts of the Federation of Malaya.

In 1948, the Communist Party of Malaya (MCP) tried to take over Malaya and Singapore. A state of Emergency was declared that lasted for 12 years.

In 1955 the first election by over 300,000 voters for its legislature was held as a measure of self-government. The Labour Front won and its leader David Marshall became Singapore's first Chief Minister. His Labour Front formed a coalition with the United Malays National Organisation and the Malayan Chinese Association.

The efforts for full internal self-government led to the Constitutional Agreement of 29 May 1958. In May 1959 the first general election for the first fully elected legislative assembly was held. The People's Action Party (PAP) won and the first Government of Singapore was sworn in with Lee Kuan Yew as its first Prime Minister on 5 June 1959.

The PAP came to power with the communists on the issue of fighting British colonialism but the communists had another agenda, which was to take control of the government. Tension between the two parties led to a break-up and the communists separated from the PAP and formed the Barisan Socialis. The Malayans, on the other hand, agreed to Singapore's merger with Malaya.

The people in Singapore agreed to be a part of the Federation of Malaysia in 1963 to include Sarawak, North Borneo (Sabah), and Brunei. Brunei refused to be a member. Malaysia was proclaimed on 16 September 1963. Singapore was crucial to Malaysia as it was like a communist dagger to it. Merger would allow Malaysia to control the situation. On the increase in the Chinese population in Malaysia in light of the communalism problem, the Malayan population of Sarawak and North Borneo could offset the Chinese dominance.

However, it was this communalist party politics that produced a threat to Malaysia. So on 9 August 1965, Singapore was removed from the Federation. Singapore became an independent nation. On 21 September 1965, it became a member of the United Nations. On 22 December 1965, Singapore became a Republic with Yusof bin Ishak as the first President. Singapore adopted a policy of survival in terms of its being the world's best trading port. Singapore also launched strategies to create a national identity and national consciousness to make people transcend their local loyalties and focus their loyalty to the Republic. Singaporeans are largely descendants of immigrants from the Malay Peninsula, China, and India.

Singapore has become Southeast Asia's most prosperous state. The people have proved to be disciplined and most trustworthy. Prime Minister Lee Kuan Yew stepped down in November 1990 in favour of Goh Chok Tong with Lee becoming a Senior Minister. In 1993, Singapore had its first elected President.

Singapore is an original member of ASEAN and is a member of the United Nations, APEC and the Non-Aligned Movement (NAM).

Singapore is an island state of about 648 square kilometres.

Singapore has 3,865,000 people as of 1998. There are three racial groups. The Chinese with 2,435,000 or 77 per cent of the population;

the Malays with 444,900 or 14 per cent, land the Indians with 239,700 or 7.6 per cent. The first Chinese immigrants came from Riau and Malacca and were followed by the Chinese from the mainland by the first junk that arrived. The Malays came from the Malay Peninsula. The Indians came from Penang and Malacca. Other people are the Europeans who came as professionals and the Arabs who came as traders.

The official languages are Malay, Chinese, Tamil and English. The racial groups are allowed to practise their respective religions. Literacy is over 93.1 per cent.

The standard of living is high.

COUNTRY PROFILE OF THAILAND

CAPITAL : Bangkok
LAND AREA : 513,115 square kilometres
POPULATION : 61.7 million
LANGUAGE : Thai, English, Chinese
RELIGION : Buddhism, Islam, Christianity, Hindu
GDP PER CAPITA (PPP) : $6,795
GDP GROWTH RATE : 4.31%
GNP PER CAPITA (NOM) : $2,450
GDP (PPP) : $412 billion
INFLATION : 0.4%
NOTE: figures as of May 1999
FORM OF GOVERNMENT : Constitutional Monarchy
HEAD OF STATE : King Bhumibol Adulyadej (Rama IX)
HEAD OF GOVERNMENT : Prime Minister Thaksin Shinawatra

KINGDOM OF THAILAND

Thai kingdoms played important roles in the politics of Southeast Asia for centuries. The Sukkothai, Ayuttha and the earliest years of the Bangkok Kingdoms controlled territories at different times from Burma to Malaya, Laos, and Cambodia.[23]

The present Chakkri dynasty started in 1782 with a general who helped the king after the defeat of the Ayutthya kingdom by the Burmese in 1767. In the kingship system where government protected the monarchy, the king was the state. The economy and administration were under royal patronage. Interstate wars between Southeast Asian kingdoms were a constant pre-occupation, but with Rama III, a new diplomatic era was born. The Europeans had come to Southeast Asian territories for their trading and political interests. The Europeans wanted free trade but Rama III was opposed to this. But the King died in 1851.[24]

Rama IV or King Mongkut ascended the throne when he was 46 years old, after being a Buddhist monk and after having studied European languages and science. He held a court group of pro-European men who understood the implications of Western expansion. Rama IV started a

70

policy of adjusting the state to the world, opened Thailand to free trade with European states and to education by Western teachers. Rama IV was the father of modern Thailand.

Rama V or King Chulalongkorn modernised Thailand. He abolished slavery and slave labour and replaced ancient personal obligations with institutional relationships of wages, rent, taxes, and conscription. Political matters were different. Both Britain in the west and France in the east were pressing on Thai borders for new territories. Chulalongkorn followed a policy of yielding a little and preserving Thai independence. While negotiating with the Europeans he made internal reforms to cope with the modern world.[25]

Rama V's son King Wachirawut became Rama VI, and then Rama VII was his younger brother King Prachathipok. Following their father's administrative reforms, these two kings developed a national consciousness in the governing class and a spirit of professionalism in the bureaucracy brought Thailand to complete legal equality in the world, and established a constitutional system. Rama VI taught love of nation and signed treaties with all powers which removed legal and fiscal limitations in the country. Rama VII believed in giving a constitution but because of resistance among his advisers it did not materialise.

In 1932, some mid-level military officials and civil servants staged a *coup d'etat* by which the absolute control of the royal family was ended and a semi-parliamentary constitution was made.[26]

This earliest experience in constitutionalism was marked by party rivalries, each representing important political ideas, dominated by nationalist tendencies.

In 1941, the Japanese started its conquest of Southeast Asian states. Thailand did not have much choice when Japanese forces landed on Thai territory. Should it be the end of Thai independence or cooperation with Japan? Thailand considered all geopolitical interests and signed a treaty of friendship and cooperation with Japan in order for Thailand to survive. However, Thai leaders formed the Free Thai Movement with an underground movement code named "Ruth". After the defeat of Japan by the Allied forces in August 1945, Thailand, assisted by the United States, projected a skillful Thai diplomacy which enabled it to become a member of the United Nations Oin December 1946 with a policy to find a great power to balance off any country that threatened its sovereignty.[27]

Since 1946 Thailand has changed its constitution several times and has held elections, until in 1999, the question was what kind of democracy should the country have. Thailand has made great advances towards a democratic system in the context of its national goals and the international environment and its great respect for the royal family and for Buddhism.

Thai foreign policy has remained for peace and stability in the region. Thailand joined Malaya and the Philippines in the Association of Southeast Asia (1961), and was the main founder of ASEAN in 1967, contributing many principles to it such as the confidence-building measures and constructive engagement.

Thailand is practically in the centre of the Southeast Asian continent and controls some important waterways that flow from the Mekong River. Thailand's neighbouring states are accessible through the Chao Phraya River plain.

The country is a rich agricultural area where 80 per cent of the populations are engaged in agriculture. Rice, fish, fruits, vegetables, and process foods are the big items of export. Industry is based on agriculture, thus agro-industrial Thailand has food security which, even without the industrial part, since the earliest history has provided stability to the households. Urban life is dominated by commerce and industry which government has regulated. There is a total log ban in the country.

There are four important factors that influence Thai attitudes. These are the King, Buddhism, nation, and democracy. The King is the symbol of national unity. Buddhism which is headed by the King is practised by 95 per cent of the people who believe that doing good is for the sake of one's own fate before everything else. Every Buddhist develops the social virtues of mercy, compassion, benevolence, and respect for others. Thai nationalism appeals for peace and tranquillity for the sake of the nation. Democracy emphasises the sense of duty in the ruling class and a fully elected parliament to control government for the people's happiness and prosperity, in a great sense, benevolence. Democracy means freedom, congruent with Buddhism which abhors regimentation and routine. "Do not be tied to the world which is the source of misery".[28]

The educational school system has expanded and has helped to create the middle class.

Thailand's population of 61.7 million is nearly homogeneous. There are small groups of Malay Muslims in the southern provinces and a small Chinese minority which is well integrated into the Thai economy and are generally assimilated into the Thai community. Groups of Shans, Thai, Lao, and other Thai-speaking people are found in the northern part of the country. They are called Thais.

Thailand has a land area of about 513,115 square kilometres.

COUNTRY PROFILE OF THE SOCIALIST REPUBLIC OF VIETNAM

OFFICIAL NAME	: Cong Hoa Xa Hoi Chu Nghia Viet Nam (The Socialist Republic of Vietnam)
GOVERNMENT	: Socialist Republic
HEAD OF STATE	: President Tran Duc Luong
HEAD OF GOVERNMENT	: Prime Minister Pha Van Kai
RULING PARTY	: Dang Cong San Viet Nam (Communist Party of Vietnam)
CAPITAL	: Hanoi
NATIONAL DAY	: 02 September – to celebrate its independence from France in 1945
LANGUAGES SPOKEN	: Vietnamese (official), French, Chinese, English, Russian
MONETARY UNIT	: Vietnamese Dong (VND)
MAJOR CITIES	: Ho Chi Minh City, Haiphong, Danang, Hue, Can Tho, Hanoi
RELIGIONS	: Buddhism, Taoism, Roman Catholic, Islam, Protestant
LAND AREA	: 331,100 square kilometres
POPULATION	: 79.4 million
POPULATION GROWTH	: 2.3 %
POPULATION DISTRIBUTION	: 21% (urban) 79% (rural)
LIFE EXPECTANCY	: 68 years
ADULT LITERACY RATE	: 91.9 %
FISCAL YEAR	: 01 January to 31 December (calendar year)
GDP GROWTH	: 4.0 %
PER CAPITA GDP (PPP)	: $1,755
PER CAPITA GNP (NOM)	: $310
EXCHANGE RATE	: US$ = VND 11,800
INFLATION	: 3.0%
EXPORTS 12 MONTHS	: $9.3 billion
CURRENCY ACCOUNT BALANCE	: -$1.8 billion
RESERVES (EXCLUDING GOLD)	: $2.1 billion

GDP (PPP)   : $131 billion
PRINCIPAL EXPORTS   : Petroleum, rice, marine
                              products, coffee, rubber,
                              coal and clothing
PRINCIPAL IMPORTS   : Refined petroleum, vehicles,
                              capital equipment, fertilizers,
                              steel and consumer goods
PRINCIPAL MARKETS   : Japan 20%, Singapore 13%,
                              China 9%, Taiwan 6%,
                              Hongkong 6%
NOTE: Figures as of 10 December 1999.

SOCIALIST REPUBLIC OF VIETNAM

Vietnam is the only country in Southeast Asia with much Chinese influence. Chinese annals in the third century B.C. mentioned the Vietnamese. In 208 B.C., the Kingdom of Nam-Viet was founded, composed of parts of Southern China and of three provinces of present day Northern Vietnam. In 111 B.C. Nam-Viet was annexed by China and became a Chinese province, Giao Chi.[29]

The Vietnamese pushed south slowly to occupy a peninsula in the shape of letter S, from the north, the Red River delta; then a little bit south where mountains are close to the sea; and farther down south to the Mekong River delta. A mountain range, the Annamite range, runs from north to south.

Chinese economic, social and political institutions, a mandarin type of bureaucracy and Confucian ethics and Chinese writing system were the features of Vietnam before 939 A.D. The people often revolted against Chinese rule. In 939 A.D., after the fall of the T'ang dynasty in China and the consequent anarchy, the Vietnamese threw off Chinese domination. Under a centralised kingship, the country was ridden with dynastic wars. In 1427 the warrior Le Loi recaptured Hanoi from Chinese forces who had held it for 20 years, and proclaimed himself emperor, starting the Le dynasty. Rivalries continued during this period, the Trinh in the north and the Nguyen in the south. Even so, the Le dynasty did not really break away from China but remained a tributary state to China, sending gold and ivory as symbolic tokens of submission in return for guarantee of support from China. The Vietnamese were already then using the Mandarinate system and the moral teachings of Confucianism. The emperor ruled with the "mandate of heaven" similar to that of China. Wisdom and scholarship were the qualities of a Mandarin who also wielded authority.

The Vietnamese moved to the southern territories, first conquering Champa in Central Vietnam and then from the area near present-day Hue, moving on to the Khmer territory in the south, until they reached the Gulf of Siam.

At this time the Europeans, England, France, the Netherlands, and Portugal had began to compete for commercial and religious privileges in Vietnam. Meanwhile the Tay Son revolt by three brothers brought a short period of unity. Then a Nguyen prince, Nguyen Anh began to reconquer his territory from the south, the region of Saigon, then to Hue, and then to Hanoi which he captured in 1802. Nguyen Anh proclaimed himself Emperor Gia Long at Hue. He unified the code of law, standardised weights and measures, and reformed land registration. His son, Emperor Minh Mang centralised the ruled and isolated Vietnam completely from Christian communities. Raised in Confucian ethics he opposed Christianity. So did the next Emperor Thieu Tri and later Emperor Tu Duc. This rule of the Nguyen Kings was the golden age of Vietnam.

The French invasion forces pushed the Vietnamese until they conquered the country but resistance to French rule continued up to the 1970s. French rule dislocated the traditional institutions and provoked a violent nationalist response. France wanted Indochina to be a cultural carbon copy of itself, putting up French-type education and French language, all of which were assimilated by the elite Vietnamese who made their careers in Europe. One reason for the success was that the traditional institutions of Vietnam placed high value on intellectual attainment and the disciplining of the mind.[30]

However, the elite became disillusioned and became nationalists, anti-French, and communists.

In the 1920s, the nationalists worked for reform. Then a revolt by the Vietnamese Nationalist Party failed. Then the Indochinese Communist Party (ICP) was organised by Nguyen Al Quoc, known better as Ho Chi Minh.[31] Although the ICP carried on the revolution of Vietnam, Ho Chi Minh was better known as the leader of the Vietnamese nationalist movement.

During the Japanese Occupation, Japan recognised French sovereignty in Vietnam under the Vichy government of France.

Emperor Bao Dai proclaimed Vietnam's independence and got from Japan the unification of the three regions. Upon Japan's surrender Ho Chi Minh put up the provisional government of the Democratic Republic of Vietnam (DRV). Bao Dai abdicated the throne in favor of the DRV which was later recognised on 6 March 1946 as a free state within the French Union.

Under the slogan of "independence and unity" to end French colonial rule, the communists transformed North Vietnam's economy into a socialist one along Marxist lines and they fought the French until the latter was defeated at Dien Bien Phu. Britain called for a Geneva Conference which signed a ceasefire on 21 July 1954, provisionally separating the North from the South at the 17th parallel.[32] North and South Vietnam governments became real. All interested countries poured assistance to the two states, the US to South Vietnam and the Soviet Union and China to the North. The war became more intractable until in 1973, the US asked for an "honourable peace". By the Paris Treaty of 1973, the US military pulled out of Vietnam, Laos, and Cambodia. By 1975, North Vietnam took over the whole country as the Democratic Republic of Vietnam. At this point, ASEAN extended its friendship to the Socialist states regardless of the political and economic systems.

Vietnam was closer to the more distant Soviet Union which gave tremendous assistance for its development and communist party activities, including fraternal and hegemonic relations over Laos and Cambodia under Hun Sen, rather than to China which was just on the northern border, a threat for any mistake in Vietnamese policy and a traditional enemy since 111 B.C. The Soviet Union supported Vietnam heavily and gained the use of Danang and Cam Ranh as bases to countervail US military facilities in the Philippine bases and in Japan. With these China felt undercut in its need to impose its influence over Laos and Cambodia, for those years alone.

With the Asian Policy of President Mikhail Gorbachev of the Soviet Union in 1986, Vietnam's control over Laos and Cambodia were practically terminated; Gorbachev dealt with the officials of the two countries separately and also stopped the assistance to Vietnam which was also its resource to control Laos and Cambodia.

When the Soviet Union collapsed in 1991 Vietnam was in a kind of isolation in Southeast Asia, with the Chinese threat on the north. Using a pragmatic foreign policy, Vietnam intensified its relations with each neighbouring Southeast Asian state and then in 1992 Vietnam acceded to the SEA Treaty of Amity and Cooperation (TAC) and then became a member of ASEAN in 1995. Vietnam Foreign Minister Mr. Nguyen Manh Cam, in describing the paradigm shift in Southeast Asia, said that his country's admission to ASEAN showed a "qualitative change in the condition of our region 50 years after the end of World War II... an eloquent testimony to the ever growing trends of regionalism and globalization in the increasingly interdependent world".

In 1999 there were about 79.4 million people living on the land of about 331,100 square kilometres. The major religions are Buddhism and Taoism but there are Roman Catholics, Muslims, and Protestants. The adult literacy rate is 91.9 per cent.

ENDNOTES

1 Flexible hegemony was Estrella D. Solidum's concept to indicate the tightening and loosening of Vietnamese control over Laos and Cambodia to suit Vietnamese interest.

2 http://www.aseansec.org/history/asn_his2htm, pp. 5-8.

3 Ibid., pp. 5-9.

4 http://www.aseansec.org/history_str2.htm. The document is reproduced in order to preserve accuracy of data.

5 The data on Brunei Darussalam is taken from the Facts Sheet of the Embassy of Brunei Darussalam in Manila, 1999.

6 Data on Cambodia's history is from the texts of Georges Coedés, E. Aymonier, L. Palmer Briggs, A. Leclére and others, all cited by Roger M. Smith, in George M. Kahin (ed.), *Governments and Politics of Southeast Asia* (Ithaca: Cornell University Press, 1964).

7 Kahin, *ibid.*, pp. 599-602.

8 *Ibid.*, pp. 605-606.

9 *Ibid.*, p. 618

10 Herber Feith, "Indonesia", in Kahin (ed.), *ibid.*, pp. 184-187.

11 *Ibid.*, pp. 188-189.

12 *Ibid.*, p. 190.

13 *Ibid.*, p. 193.

14 Kahin, *ibid.*, pp. 197-199.

15 *Ibid.*, pp. 218-220.

16 *Pantja Sila* or Five Principles are One God, Nationalism, Humanitarianism, People's Sovereignty, and Social Justice.

17 Most of this background material are from Roger M. Smith's section on Laos in Kahin, *ibid.*, pp. 527-560.

18   The data in this country profile is taken from the Facts Sheet from the Embassy of Malaysia in Manila, 1999.

19   Joseph Silverstein, "Burma", Kahin, *op. cit.*, pp. 75-76.

20   *Ibid.*, p. 77.

21   *Ibid.*, p. 79.

22   Data is taken from the Facts Sheet of the Singapore Embassy at Manila, 1999.

23   Most of the data here is taken from David A. Wilson's "Thailand" in Kahin, *op. cit.*

24   *Ibid.*, pp. 7-8.

25   *Ibid.*, pp. 10-11.

26   *Ibid.*, p.15.

27   Wiwat Mungkandi, "The Security Syndrome (1941-1975)" in Mungkandi and William Warren, *Thai American Relations* (Bangkok: Chulalongkorn University Press, 1982), pp. 67-81.

28   Kahin, *op. cit.*, pp. 30-41.

29   Data on Vietnam is taken from Roy Jumper and Marjorie Weiner Normand, "Vietnam" in Kahin, *op. cit.*, pp. 375-392; including the footnotes therein which show a wealth of readings.

30   Lucien W. Pye, "The Politics of Southeast Asia", in G.A. Almond and J.S. Coleman (eds.), *Politics of Developing Areas* (Princeton: Princeton University Press, 1960), p. 95.

31   Kahin, *op. cit.*, pp. 389-395.

32   Kahin, *ibid.*, pp. 392-399.

CHAPTER 3

Principles of ASEAN

FUNDAMENTAL PRINCIPLES

ASEAN's continued vitality comes from its "political formula" which is the basis of its existence, internal relations, intra-regional relations, and direction of its life. Indeed although "political" was not mentioned as a field of cooperation in the Bangkok Declaration of 1967, ASEAN is a political association, being run by the government officials of each member state. The principles of ASEAN have provided stability for the decisions of the leaders.[1]

Some of these principles have been taken from the United Nations Charter, the Bandung Declaration of 1955, the Declaration of the Association of Southeast Asia (ASA) of 1961 and the Manila Agreements of 1963 of the MAPHILINDO. The leaders of the ASEAN states also produced new principles to guide them in the resolution of vital problems and on new issues affecting each member and the region itself. Shared cultural values have provided the moral foundation of the principles. Asians view the world holistically and not compartmentally. Such a view proceeds from the desire to be in harmony with nature. For example, needs are always part of the whole situation because needs are identifiable with the communal nature of Asians. Every one becomes part of a situation or need and this is why Asian thought and actions acquire a moral sense. Experts have found out that Asian thinking, unlike the West, does not proceed on a linear deductive line but by induction and intuition using symbols, riddles, and feeling. In this way, there is no fear of missing some objects on the way, which might not be along the linear deductive line. Asian thought consists of enveloping moves, only focusing on a specific center whenever this is sensed.[2]

This is the process by which ASEAN's political formula has grown. Starting from a short Declaration of generally accepted principles which has become the bedrock of ASEAN, more principles have been developed and are expressed in various documents·

SOURCES OF ASEAN'S PRINCIPLES

The general principles of the ASEAN Declaration of 1967 were taken from the United Nations Charter, the Bandung Declaration of 1955, the ASA Declaration of 1961 and the Manila Agreements of 1963.

From the UN Charter came the widely accepted principles of respect for sovereignty and territorial integrity, abstention from threat or use of force, peaceful settlement of international disputes, equal rights and self-determination, and non-interference in the affairs of the other states.

The Bandung Conference of 1955, attended by Asian and African states, produced some principles which were adopted by ASEAN. These were cooperation for economic, cultural and social development, mutual respect for national sovereignty, condemnation of racialism and colonialism in all its forms and manifestations, disarmament and prohibition of nuclear weapons, respect for human rights, non-intervention, and respect for the right of self-defence "singly or collectively in conformity with the UN Charter".

The ASA (1961) and Manila Agreements (1963) contributed the ideas of emphasis on good neighbourliness, active cooperation, friendly consultations and mutual assistance, Asian solution for Asian problems, primary responsibility for the stability and security of the region, and *mushawarah* or continuous dialogue for consensus-making and arriving at consensus without the use of vote or veto. From the Manila Declaration of 1963 specifically was derived the principle on the temporary status of foreign military bases.

EMERGENCE OF NEW PRINCIPLES

Many of the principles of the 1967 Declaration were stated in general terms and remained to be operationalised in future occasions. Some of the concepts were inchoate in the early years of ASEAN, but with the emergence of new issues and conditions, ASEAN leaders had the opportunity to redefine their interests, search for new principles, and give form to their ideas.

In 1971, the Fourth ASEAN Ministerial Meeting in Manila redefined ASEAN's level of cooperation to include close consultations and cooperation among the member states' representatives at regional and international fora so that they can always present a united stand to advance their common interests. It also adopted the principle that it would engage the active participation of the private sector to achieve ASEAN goals. The Special ASEAN Ministerial Meeting at Kuala Lumpur in November 1971 produced two very important principles. The first was the declaration to secure the recognition of and respect for Southeast Asia as a Zone of Peace, Freedom, and Neutrality (ZOPFAN). The second was the need to manifest their concern for peace and stability through a meeting at the highest level and recommending therein a Summit Meeting of Heads of State or Government.

When ASEAN was in its fifth year of existence, the Foreign Ministers agreed to make an overall review of its organisation and procedural framework. From this new need, new principles were identified, such as the need for greater self-reliance, the need for coordinated and well planned strategy on both the national and regional levels for more effective cooperation, and national resilience for each member to enable it to face present changes and challenges for the future with greater self-confidence. ASEAN should also produce new guidelines and criteria for priorities for cooperation. The ministers also recognised formally the principle of consensus in decision-making by which the principle of equality became more enshrined.

DEVELOPMENT OF POLITICAL PRINCIPLES

Although the Declaration of 1967 did not mention political cooperation, it was inevitable that it would be one of the aspects of ASEAN cooperation. Some reasons may be found for this assertion. One of these is that the objectives of peace and security in the region cannot be separated from their political implications. Another is the fact that the organisation and meetings of ASEAN involved foreign ministers who are political leaders. In addition, the foreign ministers of ASEAN states were holding "special sessions" or meetings in the "corridors of ASEAN" to discuss political matters. These especial sessions were regularised in 1973. Then in 1976, political cooperation was formally provided for by the first Heads of Government meeting.

The concept of ZOPFAN in 1971 was a political principle the ideas of which were derived from the UN Charter, the Asian-African Conference at Bandung and the Lusaka Declaration which proclaimed Africa as a nuclear-free zone. In 1973 the Foreign Ministers Meeting recognised that political will as a vital precondition of ASEAN regional cooperation should be continuously developed by giving special priority to ASEAN. The ministers also established the Coordinating Committee for the Reconstruction and Rehabilitation of Indochinese states, a move to give form to the general statement of promoting peace in the region. ASEAN also took a common stand in urging Japan to review its policy of indiscriminate expansion and accelerated export of synthetic rubber. Indonesian Foreign Affairs Minister Adam Malik expressed for ASEAN on 27 November 1973 a joint view on the Middle East crisis condemning Israel's aggression and urging restoration of Palestinian rights, in support of the United Nations Resolution on the crisis.

More decisions which gave clarity to the political principles were taken even before the adoption of the Bali Agreements of 1976 which formally provided for political cooperation. In 1974, the Seventh Foreign Ministers Meeting invited the representatives from the governments of the Khmer Republic and the Kingdom of Laos to be guests of the Indonesian government. The Ministers reaffirmed the desirability of convening a conference of all Southeast Asian nations at an appropriate time. The Ministers likewise reiterated their joint views expressed at the 28th United Nations General Assembly Session to allow the Khmer people their right of self-determination by coming to a political settlement by themselves and to prevent any UN action that may prejudice the right of self-determination of the Khmer people. The Ministers also decided to remain in close consultation to obtain broad ideas of agreement on the Law of the Sea Conference.

Political principles were also modified in favour of the higher interests for peace, progress, and stability in the region. For example, while the 1967 Declaration specified similarity in aims as a condition for beneficial relationships, by 1975 the ministers at the Eighth Meeting stated their readiness to enter into friendly and harmonious relationships with the Marxist Socialist nations of Vietnam, Laos, and Cambodia based on the principles of peaceful coexistence and mutually beneficial cooperation. The original principle appeared to have been revised to express the idea that different social systems in Southeast Asia should not be an obstacle to good relations; the different social systems reflect best the character and aspiration of their respective peoples. The Ministers reiterated the principles of non-interference, respect for sovereignty and territorial integrity, equality, and justice in the conduct of their relations. They also declared that coexistence would help to relax the tensions in the region and would create favourable conditions for the establishment of ZOPFAN. This is the precondition for peace and security in Southeast Asia, to keep the region free from the rivalries and interference of outside powers.[3] This notion was further elaborated on in the following annual meeting of foreign ministers when they declared that the changed political situation in Southeast Asia, referring to the establishment of Marxist Socialist governments in Vietnam, Laos, and Kampuchea in 1975, required ASEAN states to build relations with the three states on a constructive and productive basis with the assurance of non-interference in each other's internal affairs.[4]

Continuing their discussion of political ideas, the Foreign Ministers decided again to give support to actions for a just and peaceful solution to the Middle East problem including Israel withdrawal from illegally occupied Arab territories and the recognition of the inalienable rights of the Palestinian people. In that same meeting, the ministers supported the principles of self-determination and majority rule in South Africa where the intransigence of the racist minority regime was perceived to constitute a threat to international peace and security. In their annual meeting of 1978, the Foreign Ministers called on the United Nations High Commission for Refugees (UNHCR) and other relevant agencies to take immediate measures for the expeditious resettlement of the Indochinese refugees in Third World countries.[5] The principle of cooperation for regional peace caused the ministers to also express concern over the growing tension between the People's Republic of China and the Socialist Republic of Vietnam.

Further explicit statements of principles for political cooperation can be found in the Declaration of ASEAN Concord which was signed at Bali during the First ASEAN Meeting of Heads of Government on 24 February 1976. The document reaffirms ASEAN's commitments to the Declarations of Bandung, Bangkok and Kuala Lumpur, and the Charter of the United Nations and declared that ASEAN cooperation for political stability shall take into account the following principles: 1) national and regional resilience; 2) establishment of Southeast Asia as a Zone of Peace, Freedom, and Neutrality; 3) economic and social development with emphasis on social justice; 4) assistance for relief of members in distress; 5) peaceful settlement of intra-regional disputes; and 6) mutual respect, self-determination, sovereign equality, and non-interference in the internal affairs of states. Member states shall vigorously develop an awareness of regional identity. Political cooperation as provided for in the Treaty of Amity and Cooperation in Southeast Asia (TAC), consisted of judicial cooperation and political solidarity through harmonisation of views and coordinating positions and taking common action wherever possible and desirable. Many of these principles had been adopted earlier at various times and were being reaffirmed by the Heads of Government at their Bali meeting. At this point, higher values of judicial cooperation and harmonisation were articulated. These principles became more concrete when they were embodied in the Ministerial Understanding on the Organisational Arrangement for Cooperation in the Legal Field, signed in Bali, 12 April 1986 to promote legal cooperation among ASEAN countries.

With the transformation of the general political principles into those with specific application, ASEAN's image became clearer to the world and its patterns of behaviour acquired more predictability, a factor for peaceful and orderly state relations. This fresh image gave ASEAN a new appeal to many states so that they desired to establish mutually beneficial relations with the regional association.

GIVING CLARITY AND DEFINITION TO INCHOATE ASEAN PRINCIPLES

New issues enabled the leaders of ASEAN to put its principles in clearer formulation. The principle of common action was implemented in collective approaches to multilateral trade negotiations and international fora such as those on the New International Economic Order (NIEO).

Cooperation in social fields included the principle of the basic needs strategy to effectively distribute the benefits of production to the poor in the region. Certain principles were adopted to combat the abuse of narcotic drugs. For example, each member country shall intensify its vigilance and strengthen preventive and penal measures against illicit drugs.

The Foreign Ministers also refined the concept of mutual assistance by providing principles to govern conditions of assistance in natural disasters. Each affected member country shall help the state giving assistance by undertaking immediate internal arrangements to facilitate the transit of personnel, vehicles, supplies, and equipment through its territory. A member country requesting assistance shall make internal administrative arrangements to facilitate the entry of the necessary material and personnel for rescue and relief, free from government taxes and any other charges.[6]

Still on the principle of mutual assistance, specifically on basic commodities like food and energy, member states shall assist each other by according priority to the supply of a country's needs in critical circumstances on the principle of first refusal.[7] Concrete steps have been taken towards the realisation of these principles. ASEAN has raised its Emergency Rice Reserve to a total of 53,000 metric tons under the ASEAN Food Security Reserve Scheme (AFSR) and signed two energy-related agreements, the ASEAN Energy Cooperation Agreement and the ASEAN Petroleum Security Agreement, at the 19th Ministerial Meeting. The range of cooperation on energy includes sharing in planning, development, manpower training, information exchange, conservation, supply and disposal, and a formula or scheme for ASEAN emergency petroleum sharing when at least one member state is in distress[8].

Social cooperation also aims to develop mutual understanding through cooperation in mass media and cultural activities. Exchanges of artists in the visual and performing arts and establishment of cultural institutions will hopefully lead to the discovery of more common elements in the member states' cultures. Mutual understanding is emphasised in ASEAN not with the aim to homogenise cultures but rather to develop appreciation, tolerance, and accommodation.

The principle in the Declaration of 1967 regarding collaboration for greater utilisation of agriculture and industries, expansion of trade, and raising the standards of living of the people was affirmed in the TAC (1976 Bali), and expressed in detail in the Declaration of ASEAN Concord. Member states shall cooperate to establish large scale ASEAN industrial plants, contribute to food production, increase foreign exchange earnings, and create employment. Member states shall work towards preferential trading arrangements and expansion of trade among themselves.

On the idea of developing an ASEAN community, the principle of involving as many sectors as possible, such as women, youth, private industries, and non-governmental organisations in ASEAN affairs, furnishes guidelines for an expanded cooperation.

The principle of sovereignty is the major pillar of ASEAN relations. The Declaration of 1967 enshrines this principle by making it one of the goals of regional cooperation and by providing for other principles designed to protect it. At the 19th Ministerial Meeting in Manila in June 1986, the foreign ministers reiterated that the protection of national interests and the preservation of national identities are important objectives and so there must always be an appropriate balance between the attainment of regional objectives and preservation of national interest.[9] Sovereignty or independence of the state is referred to in statements concerning equality in partnership, non-interference in national affairs, and mutual respect for territorial integrity. Its preservation is also implied in the Declaration of 1967 which does not provide for political integration as a manifestation of the consensus which was accepted by the original five states signatories that ASEAN would be a loose and flexible association wherein cooperation for mutual and regional interests of sovereign states could take place. The principle of equality among partners was intended to avoid any leader-follower relationship, even though the members have widely disparate resource endowments. For example, Indonesia is a large state while Singapore is a small island state and the rest vary in the quantity and quality of their resources.

One evidence for the pre-eminence of the sovereignty principle in ASEAN is the manner in which all their decisions are made through *mushawarah* or consensus-making. Every member becomes a participant in a process which does not require any vote and becomes committed to the resulting decisions reached as consensus.

The principle of good neighbourliness is mentioned in the Declaration of 1967 and in other ASEAN documents as a mode of conduct for members. Its operational definition includes many types of behaviour. Member states try to avoid conflict by exercising mutual restraint and tolerance when differences arise among them. Should conflicts arise, the mode of handling them would be pacific settlement, using Asian solution for Asian problems. This principle was formally stated in the 1976 agreements by the Heads of Government at Bali. Good neighbourliness also creates the expectation that member states will consult and give advice to one another when a policy that is about to be made is seen to affect the rest. This was exemplified by the round of visits which Thai and Malaysian officials made to their ASEAN partners to explain their imminent extension of recognition to China. It was also used by the Philippines when it consulted Indonesia about its Muslim problem in the southern part of the country. This principle is also at the root of another principle which is Asian solution to Asian problems. In effect it means peaceful solutions. Good neighbourliness also underlies the provisions of the TAC[10] and those of the various agreements on rescue operations in case of disasters to ships and aircrafts, on critical situations, and on the implementation of ASEAN industrial projects, by providing the norms that are to be observed regarding their behaviour with one another. The principle is mutual assistance in all cases. Moreover, crises on food and energy required another principle which is that of "first refusal". It means that any of the six states must give priority to any of its partners' emergency needs for food or energy before it places its product in the world market.

In any ASEAN project, when any of the member states is not particularly affected or is not prepared to cooperate for some reason, the principle of six-minus-one took care of the relationships. In 1978, the Committee on Industry, Minerals and Energy (COIME) recommended to the ASEAN economic ministers that implementation of the industrial complementation projects shall not be hindered or invalidated if less than five countries undertook them, provided that all five ASEAN member countries had been consulted sufficiently before then. This is the "five-minus-one" principle which assures solidarity while recognising the varying capabilities of the members. With the addition of Brunei in 1984 the principle became "six-minus-X." A member that is not ready to implement a *mushawarah* decision may be allowed the option of participating at a later stage. In another case, a member state may ask to be a participant but not in an equal status in a project after it has participated in consensus-making. For example, in the fertilizer project of Indonesia, the equities of the other three states were equal but more than that of Singapore's. Now that all the states of Southeast Asia are members, the principle is "consensus-minus-X".

Another principle for intra-regional relations is the harmonisation of national and regional interests which means that some temporary sacrifices have to be made at the national level in order that a regional interest, which in the long run would also serve the national interests of all the members, may be obtained. Harmonisation of interests can be achieved through common action, joint approaches, and a spirit of give and take.

In its relations with other states, ASEAN guides its members to respect their sovereignty and territorial integrity and to abstain from the use of force in the conduct of foreign relations. ASEAN has also expanded its relations by "dialogue relations" with friendly states and with existing international organisations in pursuance of the provisions of the 1976 Declaration of ASEAN Concord.

As one of the results of dialogue relations, ASEAN has received material assistance from economically developed Dialogue Partners. The question of the nature of foreign assistance was taken up in the early years of ASEAN when the members were particularly careful to protect their independence. After careful deliberations, ASEAN leaders defined their position on foreign assistance to be as follows: 1) any agreement with non-ASEAN countries should not be at the expense of existing bilateral arrangements of any member with other countries; 2) foreign assistance should complement ASEAN's capabilities and not supplement them; 3) foreign assistance should be for ASEAN projects that are regional in character for the benefit of all member countries; and 4) foreign assistance should be unconditional. On the other hand, dialogue relations have provided the Dialogue Partners with large ASEAN markets.

When ASEAN states are confronted by an externally generated problem, they take a common ASEAN position by consensus decision through the customary ASEAN consultations and meetings. In these meetings, the ASEAN spirit is very pervasive and influential to such a point that the positions that are subsequently adopted generally reflect regional interests and may have included some sacrifices of national interests.

The principles which were enunciated in the Declaration of 1967 and those that were adopted from time to time by ASEAN have furnished directions for its policies and projects. Although ASEAN appears to be "muddling through" to some who are impatient for dramatic results, the association refuses to be intimidated and in fact keeps steadily on its course, "making haste slowly", thanks to the collective wisdom of its leaders.

The long-term goal of ASEAN is to establish a community in Southeast Asia where peace, progress, and security will prevail. There are various paths that should lead to that goal, but ASEAN has managed to keep its orientation through its declared principles. National, regional, and international problems influence the choice of the paths to take but

ASEAN states are well-served by their principles which are conducive to orderly and balanced growth.

In order to establish a regional community which is an enunciated goal, several things must be done by the member states. One of these is that every state must develop national resilience, which is the ability to survive safely and to maintain its own identity in the face of social change.[11] Then each resilient state becomes a strong link in the chain. Another action which helps community-building is informing one another of unusual events which occur in any of them. In ASEAN, every member is aware that it should assure the rest that in spite of political changes, it will honour its commitments to ASEAN. There is a felicitous practice among the members which has become well-accepted and probably customary and it is that a Head of State or Government visits the other members to inform them of significant changes in policies and in the government for their guidance, and to assure them of his state's continuing commitment to ASEAN. Another community-building behaviour in ASEAN is mutual understanding and mutual dependability. Member states try to resolve their problems or remove their root causes by peaceful means. If the problems involve only two of the members but the outcome will affect the whole of ASEAN, any Head of State or Government can make quiet visits to the others with the hope of finding peaceful solutions, such as by encapsulating the problems and preventing their ASEANisation. In these bilateral meetings of ASEAN leaders, much can be accomplished.[12] In social and economic matters, ASEAN states continue to search for areas of cooperation where they should be most comfortable. Cooperation in ASEAN teaches each member the principle of accommodation of one another's needs. When all these practices become habitual and develop dependable expectations, then a community is in the process of formation.[13]

In the regional context, ASEAN must establish good relations with its neighbours. This is not difficult to do with states which share ASEAN's aims but it is certainly a delicate job as regards those states which are not like-minded. ASEAN adopted the principle of peaceful coexistence with the socialist states of Vietnam, Laos, and Cambodia. After developing much improved relations with these three states and with Myanmar, ASEAN has become a regional association with full membership.

Because the community must have security, ASEAN is working towards that goal through political, economic, and social policies. Its political policies are now well known but it would be useful to recapitulate them. First are the principles in the Declaration of 1967 making foreign military bases temporary in nature and giving responsibility for the security of Southeast Asia to the peoples of the region themselves. The direction for ASEAN is clearly for peace and to avoid becoming a pawn of any foreign power. This is why ASEAN has rejected suggestions for it to turn military. This direction becomes even clearer with the Kuala Lumpur Declaration of 1971 which would make the region a Zone of Peace, Freedom, and Neutrality (ZOPFAN). ASEAN refrained from being involved in the power politics of the U.S.S.R., China or any other external power, hoping that these countries would also refrain from interfering with the problems of the region. A component of the ZOPFAN was studied comprehensively by

ASEAN and this is the concept of a Southeast Asia Nuclear Weapon-Free Zone (SEANWFZ) to serve national and regional security interests. It is inspired by the South Pacific Nuclear Weapon-Fee Zone treaty signed at Rarotonga on 6 August 1985. The SEANWFZ was finally adopted by ASEAN. The SEANWFZ Treaty clearly states ASEAN's determination towards general and complete nuclear disarmament and the promotion of international peace and security. The Treaty includes the protection of the region from environmental pollution and hazards which are produced by radioactive waste and toxic materials. The ASEANWFZ Committee with its Executive Committee oversees the implementation of the Treaty's provisions.

Regarding the Japanese-sponsored Pacific community concept, ASEAN was not disposed to join it if the integrity of ASEAN would be subordinated to the interests of the developed states.[14] After going through a long search, the idea may have found itself in the Asia-Pacific Economic Cooperation (APEC). It is clear to ASEAN leaders that a community is not found just because there is trade and aid and complementarity which appears to be a conceptual trap, but that a community must be constituted by a well-bonded group of peoples who share goals, sentiments, and values. APEC is not yet a community as ASEAN leaders have said that it is only a forum.

ASEAN analysed the problem of growing reliance on the industrial states and its consequent hazards to the development of Third World countries. The leaders agreed to decrease ASEAN dependence on others by using as far as possible the resources of the ASEAN region for its development and by using external assistance only as an aid but not as a substitute for national and regional resources. Even with the trend towards globalisation, ASEAN has declared that any step or pace must recognise the cultures and conditions of the people in Southeast Asia.

THE ASEAN WAY AND THE ASEAN SPIRIT

In the first ten years of ASEAN, its leaders looked for factors that could help in community-building. The association was only a framework for cooperation but the real goal was to build a regional community where the relationships among the members and their relationships with other states are strong and secure.

The foreign ministers of the ASEAN states discussed the ways to build a community and what it should be like. The ASEAN community's character should be made clear to all sectors of society so that they could count themselves in as members of such a community and ASEAN should not be left out as an organisation apart from the people for whom ASEAN aims to bring the blessings of their cooperation. [15] A new culture of a regional community may be found. In the first few years, the leaders were surprised to find themselves behaving as if they were one family with shared values. This was very encouraging to these leaders who were just beginning to learn about one another, to learn to cooperate where just before 1967 each state had gone its own separate ways without regard to its neighbours.

This shared behaviour was happily recognised and named ASEAN Way and the enthusiasm and commitment to project the ASEAN label in all their activities was called the ASEAN Spirit.

When ASEAN was established, it was feared by the founding leaders that there would be many problems of cooperation because of the existing social and political disparities among them. But the necessity for regional cooperation for each one's survival and development as well as the region's security made the leaders observe the greatest of care during their initial meetings so that ASEAN could be nurtured by all.

It was during those days of groundwork that the similarities in culture emerged. The spirit of good neighbourliness guided Indonesian leaders in 1967 to restore relations with Malaysia which had been affected by Indonesia's *Konfrontasi* in 1963. The first step was the visit of Adam Malik to Thai Foreign Minister Thanat Khoman which led to the idea of a region-wide cooperation which then became ASEAN.

ASEAN leaders spoke of building a regional community even in the first year of the organisation. It was a pleasant surprise to the founding leaders to see that close cooperation among the ministers and employees of ASEAN was immediately experienced where this had never been evident before.[16] Adam Malik spoke of community sentiments as growing naturally from their cultural similarities. His views were shared by Philippine and Thai officials. Even in the ASA of 1961, Thanat Khoman who signed for Thailand, already proposed the word "community" which he said "underlined the neighborly and regional character of the organization".[17] Philippine Foreign Affairs Secretary Emmanuel Pelaez likewise emphasised "the need to build a strong sense of community... and sustain a bond of fraternity..." Tun Abdul Razak of Malaya said that the members of MAPHILINDO were like sister nations coming from a common stock. All these three leaders were the same architects of ASEAN and records show that they talked of a community for the region. This community is to be characterised by equality among members, interactions coming from free and voluntary association, and relationships which are not based on structures of administration but on the use of common values to sustain cooperation. There would be no need to homogenise the community. What was important in the founders' perceptions was cultural development, implying an understanding of one another's values in order to produce acceptance and comprehension among the members of the community. ASEAN elites identified and stressed values which they considered useful in making the peoples accept new modes of thought and action which could respond to and satisfy their needs.

As has been mentioned earlier, ASEAN leaders recognise a way of life which has been a big factor for the viability of the organisation. ASEAN elites are consciously and constantly invoking common values to sustain cooperation and the ASEAN Way has provided stability and a large degree of predictability in their relationships. Officials of the association acknowledge that indeed there are differences of opinion but there is a healthy feeling about these differences. As General Suharto said in Bali, those "differences clearly indicate that our minds remain active and our conceptions are developing prior to reaching a consensus". As for the problems of adjustment and learning cooperation, they have been viewed as a "necessary prelude to a new phase of consolidation – a new thrust towards more meaningful interdependence... There is a unity of thought that ASEAN's end is peace and its means are peaceful, and that politics of confrontation merely sap energy and resources better devoted to development purpose". [18]

The ASEAN Way at the elite level pervades at the moment and is now being extended to the people's level through functional cooperation for establishing a real community where members share a feeling of identity and responsibility. Functional cooperation covers the search for solutions to problems of drug abuse and trafficking, diseases, illiteracy, poverty eradication, involvement of women and youth in the development process, rural development, natural disasters, labour, health, and increasing the levels of science and technology. In this way, ASEAN can involve all sectors in a feeling of identity.

THE ASEAN WAY AS PROTOTYPE OF A CULTURE

An ASEAN culture may be seen in terms of the ASEAN Way. Culture, as defined by Ralph Linton, is an organised group of learned responses of a particular society. Culture represents an integration of past experiences and forms a configuration, all of whose parts are to some degree interrelated. The elements which compose a culture are of several different orders. The most readily accessible to direct observation are (1) material cultures; (2) behaviours which control the social relations of individuals, and consisting of conscious statements as to the way in which members should behave and generalised patterns of response called value-attitude system, and (3) individuals' patterns of overt behaviour and personality.[19] Culture consists of social integration, adjustment of traits comprising a way of life, ethos on how life should be lived, and social relationships such as drinking together, worshipping in common, organisations, organic solidarity, and desire to stay together.[20]

In the context of Linton's definition, the ASEAN Way is a prototype of an ASEAN culture.

The ASEAN Way is the configuration al all elements that have become interrelated in regional patterns of thinking, doing, and valuing in ASEAN. Thus, it consists of the beliefs, practices, structures, responses, and values commonly shared in ASEAN.

The principle of Asian solution for Asian problems was first enunciated in ASA in 1961. The founding leaders – President Carlos P. Garcia, Tungku Abdul Rahman, and foreign Minister Thanat Khoman – agreed that problems in Asia should only be solved by those who are from the region. Only Asian solutions which contain Asian values are legitimate; these must be formulated by leaders of the states involved because they understand their own problems. For example, the Asian way of solving a problem avoids fanfare before any agreement is achieved. It is suggested here that when solutions are legitimate there would be less chances for internal tensions to exist. Additionally, foreign interest cannot intrude in the solution. Accordingly, ASEAN has provided for pacific settlement of disputes but even before this document of 1976 was made, ASEAN members had been observing this principle.

Aside from this, ASEAN also upholds the principle of balanced growth which states that development must encompass both the material and spiritual realms. Under the influence of the great tradition of Hinduism, Buddhism, Islam, Confucianism and Christianity, ASEAN members do not believe that peace and happiness of the peoples can come only from material things. Justice, freedom, peace, good neighbourliness are just as important. Religious values are officially recognised, as indicated by the fact that ASEAN members implore the blessings of God Almighty for success in their meetings.[21]

When Adam Malik went to Malaya to talk of broader cooperation, Anwar Sani sought the Philippines' aid in persuading Thailand to "make some gracious gesture" to Cambodia, its traditional hostile neighbour, for it to join ASEAN. During the discussions on the nature of the proposed organisation, it became evident that there were deep-seated conflicts which were related to the short-lived ASA and MAPHILINDO. However, the spirit of "give and take" which was common to all the cultures of the five states, enabled each of them to respect the others' views by avoiding explicit references to what was objectionable to others.[22]

For example, Malaysian officials dropped their insistence on the enlargement of ASA which the Indonesians had earlier criticised; Indonesians avoided referring to MAPHILINDO which Malaysia had already denounced. Singapore, not wishing to be drawn into the religious, linguistic, or ideological problems of its neighbours, agreed to join ASEAN on the principle of equal distribution of burden and equality in their common interest.[23] Projecting another shared cultural value, Thanat Khoman and Razak emphasised in the First Ministerial Meeting of ASEAN that their cooperation was one "among members of a great family" bound together by ties of friendship and goodwill in the spirit of equality and partnership.[24]

After the First Ministerial Meeting, ASEAN leaders believed that the values which they shared and which underlay their attitudes were by now coming to the surface very naturally. During the first year, the foreign ministers "took counsel with one another in an atmosphere of informality and a real spirit of good neighbourliness". [25] Razak mentioned some common values which Malaysia shared with Indonesia and these were culture, history, and tradition. In their initial year, deliberations were conducted in a spirit of understanding and solidarity. That crucial first year brought out the value of neighbourliness which Thanat had described in this way: "They had discarded their deplorable habit of going their own separate ways and turning their backs to one another".

These values were to be more useful for the organisation in the next ten years, constituting as they did, a great part of the ASEAN Way. Of neighbourliness, understanding, and desire for peace, many examples in ASEAN's existence may be mentioned. When the Philippines' Sabah claim threatened to obstruct ASEAN's progress, Indonesian and Thai leaders went very quietly to see Malaysian and Philippine leaders to counsel them about adopting more flexible positions for the sake of ASEAN.

In another instance, when the Philippines was confronted with the problem of subversives who were taking off from Malaysia, President Marcos met with President Suharto very quietly and then the latter went to meet with Malaysian leaders. In another example, Prime Minister Lee Kuan Yew of Singapore had been reluctant to meet with other ASEAN leaders in the earlier years presumably because of his view that the endemic graft and corruption in the other four states were evidence of insincerity for development. His reluctance was soon overcome by his realisation that he had to understand the conditions in his neighbouring states. Thereafter, he made visits to Indonesia and the Philippines. Among the heads of government, the spirit of neighbourliness and understanding removed all inhibitions to meet informally which they had been doing even before the first summit meeting at Bali in 1976. ASEAN leaders visited with one another in short-sleeved diplomacy, without fanfare and protocol, in order to take counsel from one another. In later years, consultations guided the leaders when they had to make decisions on whether or not to recognise China. The specific usefulness of consultations lies in the fact that the leaders could learn of one another's position while conveying their own too, and at the same time observing one of the principles of ASEAN, which is the guarantee for the independence of foreign policy of each member.

Such neighbourliness and understanding grew in strength over the years. It was also unbelievable in the context of Malaysian-Philippines relations over Sabah that Malaysia would speak for Philippine policy towards the Muslims in Mindanao at the Organisation of Islamic Conference in Kuala Lumpur. Earlier, Muslim countries in the spirit of Darul Islam had condemned Philippine policy.

ASEAN leaders seem to share some invisible ground rules, which is an element of the ASEAN Way. Officials instinctively know when not to get involved in another's problems, even when invited to do so. When Marcos asked Indonesia for help in the Mindanao situation, Malik said that Indonesia had faith that the Philippines could solve its own problems as Indonesia did in 1965. This gesture enabled the Philippines to avoid foreign interference in its domestic problems, which, had it occurred, could have provoked more complications domestically and internationally. Similarly when Thailand was experiencing increased military pressures on its Mekong River border with Laos, Prime Minister Kraivixien went to sound out his partners in ASEAN by paying them visits. While reassuring him privately of support, ASEAN leaders announced publicly that his visit was a regular one and thus reduced its significance in the international press.

In most of the intra-ASEAN business, leaders work behind the scenes or in a very low-key fashion. Mediation activities in ASEAN bear this principle showing that the ASEAN Way relies on the personal approach in contrast to the Western way of dependence on structures and their functions. In ASEAN, mediators may be self-selected or chosen by any party and their role depends to a large degree on the predictability of loyalty to the group with whom they share their common cultural values. If they are successful in behind-the scenes negotiations, mediators can bring the conflicting parties together to agree on some pre-arranged conditions. If the mediators are not successful, neither they nor the disputants lose "face" since everything had been conducted unofficially.

The ASEAN Way depends to a large degree on the concept of kinship, kin-like relations, and brotherhood. Since the establishment of ASEAN, members have conducted their business in the spirit of fraternity. They have frequently referred to themselves as members of one family. The appeal to brotherhood as kinship is deeply rooted in Malay culture. Kinship was the basic element which ensured the cohesion of inter-sultanate relationships long before the 15th century. The concept of brotherhood was the unwritten law among the sultanates. It implicitly assumed that the kin group could be relied upon by a member at any period, all are bound to each other by specific ties of loyalty. Expectations of group solidarity are high. Thus all activities in the name of brotherhood and kinship have great significance. Predictability of behaviour is based on personal ties rather than on impersonal rules. Another element in the ASEAN Way which is rooted in Malay culture is *mushawarah*, the process of consensus-making. The participants in the negotiation or discussion come to the meeting with a disposition to agree and not to dispute. The participants avoid hard or inflexible positions in order to facilitate *mushawarah*. The points of disagreement in the business are laid aside for some future time while the points on which agreements are possible are taken up. Decisions are called consensus or *mufakat*. There is no registration of votes nor division of the house for or against an issue. There is no veto, no vote, no conflict between opposing views, no taking of sides. The decision is contributed to by all. No one is seen as a loser. In ASEAN, flexibility accompanies *mushawarah* and *mufakat*, for even if everyone had agreed on a certain matter, not everyone is obliged to actually implement it because ASEAN allows bilateral and other arrangements in cooperation. If a member is not ready to participate, his participation in the consensus does not oblige him to act on it. All that is needed is his agreement in principle. Some exceptions to this are the cultural projects in which every partner must participate and the ASEAN positions in relation to international issues. *Mushawarah* was first used by Asian leaders in MAPHILINDO where frequent and regular consultations were held at all levels.

But *mushawarah* is based further on another underlying factor in cooperation. This is collective activity, known in Indonesia and Malaysia as *gotongroying* and in the Philippines as *bayanihan*. It is deeply rooted in the cultures of the people of these three countries, and even of Thailand, as can be seen in their daily lives at harvest-time, planting time, or house construction. Everyone in the neighbourhood comes to help accomplish work that needs to be done right away without expectation of material reward. For example, rice has to be harvested fast before the stalks come loose, the grains rot, the locusts arrive, or the rains destroy the ripe grains. This can only be done collectively.

Similarly, building a house needs labour that can only be supplied by the community. The spirit of mutual assistance is greatly aided by the fact that many are kinsmen by blood and marriage and as explained earlier, there are great expectations from kinship. In the tradition of such deeply rooted concepts of cooperation, decisions are implemented through collective action in ASEAN. When Malaysia and Indonesian rubber industries stood to be harmed by the large-scale production of synthetic rubber by Japan, the rest of the ASEAN member states, even if they had no rubber industry to speak of, joined in the negotiations with Japan. Similarly, all the ASEAN partner states supported Singapore in its position vis-à-vis Australia's low-air fare programme which harmed Singapore's air travel business.

Hand in hand with mutual regulation of behaviour and taking counsel from one another is the practice of exercising voluntary restraint in their behaviour. The members agreed in Bali not to take advantage of one another's crisis situations. But even before Bali, there had been an observable use of voluntary restraint among the members. In the Malaysia-Philippines and Malaysia-Singapore conflicts, the countries concerned behaved with moderation. When Singapore delivered its ultimatum to Malaysia regarding the delineation of routes for the Singapore International Airways and Malaysian Airways System, Singapore withdrew the ultimatum in the interest of ASEAN relations as soon as it was realised that the ultimatum would be prejudicial to the organisation. Referring again to Malaysia, it refused to discuss or even recognise problems in public to avoid escalation of intra-regional problems.

ASEAN members have also agreed to use their resources first before asking for external help which when given should only be complementary to their resources and not used as a substitute. This principle was later conceptualised by Indonesia as regional resilience, arising from an Indonesian concept of national resilience. In many ways these principles have served to regulate their collective behaviour.

It has been mentioned earlier that ASEAN leaders do not believe in homogenising the community but that they see the value of understanding one another's culture. It has been a practice to welcome visiting ASEAN delegates with traditional ceremonies featuring flowers, dances, or some other cultural presentations. To further encourage cultural understanding, ASEAN has organised cultural groups composed of representatives of all member-states to tour the member-states. Painters, singers, actresses, models, radio-television artists, and others have visited to expose the people to the various cultures. During an early ASEAN film festival in Manila, Filipino viewers commented on the similarities in some words, in humour and in the responses to situations which occur in ordinary people's lives such as love, marriage, going to school, raising families, and meeting friends. In the realm of academic pursuits, joint research in archaeology and museum work have brought to light great similarities in cultural traditions.

ASEAN leaders have experienced that communication among them is getting easier. There are multiple ranges of communication, including formal language, cues and signals, symbols, and traditional behaviour. In formal language, ASEAN is expressed in such concepts as family, brotherhood, fraternity ties, community feeling, and others. Cues and signals are expressed in symbolisation which stand for regionalism or community. Informal visits, restraint in behaviour, mutual respect, tolerance, self-effacement, prayer before meetings, consultation, interchange of group roles, mutual assistance, and others are expressions of shared value. There is increasing frequency and comfort in the use of these cues and signals, implying the growing intensity of sharing, and therefore the growth of the ASEAN Way. Needs are perceived among the members without much explanation while responses are made in the same spirit. Communication in the ASEAN Way has facilitated the strengthening of the political will and the ASEAN Spirit, the resolution of all outstanding issues, and the attainment of consensus and community of interests. All ASEAN meetings are recorded as having been held in the traditional spirit of cordiality, friendship, and hospitality of the host country. This consistent recognition of the traditional values holds the leaders together, even in times of difficulties.

ENDNOTES

1   Most of the texts here are excerpted from Estrella D. Solidum, "ASEAN's Political Formula" in *Foreign Relations Journal* (Manila, Vol. I no. 3, 1986).

2   Leonardo Mercado, *Elements of Filipino Philosophy* (Manila: Divine Word University, 1976), pp. 8-88, citing studies of Lily Abegg in *The Mind of the East* (London, 1952).

3   Ninth ASEAN Ministerial Meeting, Manila, 24-26 June 1976.

4   Tenth ASEAN Ministerial Meeting, Singapore, 5-8 July 1977.

5   Eleventh ASEAN Ministerial Meeting, Bangkok, 14-16 June 1978.

6   ASEAN Declaration for Mutual Assistance on Natural Disasters, Manila, 26 June 1976.

7   Declaration of ASEAN Concord, Bali, 24 February 1976.

8   ASEAN Energy Cooperation and ASEAN Petroleum Agreement, Manila, 24 June 1986.

9   H.E. Professor Mochtar Kusuma Atmadja, Foreign Minister of Indonesia, Opening Statement, Manila, 23 June 1986.

10   Signed at Bali by the five Heads of Government of Indonesia, Malaysia, Philippines, Singapore and Thailand, 24 February 1976.

11   President Suharto, Statement at the Opening of the Meeting of Heads of Government, Bali, 26 February 1976.

12   Estrella D. Solidum, *Bilateral Summitry in ASEAN* (Manila: Foreign Service Institute, 1983).

13   Amitai Etzioni says that a community is characterised by its ability to maintain its existence and form through the use of its self-sufficient mechanisms and processes and will not be dependent upon those of external systems. (Amitai Etzioni, *Political Unification*, New York: Holt, Rinehart and Winston, 1965). Ernst Haas adds that there is a cumulative pattern of accommodation in which the participants seek to attain agreement by means of compromises to upgrade common interest. (Joseph Nye, ed.) *International Regionalism: Readings* (Boston: Little, Brown, 1968).

14   Estrella D. Solidum, "The Pacific Community in Search of a Form", in *Asian Perspective*, Fall-Winter, 1985, Korea and in *Foreign Relations Journal* (Manila, 1986).

15   Estrella D. Solidum, "The Role of Certain Sectors in Sharing and Articulating the ASEAN Way", in *ASEAN Engagements for Peace* (Manila: Yuchengco Center for East Asia, de la Salle university, 1999), pp. 52-71.

16   Solidum, *op.cit.* p. 78.

17   *Ibid*, p. 82.

18   Statements by President Suharto and Prime Minister Hussein Onn at Bali, 1976.

19   Ralph Linton, *The Tree of Culture* (New York: Alfred A. Knopf, 1957), Chapter IV.

20   John J. Honigmann, *Understanding Culture* (New York: Harper and Row, 1963).

21   Opening statements by Heads of Government Meeting at Kuala Lumpur, Malaysia, 4 August 1977.

22   Solidum, *Towards A Southeast Asian Community* (Quezon City: University of the Philippines, 1974), p. 58.

23   *Antara News Bulletin*, 23 March 1967, as cited in *ibid*.

24   ASEAN/Doc/3. Opening statement of Thai Foreign Minister Thanat Khoman, 5 August 1967.

25   ASEAN/MM/11DKT. Report of the Proceedings of the Second Ministerial Conference, Djakarta, 8 August 1968.

4

Political Dimensions
of ASEAN

The Bangkok Declarations of 1967 on the formation of ASEAN mentioned the association as a framework for cooperation and "represents the collective will of the nations of Southeast Asia to bind themselves together in friendship and cooperation" and through joint efforts secure for their people and for posterity the blessings of peace, freedom, and prosperity.[1] The declaration stated cooperation in the social, economic, cultural, and scientific fields but not in the political. It was only at the First Heads of Government Meeting (Summit) at Bali in 1976 that political cooperation was provided for with the Declaration of ASEAN Concord of 24 February 1976.

The First ASEAN Summit in Bali stated the principles for achieving ASEAN's objectives. These are: 1) taking a common ASEAN stand in international fora on matters affecting the region; 2) promoting friendly relations and cooperation with other nations; 3) intensifying government and private efforts to develop a regional identity; and 4) placing military cooperation outside the framework of ASEAN.

Political cooperation focused on both resolving disputes and the more positive aspect of showing the direction to peace and stability in the region.

This is to be understood in terms of the deep yearnings of the member states of ASEAN to have meaningful cooperation among themselves as they had not had close relations before 1967 and because political manoeuvrings or "high politics" is fraught with conflict and distrust and could break the learning of cooperation among themselves.

On the other hand the Association of Southeast Asia (ASA, 1961) taught them that functional cooperation or "low politics" is more conducive to success. As noted by David Mitrany, to move from political to a technical framework of cooperation is to eliminate the potential for conflict.[2]

It does not mean, however, that ASEAN left out of its attention the various political problems in and around ASEAN. ASEAN is political, to begin with, as it functions through the government leadership and administrations of the member states. In the earliest admission of political attention to issues, ASEAN officials said they discussed those "in the corridors of ASEAN".

At the start of its existence, ASEAN was faced with intra-regional conflicts. These included the strained relations between Malaya and Singapore which had resulted from historically difficult relationships; Indonesian-Malaysian conflict due to the former's opposition to the establishment of Malaysia; Thai-Malaysia problems on the common border concerning the "hot pursuit" by Malaysian troops of the Communist Party of Malaya (CPM) fleeing into Thai territory, and the Muslim separatists in southern Thailand; strained relations between Malaysia and the Philippines over conflicting claims on Sabah (North Borneo); and problems of overlapping claims on territories along common borders.[3]

These issues were approached with the principle of Asian solutions to Asian problems as the legitimate way because the peoples involved knew their interests best and how to resolve the conflicts. Thus in the earliest period of ASEAN, the use of low-key diplomacy and bilateral summitry led to agreements which resolved territorial problems. Parties to the conflicts and problem-solvers approached the conflicts with respect for one another's views, with a spirit of "give and take", and with a spirit of understanding and good neighbourliness. On the spirit of neighbourliness, Thai Foreign Minister Thanat Khoman said in the first year of ASEAN that "they had discarded their deplorable habit of going their own separate ways and turning their backs on one another". Thanat was himself very much a problem-solver among Malaysia, the Philippines and Indonesia.

Most of these issues were resolved by border agreements and none of these had erupted into violence. In the 1990s, Vietnam settled its border disputes with Malaysia and Laos. Myanmar has also committed to solve its problems by negotiations. In the case of Malaysia and Indonesia, they had agreed to bring the dispute over Ligitan and Sipadan Islands to the International Court of Justice, which awarded the two islands to Malaysia in December 2002.

The Bangkok Declaration has provided that "the countries of Southeast Asia are determined to ensure their stability and security from external interference in any form or manifestation in order to preserve their national identities in accordance with the ideas and aspirations of their peoples".

On 27 November 1971, ASEAN adopted the Kuala Lumpur Declaration, known as the Zone of Peace, Freedom, and Neutrality Declaration (ZOPFAN) to bring about relaxation of international tensions. The ZOPFAN Declaration recognised the principle of a nuclear weapon-free zone and the neutralisation of Southeast Asia as a desirable objective. Originally in 1968 Malaysia had hoped that with ZOPFAN Southeast Asian countries could be insulated from the Great Powers' competition for power. The proposal went through several revisions. Some states wanted steady disengagement by the Great Powers.

ZOPFAN later included the concept of national and regional resilience, also known as the Suharto Doctrine. This was the concept of Indonesia for its national security which was defined as comprehensive security because it included political, socio-cultural, economic, and military components which are all interrelated. [4] In 1983, the ZOPFAN incorporated the principle of the Southeast Asia Nuclear Weapon-Free Zone (SEANWFZ). In 1995, the Treaty on the SEANWFZ was signed by the Heads of Government of the ten Southeast Asian countries. ASEAN senior officials are consulting with Nuclear Weapon States to obtain their support for the Treaty on the SEANWFZ by signing its Protocol. The Treaty's Protocol has implications for port visits of foreign ships and aircraft in the SEANWFZ.

The impending take-over of governments by communist parties in Vietnam, Laos, and Cambodia in 1973 created fear among the peoples which made them leave their respective countries either by boat or by land. Thus, the "boat people" took great risks on the high seas which abounded with deadly pirates who sank the boats of the refugees and robbed them. "Land people" had similar risks. If they had no admission to other countries, the refugees were as good as dead. ASEAN took cognisance of the refugee problem. By arrangements with the UNHCR and with possible host countries in Europe, the United States, in South America, Australia, and elsewhere, ASEAN states took the responsibility of accepting the boat and land peoples as countries of first asylum. The fleeing peoples were given designated areas where they were given shelter, food, medicines, education, and other necessities while training for skills that could make them acceptable to probable host countries. The principle involved was that no refugee would be residual in the first asylum countries at the end of the designated period. One of the consequences of this arrangement is that many Vietnamese, Cambodians, and Laotians acquired high technological and scientific skills in their host countries which provided them with food, clothing, shelter, education, training, and jobs. Many returned to their countries to train the people who were left behind and to contribute to the development of their own respective countries.

As the Vietnam War had ended in 1973 by the Paris Peace Treaty and the communist parties had come to power in 1975 in Vietnam, Laos, and Cambodia, ASEAN decided to establish relations with each of them rather than get external military support to confront them. ASEAN's new strategy was a diplomatic initiative of confidence-building measures to create amity rather than enmity and was a development from low-key diplomacy. But peace was not to be. Vietnam took the initiative in Laos and Cambodia, bringing with it the support of the Soviet Union which was designed to undercut China in the region. Meanwhile, ASEAN member states strengthened themselves economically and socially to forestall internal communist insurgencies and propaganda.

ASEAN POLITICAL PROCESSES TO COPE WITH THE CAMBODIAN PROBLEM

The Cambodian problem became more complicated in 1978 when Vietnam sent occupation troops into Cambodia and the three Cambodian groups that opposed the Hun Sen government which Vietnam had installed in their country were unable to gather strength to form a tentative grouping to work for self-determination. ASEAN had a real stake in Cambodia's stability because foreign intervention in the region could present a much bigger threat.

ASEAN used legal and diplomatic means on Vietnam to remove its occupation troops from Cambodia. At times diplomacy seemed to promise results but Vietnam was changeable and belligerent from time to time. In 1979 ASEAN presented a resolution to the United Nations Security Council for non-interference in the internal affairs of Cambodia and for the withdrawal of Vietnamese troops. The Soviet Union expectedly vetoed the resolution. When the General Assembly started its fall session, ASEAN secured the recognition of Pol Pot's Democratic Kampuchea as the legitimate government instead of the

Vietnamese-installed Hun Sen government and the passage of ASEAN Resolution 34/22 for the withdrawal of all foreign troops from Cambodia. In 1980, Malaysia's Hussein Onn and Suharto met in Kuantan and released the Kuantan Initiative which recognised Vietnam's legitimate security interests and restrained harsh actions against the country to prevent it from rushing to Soviet arms once more. But Vietnam was impatient with ASEAN's diplomacy where its members appeared to be divided by the prospect of China's growing influence over Thailand.

Vietnam attacked refugee camps in Thailand which it had suspected of arming Cambodian refugees and sending them back to help Pol Pot's soldiers against the Hun Sen government. Thailand had become a "frontline state" in the war. China offered military assistance to Thailand and was considered a threat to ASEAN but ASEAN fully supported Thailand's position.

In 1982, Singapore and Thailand helped to form a coalition of Cambodian resistance forces namely the Khmer Rouge, the KPNLF and Sihanouk's FUNCINPEC to struggle for Cambodia's right to self-determination. Indonesia also made its initiative as "interlocutor" to Vietnam to make a common stand against China even as Thailand developed a closer relationship with China. Singapore took a middle path of sending strong words to Vietnam. The ASEAN process seemed to be in confusion but Singapore's Lee Kuan Yew said that Malaysia's and Indonesia's dialogue with Vietnam was useful so that more information could be gathered on Vietnam's intentions. Indonesia's comment on Singapore's tough stand was that it was useful for ASEAN where different attitudes are an asset.

What appeared to be differences within ASEAN were transformed into division of labour and preservation of national identities through their independent foreign policies.[5]

Indonesia took another initiative to help Cambodia's search for self-determination by sponsoring Jakarta Informal Meetings I and II (JIM I & II). ASEAN helped to get the United Nations Security Council to take action which resulted in the Paris Peace Treaty of 1991, the formation of the UN Transitional Authority in Cambodia (UNTAC) and finally the setting up of the royal government of Cambodia with elected King Norodom Sihanouk, all under the comprehensive Political Settlement of the Cambodian Conflict of the Paris conference on Cambodia.

ASEAN's political processes have provided potential expressions for each of its members but have transformed every situation to advantage for the image of solidarity.

It seemed impossible that the three Marxist Socialist states of Laos, Cambodia, and Vietnam could ever be members of ASEAN. The three states were isolated politically and economically from their patron, the Soviet Union when Mikhail Gorbachev announced his New Asia policy. From ideological camp to isolation, Vietnam adopted a pragmatic policy which Laos soon followed to develop relations with their neighbours in Southeast Asia. However, ASEAN's own development as a viable and attractive regional association and its non-military strategies to create peace in Southeast Asia could have made the three states consider joining it. Vietnam and Laos acceded to the TAC in 1992. Vietnam became a member of ASEAN in 1995 and Laos with Myanmar in 1997. Cambodia became the tenth member in 1999. Vietnam's Minister of Foreign Affairs Nguyen Manh Cam said that Vietnam's admission was a "qualitative change in the condition of our region 50 years after the end of the World War II... an eloquent testimony to the ever-growing trends of regionalization and globalization in the increasingly interdependent world". Indonesia's Foreign Minister Ali Alatas said that Vietnam's admission was more than an increase in membership. Vietnam will enhance the vitality and collective strength of the Association and deepen the meaning of ASEAN cooperation.

Myanmar was also a concern of ASEAN in the region. Myanmar according to outsiders had a high record of human rights violations, the military rulers had refused to recognise the victory of the National League for Democracy in 1990 under Daw Aung San Suu Kyi, and was under pressure from China which needed to influence it as its leverage in its rivalry with India in the Indian Ocean. With its isolationist and neutralist policy, Myanmar could be out of ASEAN, looking in with its sights unknown. ASEAN leaders tried to attract Myanmar to join ASEAN as Myanmar could derive union strength for its national interest.

ASEAN developed a new strategy called constructive engagement by which Myanmar leaders were invited to ASEAN meetings to see for themselves what benefits their country could derive from being with ASEAN or what risks it had by standing alone. Myanmar was a "Guest" of ASEAN in 1994, acceded to the TAC in 1995, became Official Observer in 1996 and became a member in 1997.

The TAC was contained in the Bali Agreements of 1976 made during the First Heads of Government Meeting of ASEAN. TAC represents a code of international conduct governing peaceful relations among countries in the region in accordance with the Charter of United Nations, the Ten Principles of the Bandung Conference of 1995, the ASEAN Declaration of 1967, and the Declaration on the Zone of Peace, Freedom, and Neutrality of 1971.

The High Contracting Parties of the TAC shall develop and strengthen the traditional, cultural and historical ties of friendship, good neighbourliness and cooperation which bind them together and shall fulfil in good faith the obligations assumed in this Treaty. The High Contracting Parties shall cooperate in all fields of endeavour. They will also cooperate with all peace-loving nations for world peace.

Settlement of differences or disputes should be regulated by rational, effective and flexible procedures, avoiding negative attitudes. Settlement of disputes shall be through friendly negotiations. To settle disputes through regional processes a High Council shall be constituted to take cognisance of the dispute and recommend to the parties in the dispute means of settlement such as good offices, mediation, inquiry, or conciliation. Parties to the disputes should be well disposed to the means and offer of assistance from the other High Contracting Parties.

The UN General Assembly endorsed the TAC in 1992. In 1998, the second Protocol amending the TAC was signed by the High Contracting Parties to enable non-Southeast Asian countries to accede to the TAC.

The Declaration of ASEAN Concord (1976) contains the principles and framework for ASEAN cooperation in the political, security, economic, and functional fields. The ASEAN Concord provided for cooperation in political matters and for cooperation in security (military) matters on a non-ASEAN basis and according to the mutual needs and interest of the parties concerned.

Even as the functional committees and ministerial level meetings handle the work of ASEAN with the full support of the revitalised ASEAN Secretariat, it was realised in the earlier years of the association that there were certain matters which could not be handled at the structural level. The peculiar nature of those matters necessitated some other levels of communication because they were of far-reaching consequences. These were issues that were important to ASEAN and its regional objectives.

The response to such necessity were the bilateral meetings of Heads of Government which have been called bilateral summitry. The Heads of Government met with one another informally to discuss the issues and make political decisions. Even after the First Heads of Government Meeting in Bali (1976) bilateral summitry continued, at least until the structure of ASEAN could accommodate all the needs.[6]

From 1967 to 1981 there were about 96 of those meetings. The most number of bilateral summitry meetings were in 1976 (16), 1978 (12), 1975 (11), 1979 (9) and 1980 (8). The countries most involved were Thailand, Malaysia, and Indonesia.

The subjects covered were threats from the regional and international environment, border problems, need for a first ASEAN Summit, developments in Vietnam, Laos, and Cambodia after the war, and communist activities. Economic cooperation was always mentioned as it was a welcome take-off point, producing agreeableness among the parties which had hoped that the spirit could spill-over to the more sensitive matters.

We can see some examples of the sensitive issues. Singapore's Prime Minister Lee Kuan Yew visited President Marcos of the Philippines, Prime Minister Thanin of Thailand and President Suharto of Indonesia. Lee's urgent message was for the governments to look after the problems of food, shelter, and employment, set the houses in order, and speed up the ASEAN programme for the development by reducing the problem of corruption.

In 1978 Thailand's Prime Minister Kriangsak visited Suharto, Hussein Onn, and Lee to expand trade and political cooperation. Soon the oil crisis threatened the stability of non-oil states. Kriangsak went to Indonesia to get an assurance of oil supply. When Kampuchea (Cambodia) was invaded by Vietnam in 1978, Thailand was the most pressured ASEAN state. Kriangsak went to see Lee in Singapore to ask him to sell surplus oil to Thailand.

In 1968, the Sabah problem had strained Philippine-Malaysian relations. Thai Prime Minister Thanom Kittikachorn visited Malaysian leaders whose position was for ASEAN leaders to persuade the Philippines to give up its claim to Sabah or suffer the consequences. Thai leaders were at all times willing to help in the resolution of conflicts as a "good neighbor and good friend" but were not willing to get involved in the problem. Thai Foreign Minister Thanat Khoman rejected the Malaysian proposition while expressing a general desire to limit the conflict to the two parties and help eliminate conflict situation in ASEAN by presenting an openness to new solutions and by reiterating a willingness to help.

All in all, bilateral summitry issues according to importance by frequency of mention, were:

1. ASEAN cooperation, the need for mutual understanding and unity in all matters;
2. Intra-ASEAN problems that were too sensitive for formal ASEAN-wide discussions such as secessionism problem, territorial claims and border problems;
3. Foreign policies on non-alignment and neutralisation, and explanation of new policy shifts;
4. Security problems including US military in Philippine bases, SEATO, military cooperation in ASEAN, bilateral military cooperation outside of ASEAN, ethnic insurgencies;
5. International developments;
6. ASEAN organisation itself; summit meetings, restructuring of ASEAN.

The topics were highly sensitive, delicate, counterproductive if taken ASEAN- wide, too specific in impact, and broad in dimension, enough to cut into national or regional or political interests of the members.

Bilateral summitry was easy to set up and was quite acceptable to all because the action was embedded in cultural values.

In the 1980s the problem of overlapping claims on the Spratly Islands in the South China Sea was becoming critical. Some incidents nearly erupted into military confrontations which could have plunged Southeast Asia into a new crisis. The claimants to some of the islands are Malaysia, Brunei, Vietnam, and the Philippines, while China and Taiwan separately claim all the islands. They are seen to be of strategic value as they straddle the sea lanes of communication (SLOC) and may have prospective marine and mineral resources.

In November 1991, Philippine and Thai foreign ministry officials hosted security-oriented conferences with ASEAN states, Dialogue Partners, Laos, Vietnam, Myanmar, Russia, and China attending. On another initiative, Indonesia organised workshops on "Managing Potential Conflicts in the South China Sea" on a non-governmental level. The first workshop was in Bali in January 1990, then it was followed by the Bandung meeting in July 1991; and the fifth was in Sumatra in October 1994.

This process is a building block for security by creating space for mutual understanding. This process is called preventive diplomacy.[7] It is informal, develops goodwill, and preserves friendly relations for the present and for the future.

In February 1992, China's Congress authorised military action against maritime violations of Chinese sovereignty. The response of ASEAN later that year was the Declaration on the South China Sea or the Manila Declaration of 1992 which calls on all parties to exercise restraint and to use peaceful resolution on the problems of the Spratlys. China has agreed to such references in the ASEAN Regional Forum (ARF) Chairman's Statement and in the Summary Record of ASEAN-China Political Consultation.

THE ASEAN-CHINA SUMMIT

Declaration on the Conduct of Parties in the South China Sea, 4 November 2002[8]

One of the most significant outcomes of the Eighth Summit Meeting was the signing of the Declaration on the Conduct of Parties in the South China Sea. The signing, according to Philippine Foreign Affairs Secretary Blas F. Ople, "was a major leap for peace, stability, and development in our region".

To go back briefly to the roots of the South China disputes, one has to see the bases for the conflicts over the Spratly and Paracel Islands, namely, sovereignty, jurisdictional, and historical claims. Some strategic factors such as control of the sea lanes of communication (SLOC), intrusion of ambitions by states outside of Southeast Asia over the same sea lanes, possible presence of oil and mineral products under the sea, and new developments in the competing foreign interests and policies of large states in Asia and the Pacific, have produced much anxiety among the claimant states, namely, China, Taiwan, Vietnam, the Philippines, Brunei and Malaysia. In those days, these were not yet problems of ASEAN.

In the early 1990s, Indonesia and the Philippines separately sponsored conferences for the possible peaceful handling of the territorial and jurisdictional disputes. There were hopes but there were physical

110

actions by claimant states that could have led to actual conflicts. Ships were positioned threateningly, structures were being constructed in the challenged islands, and unilateral occupation by stronger states seemed to lead to worse conditions. On the US side, all it was interested in at that time was freedom of navigation and of the sea-lanes of communication (SLOC).

In 1998, ASEAN adopted the Hanoi Plan of Action which made reference to a code to govern ASEAN-China relations vis-à-vis the South China Sea. Work on such a code continued, until at the Eighth ASEAN Summit on 4 November 2002, the Declaration on the Conduct of Parties in the South China Sea was signed.

Meanwhile the Asia-Pacific region had been a picture of changing power directions involving strategic policy choices of the US, China, Japan, and lesser states. For example leaders in China have perceived that their country should have regional military and economic supremacy.

With the declining economies in Japan, US, and ASEAN states since 1997, and China's entry into the World Trade Organization (WTO), China's low-priced goods in the world market has enabled a 9 per cent economic growth in the country.

But Chinese leaders also perceive that the US has frustrated China from becoming the power in the Asia-Pacific region as the US has kept unlimited access to the other states through their bases, missiles, and weapons of mass destruction. The growing power of the US is seen as encirclement of China.

China has adopted a flexible, realistic policy. Its military spending has been increased by 18 per cent to meet the global changes and prepare for high technology defence. China's Defence White Paper of October 2000 saw the US as the obstacle to China's regional military supremacy. To consolidate its policy and power directions vis-à-vis the kind of role the US would play as a unilateral world power, China countered US initiatives in Central Asia and South Asia with its own foreign policy actions. To meet US military presence in Central Asia, China offered to provide military and security services to Kazakhstan, Kyrgystan, and Uzbekstan. On India-US cooperation, China strengthened its military cooperation with Pakistan on nuclear capability. China has also signed a treaty with Russia on economic and strategic cooperation.

China has expanded its scope of relations with other countries to address newer problems in the world, such as drug trafficking, terrorism, transnational crimes and non-traditional security issues.

In this heightened-risk condition, the South China Sea, a grand artery that reaches all directions, has become a security leverage for all interested parties. ASEAN is fixed in its declared goals of peace, progress and prosperity in the region. China as well would need a peaceful neighbourhood that will at least not put pressures on its national policies at this time.

It is really of great significance that the People's Republic of China has joined ASEAN in the Declaration on the Conduct of Parties in the South China Sea. The Declaration provides, among others,

1. The Parties reaffirm their determination to consolidate and develop the friendship and cooperation among them to promote a 21st century-oriented partnership of good neighbourliness and mutual trust.

2. The Parties need to promote, friendly and harmonious environment in the South China for the peace and prosperity of the people.

3. The Parties desire to enhance favourable conditions for a peaceful and durable solution of differences and disputes among countries concerned.

4. The Parties are committed to the purposes and principles of the Charter of the United Nations, the 1982 UN Convention on the Law of the Sea, the Treaty of Amity and Cooperation in Southeast Asia, the five Principles of Peaceful Coexistence and other universally recognised principles of international law which serve as the basic norms of state-to-state relations.

5. The Parties affirm their respect and commitment to the freedom of navigation in and over flight above the South China Sea as provided by the principles of international law.

6. The Parties concerned shall resolve their territorial and jurisdictional disputes by peaceful means, without resorting to the threat or use of force, through consultations and negotiations by sovereign states directly concerned in accordance with the principles of international law.

7. The Parties shall exercise self-restraint in the conduct of activities that would escalate disputes and affect peace, refrain from action or inhabiting the presently uninhabited areas, and handle their differences in a constructive manner.

8. Pending the peaceful settlement, the Parties concerned will seek ways to build trust and confidence among them, including dialogues

between their defence and military officials, just and humane treatment of all persons in distress.

9. Pending settlement of the disputes, the Parties concerned may undertake cooperative activities. These include
   a. marine environment protection,
   b. marine scientific research,
   c. safety of navigation and communication at sea,
   d. search and rescue operations
   e. combating transnational crime, such as illicit drug-trafficking, piracy, armed robbery at sea, and illegal traffic in arms.

10. The adoption of the Code of Conduct in the South China Sea will promote peace and stability in the region and the Parties concerned agree to work on the basis of consensus.

ASEAN'S SOLUTIONS

ASEAN's solutions for its intra-regional problems and its means for increasing multilateral ties have been summed up by Michael Antolik as "diplomacy of accommodation". Indeed, this diplomacy of accommodation is made up of not only Asian solutions for Asian problems but also of actions to foster rapport and develop regional solidarity.

As in the bilateral visits among Heads of Government which were made very privately and in very low-key fashion, these meetings were customarily done as *empatmata* (four eyes) for direct consultation and mutual understanding. There were also continuous visits among officials of ASEAN at all levels which have served to acculturate or socialise new officials into the ASEAN Way and to vitalise the process of continuous consultations in multi-channels to prevent the setting in of, distancing or remoteness among political, social, economic, and other sectors, and to strengthen the mechanism of accountability. Understanding and accepting credibility and empathy have nearly banished any thought of bureaucratic accountability as consultation-accountability is accepted as the means for ASEAN peace and stability. Tolerance for each member's domestic system has led to confidence in one another's goodwill, which in turn, has become a foundation for the practice of mutual restraint and accountability. A strong commitment to ASEAN and the accompanying responsibility is the important element of accommodation because one has to be responsible for the effects of his actions on the others. [9] As Thai Prime

Minister Kukrit Pramoj said, "…we have to learn to live together and to adjust to one another in the spirit of tolerance".

In addition to the diplomacy of accommodation to meet intra-regional problems, ASEAN also had to use formal processes to meet real economic threats from the environment which could damage the economic and social fabric of ASEAN member states. At the Sixth ASEAN Summit held in Hanoi on 15-16 December 1998, the ASEAN leaders adopted the Hanoi Declaration which outlined ASEAN's policy directions and priorities in the context of the current problems. [10] The Sixth Summit also adopted the Hanoi Plan of Action (HPA), the first of a series of plans of action that should lead ASEAN to realise its ASEAN Vision 2020 which had been earlier adopted in December 1997. Vision 2020 laid out the ideal of ASEAN in the 21st century: "a concert of Southeast Asian Nations, outward-looking, living in peace, stability and prosperity, bonded together in partnership in dynamic development and in a community of caring societies".

ASEAN'S political processes include a human dimension particularly that of personal familiarity. A scholar of Southeast Asia, Robert Pringle wrote "that the mere process of contact breeds a desire to be helpful, to see those we know personally succeed…this is true in Southeast Asia where personal charm is endemic and hospitality has been developed to a fine art". Indonesian leader Ali Moertopo said that consultations are successful because leaders have been old friends who know one another so well. Ghazalie Shafie, a Malaysian leader said that ASEAN is an "almost telepathic community". In trying situations, silence or restraint, couching policy in terms of ASEAN or ambiguity can convey the meanings of actions and yet provide "safety nets" in relationships. [11]

During times of changing roles in Southeast Asia among China, the Soviet Union, the U.S., and some members of ASEAN, such as in the period of US withdrawal from Vietnam and the rise of China as a power, ASEAN members expressed their policies in unity which are restrained underneath their differences in approaches and covered them by some concepts such as "common interests". [12]

ASEAN has successfully resolved the intra-regional and regional issues that confronted it. ASEAN used non-military measures to resolve problems, prevented them from becoming disputes and prevented the occurrence of violence. ASEAN has increased and improved available strategies to preserve peace and stability in Southeast Asia, using innovative Asian solutions for Asian problems. Most of all ASEAN has eschewed the use of military force.

ENDNOTES

1   The ASEAN Declaration (Bangkok Declaration, 8 August 1967).

2   James E. Dougherty and Robert C. Pfaltzgraff, Jr., *Contending Theories of International Relations* (New York: Harper and Row Publishers, 1981), p. 19.

3   Chan Heng Chee, "Intra-ASEAN Political, Security, and Economic Cooperation" in Sandhu and Siddique (eds.).*The ASEAN Reader* (Singapore: ISEAS, 1992), pp. 101-105.

4   Bilveer Singh, *ZOPFAN and the New Security Order in the Asia-Pacific Region* (Malaysia: Palanduk Publication (CM) SDN Bhd., 1992), pp. 55-59.

5   Michael Antolik, *ASEAN and the Diplomacy of Accommodation* (New York: M.E. Sharpe, Inc., 1990), pp. 103-104.

6   Estrella D. Solidum, *Bilateral Summitry in ASEAN* (Manila: Foreign Service Institute, 1983).

7   Michael Antolik, "ASEAN and the Utilities of Diplomatic Informality", in Sereno and Santiago (eds.) *The ASEAN: Thirty Years and Beyond* (Quezon City: Law Center, University of the Philippines Press, 1997), pp. 441-445.

8   Declaration on the Conduct of Parties in the South China Sea, 4 November 2002, Phnom Penh.

9   Michael Antolik, *ASEAN and the Diplomacy of Accommodation, op cit.*, pp.90-107.

10   Association of Southeast Asian Nations Annual Report 1998-1999, Jakarta: Central Secretariat, pp. 10-11.

11   Michael Antolik, *op.cit.*, pp. 108-115.

12   *Ibid.*

CHAPTER 5

Functional Cooperation in ASEAN

FOUNDATION OF FUNCTIONAL COOPERATION

Bangkok Declaration of 1967

To know the aims and purposes of ASEAN, one has to go to the ASEAN Declaration of 8 August 1967. The over-arching milieu of the times was the urgent need for cooperation in Southeast Asia. The milieu consisted of (1) the existence of mutual interests and common problems among countries of Southeast Asia and the felt need to strengthen existing bonds of regional solidarity and cooperation; (2) the desire to establish a firm foundation for common action to promote regional cooperation in the spirit of equality and partnership for peace, progress, and prosperity in the region; (3) the consciousness that the ideals as stated in 2) may best be attained through good understanding, good neighbourliness and meaningful cooperation among these countries which are already bound by ties of history and culture; (4) the primary responsibility of the countries of Southeast Asia for the stability, national development, and security in accordance with the ideals of their peoples; and (5) the commitment that foreign military bases are not to be used to subvert the national independence and orderly processes of national development of each country.

Thus ASEAN was established with the following specific aims and purposes:

1) Economic growth, social progress, and cultural development in the region through joint endeavour in the spirit of equality and partnership;
2) Respect for the rule of law;
3) Active collaboration and mutual assistance on matters of common interest in the economic, social, cultural, technical, scientific, and administrative fields;

4) Assistance to each other in the form of training and research facilities in the educational, professional, technical, and administrative spheres;

5) Collaboration in agriculture, industries, expansion of trade, transport and communication facilities, and raising the standard of living of the people;

6) Promotion of Southeast Asian studies; and

7) Beneficial cooperation with existing international and regional organisations with similar aims and purposes.

In the course of time, ASEAN separated the cooperative projects into manageable fields, namely economic, political, security, and functional cooperation. Even with this apparent disaggregation, ASEAN finds this more convenient and useful.

THEORETICAL UNDERPINNING FOR FUNCTIONAL COOPERATION

The formation of commercial leagues such as the Hanseatic League in the Middle Ages led to the idea of functionalism for world cooperation. In modern times, the earliest use of the concept functionalism in integration theories by David Mitrany has influenced greatly the thoughts of contemporary integration theorists. Mitrany developed this concept during the years between the two World Wars (1918-1937) and in the few years after World War II. Looking at the complex problems facing governments, especially technical and non-political problems that demanded government attention, Mitrany said that such problems needed highly trained specialists at the national level who could also contribute to solving essentially technical problems at the international level. The solutions to such problems lie in the collaboration among technicians rather than with political elites. This has a corollary, that the political has potential for conflict, so a framework for international cooperation can move away from the political to the technical. Mitrany's strategy was to shift political cooperation to cooperation in non-controversial technical problems.[1]

Mitrany said that "functions" refer to "vital social activities" that are necessary to the survival of modern societies. Such activities are cultural, educational, social, political or legal. Functionalist focus on scientific, technological, and economic activities. Functionalists view issues like educational, cultural, and social isues as "low politics" while activities that impinge on a state's sovereignty which are conflict-prone are "high politics".

Mitrany's theory has a doctrine of "ramification" which means that collaboration in one field leads to collaboration in other technical fields. Functional cooperation in one sector results from a felt need and generates a felt need for functional cooperation in another sector. For example, today in ASEAN, cooperation in poverty eradication could lead to cooperation in social development and drug abuse prevention. Mitrany assumed that functional cooperation could lead to world peace and would even encroach upon the political sector.[2] This is because the nation-state lacks the ability to preserve peace or to improve the social and economic well-being of its inhabitants.

Later, integration theorist Ernst Haas tried to refine Mitrany's theory. Haas said that power is not separable from welfare. Haas enlarged Mitrany's "ramification" and called it "spill-over" such as when, in the process of functional cooperation, the rates of transactions are high, functionalism will spill-over to the political field especially when crises occur and would need an authoritative hand to manage them. His example was the European integration movement in the 1960s. The progress of the common market to common external tariff, to uniform rules of competition, on to a common agricultural policy would need to be directed by some form of authority beyond the nation-state, or a supranational structure.[3] This is the spill-over to the political from functional cooperation for which theories Haas and others like Philippe Schnitter and Joseph Nye are known for "neofunctionalism".

Although the use of functionalism was for developing integration theories, it is useful to study it here because cooperation is a first step to integration. But even if no supranational structure for a common loyalty which transcends local or national loyalties occurs as in integration, still functional cooperation is a useful classification for ASEAN activities that are seen to bring about good understanding and solidarity to achieve social progress, cultural development, national development, and stability in the region.

DEVELOPMENT OF FUNCTIONALISM PRINCIPLES IN ASEAN

ASEAN's decisions for functional cooperation were made over the years.[4] In addressing the stated aims of the ASEAN Declaration of 1967, officials focused on cooperation to provide progress and development for the people in general and for national development and regional identity. In 1967, political cooperation was not mentioned in the Declaration because what was political was known from earlier experiences to be fraught with conflict. Since 1967 ASEAN had looked to the external environment, this is to say, to countries, inter-governmental organisations, non-governmental organisations, international organisations and individual experts, for promoting cooperation with them on the basis of mutual respect and benefits. ASEAN countries particularly needed transfer of technology and scientific experience for national and regional economic and social development.

By the First ASEAN Summit in Bali in 1976, the principles for achieving its objectives were stated. These principles included 1) taking a common ASEAN stand in international fora on matters affecting the region; 2) promoting friendly relations and cooperation with other nations on the basis of mutual respect and benefits; and 3) intensifying the efforts of the government and private sectors for the development of a regional identity.[4] On this last one, ASEAN officials also agreed on the use of the ASEAN label whenever a cooperative project was being planned and implemented. The First Summit also provided formally for the first time a platform for political cooperation.

The Second ASEAN Summit in Kuala Lumpur in 1977 planned for expanded cooperation on human resource development, the integration of women and youth in the development process; the elimination of poverty, disease and illiteracy; the integration of population with rural development policies; the provision of productive employment opportunities for low-income groups especially in the rural areas; and the concerted action to curb the abuse and traffic in narcotics and drugs.

International developments in the 1970s already revealed the increasing problems of states and their peoples and ASEAN had to face these problems through expanded cooperation regionally and internationally. Obviously, the problems were not substantively political in nature.

119

The Third ASEAN Summit held in Manila in 1987 reiterated the importance of functional cooperation to promote awareness of ASEAN, increased participation and involvement of peoples in ASEAN, and development of its human resources. ASEAN resolved to eliminate drug abuse and illegal trafficking, all of which threatened the fabric of ASEAN societies and peoples. These areas of interest were classified into functional cooperation.

The Fourth ASEAN Summit in Singapore in 1992 clarified and explained the different purposes and modalities of functional cooperation, now to include the expansion of ASEAN studies in school curriculum and the introduction of student exchange programmes; the enhanced role of NGOs, women and children; intensification of the fight against drug and illicit trafficking at the national, regional, and international levels; efforts to curb the spread of AIDS through exchange of information on the disease; protection of the environment, and promotion of sustainable development. Functional cooperation in ASEAN was made more specific by the 1995 Bangkok Summit Declaration.

The Fifth Summit held in Bangkok in 1995 elevated functional cooperation to a higher plane, the aim of which was to bring shared prosperity to its members. The theme is "shared prosperity through human development, technological competitiveness, and social cohesiveness".

The framework for elevating functional cooperation to a higher plane of shared prosperity lists down six measures to guide the activities of the functional committees. These are:

1) Selected programmes and activities shall be prioritised in line with the 15-point consensus on functional cooperation as contained in the 1995 Bangkok Summit Declaration.
2) High profile or flagship projects shall be developed by the functional committees.
3) Greater publicity shall be given to functional cooperation activities of ASEAN through the publication of a newsletter.
4) The public profile of functional cooperation activities shall be raised by the presentation of ASEAN Awards to industries and organisations.
5) The functional committees shall develop projects using various cost-sharing schemes.
6) The Functional Cooperation Bureau of the ASEAN Secretariat shall be strengthened.

It may be noted at this point that cooperation that is not political, economic, and security have been placed under the class of functional cooperation.

FUNCTIONALISM IN ASEAN

In ASEAN, functional cooperation includes 1) poverty eradication, 2) social development, 3) science and technology, 4) environment, 5) drug matters, and 6) culture and information.

1) Poverty Eradication [5]

The financial and economic crisis in Southeast Asia since 1997 brought about great economic and social difficulties to the already poor and disadvantaged. ASEAN officials were alert to respond to the impact of the crisis not only on the poor but also on the various economic levels of societies. But the plight of the poor had to be attended to immediately.

The Sixth ASEAN Summit held in Hanoi in December 1998 resolved to safeguard the welfare of the poor and the disadvantaged. The Summit adopted the Hanoi Plan of Action which mandates ASEAN to implement the Plan of Action on ASEAN Rural Development and Poverty Eradication and to implement the ASEAN Action Plan on Social Safety Nets to protect the most vulnerable sectors of society. In its informal meeting, the ASEAN Ministers on Rural Development and Poverty Eradication (AMRDPE) was made in charge of coordinating the implementation of the relevant measures.

The Action Plan on Social Safety Nets (SSN) as adopted by the AMRDPE in its Informal Meeting in Jakarta in December 1998 aims to build the capacity of participating countries in 1) assessing and monitoring the social impact of the economic and financial crisis and identifying target groups that have been affected and their needs; 2) developing and implementing social safety net programmes for the disadvantaged and vulnerable; 3) monitoring and improving the effectiveness of economic and social services delivery; and 4) promoting public awareness of the impact of the crisis on the poor. Several international agencies such as the UNDP, the Asian Development Bank (ADB), and the World Bank attended this meeting and they were urged to support ASEAN in implementing the Action Plan on Social Safety Nets.

An ASEAN task force on social safety nets created in 1998 by the meeting of the Senior Officials on Rural Development and Poverty Eradication in Kuala Lumpur will develop a comprehensive regional work plan for the SSN and other forms of social protection and mobilise resources and technical assistance from international agencies, ASEAN Dialogue Partners, the ASEAN Foundation, and the private sector.

Meanwhile, the framework for the ASEAN Plan of Action on Rural Development and Poverty Eradication of 1997 was operationalised initially into a short-term work programme with three projects.

These are 1) Building and/or Enhancing Capacity for Research; Assessment, and Monitoring of Poverty Incidence in ASEAN Countries (coordinated by Malaysia); 2) Regional Training Programme for Facilitators to Work in Anti-Poverty Programmes in the Rural Areas with Skills in Economic Management, Communications, Agricultural Extension, and Microcredit Services (coordinated by Indonesia); and 3) Campaign for Enhancing National and Regional Public Awareness on Rural Development and Poverty Eradication (coordinated by the Philippines).

As of the year 2000, the operationalisation of the ASEAN Plan of Action was going through various national levels of study for final consensus and implementation by ASEAN units.

2) Social Development

The Meaning of Social Development

ASEAN documents have not given a precise definition of social development. Instead the programmes are centred on concerns about the people in the society and on the increase in the people's capabilities to enable them to improve their quality of life and to be responsible members of a strong, caring, educated, and cohesive society.

A definition is posited here. Social development is any perceptible change in the peoples' lives in a community, which change is directed to the achievement of the common or shared goals of the collectivity of people.

Not every change is development. The criterion for development is that the change leads to the increase in capabilities for achieving goals.

The ASEAN Declaration (Bangkok, 8 August 1967) has declared that the aims of the association are 1) to strengthen the foundation for a prosperous and peaceful community in Southeast Asia; 2) to promote regional peace and stability; 3) to promote active collaboration and mutual assistance on matters of common interest in the economic, social, cultural, technical, scientific, and administrative fields; and 4) to establish a community in the region where the relationships are based on justice and the rule of law.

The Bali Declaration of 1976 (under "social") enumerates the forms of cooperation in social development to include 1) emphasis on the well-being of the low-income group and of the rural population through more opportunities for employment and fair wage; 2) support for the active involvement of all sectors and levels of the ASEAN communities especially the women and the public in development efforts; and 3) intensified efforts to met the problems of population growth in the ASEAN region.[6]

The Singapore Declaration of the 1992 Singapore Summit stated some priorities for cooperation in social development, such as expansion of ASEAN Studies as part of Southeast Asian studies in the school and university curricula, student exchange programmes to promote awareness of ASEAN at the secondary and tertiary schools of education, stronger network of cooperation among leading universities with a view to establishing an ASEAN University, exchange on information among NGO's on intra-ASEAN cooperation, and coordinated efforts to curb the spread of AIDS.

These broad mandates are strengthened by the following specific statements on principles and modes of cooperation:

1. ASEAN Declaration on Mutual Assistance on Natural Disasters. (Manila, 26 June 1976).
2. Meeting of ASEAN Ministers Responsible for Social Welfare (Jakarta, 18-19 July 1977).
3. Various resolutions of ASEAN Health Ministers (Manila, 1977 and 1980, Pattaya, 1984.
4. Declaration of Principles of Strengthening ASEAN Collaboration on Youth (Bangkok, 24 June 1983).
5. Various ASEAN communiqués of ASEAN Labour Ministers.

The focus of social development is the people, whether individual or groups, young or old, men and women, poor or rich, healthy or sick. Each one of these has to be developed to make him a responsible member of society or community that seeks to achieve a good life.

Cooperation for Social Development in ASEAN[7]

ASEAN cooperation for social development is under the Committee on Social Development (COSD) which was established in 1978 to formulate and recommend policies, programmes and strategies for social development. COSD also secures external support for the implementation of its activities.

From the directions of all the summit meetings, COSD has identified the priority areas of cooperation and created ASEAN Sub-Committees to be responsible for the activities. These are the:

1. ASEAN Sub-Committee on Education (ASCOE)
2. ASEAN Population Programme (APP)
3. ASEAN Sub-Committee on Health and Nutrition (ASCHN)
4. ASEAN Sub-Committee on Youth (ASY)
5. ASEAN Women's Programme (AWP)
6. ASEAN Committee on Labour Affairs (ASCLA)
7. ASEAN Experts Group on Disaster Management (AEGDM)

According to the 1995 Bangkok Summit, the following goals are to be achieved by ASEAN:

1. Upgrading of its human resources by building institutional capacities for education training and research;
2. Strengthening of the networking of HRD institutions;
3. Increased efforts to improve the quality of life of its peoples through ensuring social justice, improving the quality of and access to social services, and working towards the reduction of poverty;
4. Total eradication of illiteracy;
5. Better informed and educated societies through cooperation in educational development on an interdisciplinary basis and provision of a strong, caring, and cohesive society;
6. The equitable and effective participation of women in all fields and levels of society;
7. Enhanced regional cooperation for the survival, protection, and development of children and for youth development;
8. Strong collective response to the problems and challenge posed by HIV/AIDS.

ASEAN's COSD has formulated the following Plans of Action and Work Programmes:

1. ASEAN Plan of Action on Children (1993)
2. ASEAN Plan of Action on Social Development (1994)
3. Work Programme of the ASEAN University Network
4. ASEAN Regional Programme on HIV/AIDS Prevention and Control (1995-2000)
6. Four Year Plan of Action of the ASEAN Occupational Safety and Health Network (1997-2000)

State of Social Development in ASEAN

A. Population

Urbanisation

Urbanisation is growing among the population of ASEAN member states and has increased substantially from 1960-1990. Indonesia's urbanisation increased from 15 per cent in 1960 to 40 per cent in 2000. Annual growth rate is 4.4 per cent from 1990-2000. In Malaysia, urbanisation was at 5 per cent in 1980-1987. In Thailand, Singapore and the Philippines, urbanisation rate decreased by around 1 per cent. These are according to ESCAP 1992 data.

Urbanisation has produced many problems. It is not the case that urbanisation in Southeast Asia is an indicator of rapid industrialisation and real economic progress because these have not really occurred in the region. In most cases, people go to the urban areas to find odd jobs because population has increased and there are no corresponding sources of livelihood for the people. Farm areas have been reduced by conversion to residential use, golf courses, and commercial purpose, thus people have to seek jobs in the urban areas.

Besides the problems of congestion, slum life, environmental pollution, poor sanitation, diseases, traffic congestion, pressures on demand for water, electricity, and road use, and big problems of crime including drug abuse have been experienced.

Youth

The youth group has been the fastest growing age group in ASEAN countries. The increase in youth population increases un-employment problems, the need for skills training in gainful occupation, and problems of crime. There is also the problem of dropouts from schools. For the 12-18 age group there is a drop in enrolment ratios from the primary level. In the 12-18 age group, 28 per cent in Thailand, 54 per cent in the Philippines and 41 per cent in Indonesia are enrolled in secondary schools. The ASEAN Sub-Committee on Youth (ASY) is working on the Kuala Lumpur Agenda on Youth Development (1977) on the following aspects: 1) entrepreneurship (Indonesia), 2) social/ civic responsibility (Lao PDR), 3) leadership development (Malaysia), ASEAN Awareness (Philippines), 4) science and technology (Philippines), 5) sustainable development and rural youth (Thailand), and 6) skills training for out-of-school youth (Vietnam). The countries are the respective coordinators of work plans.

The skills training of out-of-school youth has been given sustained attention in the 1998 Hanoi Plan of Action. Under a project funded by the Japan-ASEAN Exchange Projects, an ASEAN SKILLS NET will be established as a network of national skills training centres or agencies for out-of-school youth to share information on curriculum, job placement arrangements, and expert resources.[8]

An ASEAN Youth Day Meeting (VII) was held in Hanoi in August 1998. ASEAN delegates and the Council for ASEAN Youth Cooperation discussed the concerns of the youth in the present socio-economic situation and the formulation of national policy on youth. The theme was "National Policy on Youth". The Youth Day Meeting was funded by the Japan-ASEAN Exchange Projects.

The other projects for ASEAN Youth Development are Youth External Cooperation, Youth Cooperation with Youth NGO's Youth Exchange Programme, and the ASEAN Volunteer Corps Exchange Programme to develop the talents of ASEAN youth in international development. These projects aim to develop understanding of training approaches, methodologies, and techniques in youth development.

Educational scholarships funded by Japan for ASEAN Youth, tenable for 15 years, are available for nation building through development of human resources. The fields of training include:

1) Brunei Darussalam – country planning, housing development, customs, fire brigade, etc., to be trained in ASEAN countries and the United Kingdom;

2) Indonesia – training in country or abroad on post-harvest production, agriculture, computer management, integrated cooperatives, English and Japanese languages, leadership training for rural youth;
3) Malaysia – for degree courses and for professional and non-professional courses;
4) Philippines – as screened by the National Economic Development Authority (NEDA);
5) Singapore – for undergraduate, post-graduate studies and non-degree technical professional courses;
6) Thailand – scholarships to develop human resources in engineering, science and technology, tenable only in Japan.

Elderly

Advances in health, nutrition, and sanitation have increased peoples' life expectancy. A second result is a large population of elderly people. An estimate says that in five ASEAN countries, the number of elderly people will double from 1990 to 2005. For example in Singapore it is expected that by 2020, 14.5 per cent of its population will be elderly, and by 2033, almost 20 per cent will be 65 years and older. This condition will have implications for housing, health care, recreation, and other social services.

On the other hand, because of government population policies and population awareness of the people, there could be decreasing family size, nuclear family arrangements, and single parenthood. More problems will arise from a declining population sector that pays taxes to take care of social security for the elderly, for day care, counselling, and other social needs.

Changes in population size are also due to changing lifestyles of people. Therefore governments may not be able to rely on long-term policies for meeting population challenges.

ASEAN has been implementing the Work Programme on Community-Based Care Programmes for the Elderly since 1997.

Women

Women in ASEAN states have lagged behind men in employment, literacy, and education[9]. Even if there is increased female participation in the labour force, there are resulting problems such as stress in the traditional family arrangement, women having double full-time roles in the home and at work, neglect of children, child abuse, and other crimes. Women labour abuses need to be monitored and prevented. The Convention on the Elimination of Discrimination Against Women needs to be implemented.

The ASEAN Sub-Committee on Women (ASW) is monitoring the implementation of the 1988 Declaration on the Advancement of Women. The ASW prepares a report every three years on its implementation. There is also the ASEAN Network for Women in Skills Training (1988) and the ASEAN Network of Clearinghouses for Women in Development, coordinated by Indonesia, to provide necessary action on the status and role of ASEAN Women. July 5 has also been designated as ASEAN Women's Day.[10]

The other projects for women development are:

1. Programmes on Art and Culture
2. Women's Vocational Centre
3. Population Development Project on Literacy and Legal Aid
4. Network on Indicators and Statistics on Women
5. Prevention of Family Violence

B. Health and Nutrition

In general people in ASEAN states had improvements in their nutritional status during 1960-1985. The average level of nutrition in ASEAN has exceeded internationally recommended requirements (UNDP 1992).

There has also been much progress in health as seen in increased life expectancy from 70 to 73 years (1987) in Malaysia and Singapore and decreased infant mortality rate.

Crude death rates per thousand also decreased in Indonesia, Malaysia and Thailand, and in the Philippines and Singapore, there was a very slight increase. In 1999 a Plan of Action For Strengthening Disease Surveillance was funded by the WHO within the framework of the WHO-ASEAN Memorandum of Understanding on collaboration on health and nutrition. The projects aimed at regional self-reliance in disease surveillance and control of communicable disease. A programme for tuberculosis control was also approved in 1999 to mobilise resources for the implementation of the Directly Observed Treatment, Short Course Strategy in Treating Tuberculosis.

There was also a Seminar on Ageing in 1998 for the care of the elderly to meet their social and health needs; reaffirming the current policies of keeping the elderly at home and in the community for as long as possible with the support of community-based and home-based services and emphasising the virtues of strong religious, cultural, and family ties in order to avoid institutionalisation of the elderly. Brunei was the country coordinator.[11]

C. Education

An ASEAN Network of Development Education Centres to carry out cooperative projects in education was decided on by the ASEAN Ministers of Education in 1977. In 1979, with Australian funding, the ASEAN Development Education Project (ADEP) was established to implement projects aimed at enhancing the contributions of education in national development. ADEP's sub-projects and country coordinators are: 1) Special Education (Indonesia), 2) Education Management Information System (Malaysia), 3) Test Development (Thailand), 4) Teacher Education (Philippines), and 5) Work-Oriented Education for In-School and Out-of-School Youths (Singapore). These sub-projects were completed in 1986.

The Hanoi Plan of Action (1998) called for the strengthening of the educational systems in member countries so that all groups of people including the disadvantaged can have equal access to basic and higher education. Strategies for these and collaboration with SEAMEO are being explored to ensure that HPA directives on basic and distance education will be implemented.

The ASEAN Sub-Committee on Education (ASCOE) has been promoting ASEAN Awareness in primary and secondary schools through the integration of ASEAN studies in the school curriculum and running student exchange programmes. ASCOE's flagship project on Integrating ASEAN Studies in Primary and Secondary Schools Curricula aims to produce a source book on ASEAN studies to help in the development of an ASEAN studies curriculum.

The ASEAN University Network (AUN) Secretariat assisted ASCOE in compiling a bibliography of ASEAN studies to serve as the common basis for textbooks on ASEAN Studies for primary and secondary school students. The first draft of the source book has been completed in book and CD-ROM formats. More workshops for curriculum planners will be held to study the implementation approaches to integrating ASEAN studies.[12]

ASEAN University Network (AUN)

There has been steady development of the AUN activities in the identified priority areas in ASEAN Studies, student and faculty exchange, collaborative research, and information networking. At this higher education level, the participating universities of AUN engage in faculty and student exchanges, development of executive education, and continues development of the quality of education offered by universities in ASEAN.

Myanmar hosted the ASEAN studies workshop in April 1999 which discussed a list of core courses for an ASEAN Studies Programme, a common curriculum and course materials for the core courses in ASEAN Studies and possibly designate a resource centre for that purpose. All these projects were ongoing in 1999. The second AUN Educational Forum was hosted by the Vietnam National University in Hanoi on 17-31 May 1999 on the topic of Student and Faculty Exchange. The AUN Distinguished Professors Programme for faculty exchange was scheduled for 1999. The AUN will develop a common standard of quality of education. The AUN will also develop an Executive Development Programme. The Hanoi Plan of Action directs the transformation of the AUN into the ASEAN University. This was to be discussed in the Philippines by the ASEAN Ministers Responsible for Higher Education in 2000. University networking beyond the ASEAN region is in progress. Networking with European universities is being prepared and will be funded by the European Commission.[13]

D. Labour

Labour is very sensitive to changing economic conditions, especially if the work force is unskilled and not adequately educated. In ASEAN member states, the financial crisis since 1997 and world developments that show contradictory trends like globalisation and regionalism, and free trade to the detriment of newly industrialising countries, have brought to the fore the weaknesses of labour. As the economy slowed down, workers were retrenched. The available work in the market is not accessible to these workers because they lack education, skills, knowledge, and resources to enable them to capture the labour market. On another point, ASEAN countries are labour-exporting countries, and when these workers return home, they cannot find gainful employment because of the slowed down economy.

Cooperation in the field of labour started in 1975 when the ASEAN Labour Ministers held their first meeting. Since then the Labour Ministers have met regularly and have organised seminars and projects on labour and manpower development. The ASEAN Labour Ministers meeting in Yangon discussed these issues in connection with Regional Project on Human Resources Development Planning, the ASEAN Plan of Action in Informal Sector Development, and the operationalisation of the ASEAN Occupational Safety and Health Network (ASEAN OSHNET). A framework regional programme by the ASEAN Secretariat for ASEAN names the following pilot activities: 1) sharing and exchange of experience and the best practices in designing social protection and social security systems/practices; 2) promoting tripartite cooperation through increased consultations among government, corporate management, unions, and workers for economic restructuring and mediation/conciliation machinery; and 3) enhanced capacity for designing programmes/policies on employment generation, focusing on active labour market policies and job training.

An ASEAN Skills Competition was first held in Malaysia in 1995 by skilled workers on a wide range of trade areas. It is now held every two years by member countries. In 1998, in Thailand, the third skills competition listed 13 trade areas.[14]

E. Disaster Management

The need for ASEAN cooperation on natural disaster and calamities was first stated in the ASEAN Declaration on Mutual Assistance on Natural Disasters in 1976. Since 1991 the ASEAN Natural Disaster Information Network has been promoting awareness on natural disaster through the newsletter published twice a year, two years in each country by alphabetical rotation. Japan is funding the project.

3) Science and Technology

Although the start of ASEAN cooperation in Science and Technology (S and T) was in 1973, the terms of reference for the ASEAN Permanent

Committee on S and T was formulated in 1974. In 1978 the ASEAN Committee on Science and Technology (COST) was established to accelerate the development of scientific and technological expertise and human resources and facilitate transfer of technology from the more advanced countries to ASEAN states.

In 1983 COST made a Plan of Action for S and T, which should last until 1987. This was revised in 1987, followed by another Plan for 1989-1993, and an updated Plan of Action in 1994 on S and T. Under this 1994 Plan of Action on Science and Technology, the following objectives are to be achieved:

1. A high level of intra-ASEAN cooperation on S and T which is self-sustaining and involves the private sector;
2. A network of S and T infrastructures and programmes for public and private sectors of human resources development;
3. Enhanced public awareness of the importance of S and T to ASEAN's economic development;
4. An expanded S and T cooperation with the international community.

In line with the goal of technological competitiveness articulated in ASEAN Vision 2020, COST continues its activities. In 1998, the ASEAN Ministers for Science and Technology decided to increase the ASEAN Science Fund, to meet regularly every three years and meet informally in-between, and develop innovative systems for project management and resource generation to support S and T activities.

COST has eight sub-committees which handle its programmes. These sub-committees are 1) Food Science and Technology, 2) Biotechnology, 3) Microelectronics and Information technology, 4) Materials Science and Technology, 5) Non-conventional Energy Research, 6) Marine Sciences, 7) Meteorology and Geophysics, and 8) Science and Technology Infrastructure and Resources Development.[15]

In 1998-1999, 23 projects were undertaken of which six were completed and 17 are continuing. Thirty-four proposals need further development or funding.[16]

Under development is a sub-programme element in strategic and enabling technologies. The proposal includes networking of institutions, enhancement of ASTNET, development of new S and T indicators, and activities to emphasise the role of S and T for sustained economic growth.

COST formed linkages to ensue continuing exchange of information with SOM-AMAF and the Senior Officials Meeting on Energy (SOME) for technology development. Cooperation with ASOEN on practical terms was strengthened through the services of the ASEAN Specialised Meteorological Centre to the regional haze programme.

Cost also recommended a policy on intellectual property rights (PR), sharing on research projects with Dialogue Partners.

The ASEAN Science and Technology Information Network (ASTNET) is expected to provide up-to-date information on S and T manpower, R and D, technology offers and request in each ASEAN member country, and technology – specific databases relevant to R & D and business communities.

Because of the growing difficulty of obtaining funding for science and technology projects, the Ministers agreed to increase the ASEAN Science Fund (ASF) by a target contribution of $1 million per country over a period of ten years.

There is continuing cooperation between the Dialogue Partners and eight sub-committees and the ASEAN experts group on Remote Sensing. The eight Sub-committees are the following:[17]

1. The Sub-Committee on Food and Science and Technology (SCFST) is implementing the training network for the development of the food industry in the region and the quality assurance systems for fruits, and the waste water treatment. An ASEAN Food Conference will be held every three years to be funded by the Federation of International Food Science and Technology Associations (FIESTA).

2. The Sub-Committee on Meteorology and Geophysics (SCMG) is now implementing the ASEAN Network for Rapid Exchange of Strong Earthquake Data. The project hardware and software have been distributed to the node institutions in member countries. Two Japanese experts from the Japan Meteorological Agency have provided training and technical advice to the project participants. The SCMG is developing new project proposals such as exchange networks for marine meteorology and oceanography, climate information and prediction services, climate change, and assessment of solar energy and daylight resources.

3. Sub-committee on Microelectronics and Information Technology
Around 30 short courses were delivered by the Telecommunications
Cooperation and Training Project (TCTP) on Telecommunications
Business Management; Telecommunications Strategic Policy
Planning Regulation; Telecommunications Network, Planning and
Implementation, Telecommunications Transmission Systems; and
Telecommunications Business Practice. There is need for further
training to meet the human resources and telecommunications and
infrastructure development needs.

The ASEAN-India Digital Archive Project (AIDA) was
completed in early 1999 and produced a multi-lingual, multicultural
archive of fonts, text, voice, pictures and video clips of common
words, phrases on events from India and the ASEAN member states.
The archive is available to prospective users.

4. Sub-Committee on Materials Science and Technology (SCMST)
Substantial progress was made by the SCMST in cooperation with
India and New Zealand. Training was given to eight scientists for
the ASEAN states at a Department of Defence Facility in
Hyderabad. Of the eight, five were specialists in rare-earth magnets
and three surface engineering. In New Zealand, two scientists from
each of the ASEAN Member Countries participated in the course
of corrosion prevention in infrastructure through the application
of life-cycle analysis techniques conducted at the University of
Auckland School of Engineering.

5. Sub-Committee on Biotechnology
The "ASEAN-Korea Workshop on Formulation of Biotechnology
Atlas" will provide information on national biotechnology programmes
of ASEAN countries and Korea, their expertise and their facilities in
both public and private institutions. Possible R and D biotechnology
projects will be identified for cooperation from 1999 onwards.

6. Sub-Committee on Non-conventional Energy Research
The ASEAN-New Zealand Cooperation in Natural Gas Utilisation
in Transport and the ASEAN-EC Energy Cogeneration Programme
(COGEN) Phase II have been completed. Energy from Biomass
Residues Project, Phase III was going in the year 2000. The EU
has agreed to extend COGEN for another phase.

7. Sub-Committee on Marine Science
The Sub-Committee completed the Coastal Zone Environment
and Resource Management Project (Phase III). A National

Environment Resource Information Centre to collect and manage data on coastal zones was established. The ASEAN-Canada Cooperative Programme on Marine Science (Phase II) which focuses on the development of safe standards for the marine environment was completed in 1999. Other projects of the ASEAN-Canada Programme are preparation of Marine Water Quality Criteria and Publication of Manuals in Pollution Monitoring and Environmental Management. A new project proposal "Coastal and Ocean Environment Management for Economic Development, Human Health Protection and Resource Sustainability in ASEAN" has been submitted to COST for approval. The ASEAN-EU project on Interdisciplinary Methodologies for the Sustainable Use and Management of Coastal Resource System has developed an expert system for it (SIMCOAST).

8. Sub-Committee on Science and Technology Infrastructure and Resource Development

This sub-committee started some initiatives to develop S and T management and networking, S and T human resources, technology transfer and commercialisation, information dissemination, and the ASEAN Science and Technology Network (ASTNET). Funding is still a problem for the project ASTNET so the sub-committee is inviting private sector support.

ASEAN Experts Group on Remote Sensing[18]

This Group has drafted and discussed a "Framework for Enhancing ASEAN Collaboration on Remote Sensing and Related Space Technologies". This may be the basis for an ASEAN Space Agency. Proposals have been received from the European Space Agency, the Saskatchewan Research Council, and Radarsat International. A pilot project on technology for updating maps using remote sensing has generated results in a workshop in Kuala Lumpur in 1998. This is supported by Australia.

ASEAN member states, being in the class of developing states, have aspired to be in the category of newly-industrialised countries (NICs). Aware that NICs depend on scientific advances, technological innovations, and the presence of supportive institutions, ASEAN, as early as the Bangkok Declaration of 1967 stated that one of its principal aims is "to promote active collaboration and mutual assistance on matters of common interest in the economic, social, cultural, technological, scientific, and administrative fields".

ASEAN Secretariat documents say that the ASEAN Committee on Science and Technology (COST) which was established in 1978 has five flagship or high profile projects by the year 2000 namely:

- ASEAN S & T Fellowship/ HRD Programme;
- Development of Technology Scan Mechanism;
- ASEAN Science and Technology Week;
- ASEAN Science and Technology Information Network;
- ASEAN Food Conference.

The principal sources of funds for programmes/ activities of ASEAN COST are the Dialogue Partners. ASEAN Member Countries make substantial counterpart in-kind contributions to match the aid-funding provided by the Dialogue Partners.

In every summit meeting, ASEAN collaboration in S & T has been emphasised. The Manila Declaration of 1987 stated that "ASEAN shall emphasize developing an intelligent and highly productive workforce by providing effective training in order to facilitate effective transfer of technology". The Singapore Declaration of 1992 pledged to continue to step up cooperation in other economic related areas, such as science and technology transfer and human resource development.

The Singapore Summit's Programme of Action for the member states include:

1) Building R & D infrastructure including training to develop indigenous technology and innovative capability;
2) Promoting private and public sector collaboration in R & D in key technology areas that have potential for commercialisation;
3) Continuing active collaboration with Dialogue Partners in S & T development and management, especially those needed in industry.

To operationalise these, meetings of the ASEAN Ministers of Science and Technology and sometimes in cooperation with the ASEAN Economic Ministers have been held. Limited available data on S & T in ASEAN countries show that ASEAN had adopted the following indicators of the state of S & T in the areas:

1) Percentage of resources allocated to education. On the whole, ASEAN countries have done well. Indonesia upgraded its literacy by 4.5 per cent in 1970-1974 to 8.3 per cent in 1975-1979 and so on, to more than 12 per cent in 1988.

2) Enrolment rate of students in science and technical fields in ASEAN states is rather low.

3) Share of private sector in R & D expenditures. The average share in US, Japan, and Germany is about 60 per cent. In ASEAN states it is about 14 per cent.

4) Priority for development plans for S & T and human resources, such as skills training, indigenisation of S & T, technology imports, and industrial restructuring.

Some Successful Projects in Science and Technology [19]
The following list contains a number of the projects in S & T that have had success.

1. ASEAN Protein Project to solve malnutrition and to develop technology for protein foods; a number of acceptable protein-rich food formulations have been developed and standardised such as baby food, noodle products, textured vegetable protein, fermented products, soy beverages and snacks.

2. Research on food habits, such as natural food flavours.

3. Management and utilisation of food waste material research resulted in developing technologies such as organic tanning of shark skins to shark leather, production of organic products from solid waste materials such as banana peelings and pineapple, production of food for tropical ornamental fish, pineapple juice concentration by reverse osmosis, recycling of waste water from softdrinks industries using membrane process, citric acid production from food waste material, and important technical publications.

4. Seminar on ASEAN Food Technology to include food processing and preservation, new product development, and nutrition and safety aspects of food products.

5. ASEAN Climatic Atlas and Compendium of Climatic Statistics Project has produced a two-volume set publication which is now available. A user's manual is also available. Both are at the ASEAN Secretariat.

6. ASEAN Specialized Meteorological Centre to refine models analysis and forecast.

7. Workshop in Geology and Geophysics to analyse the movements of the deep tectonic plates around the Indonesian and Brunei Seas and to discover the mechanisms and reasons of earthquake and other natural disasters in the area. Three project proposals have been submitted for funding possibility by the EC.

8. Biotechnology for Plant Extract and Carbohydrate Biotechnology (ASEAN-Australia). Programmed for training and exchange of information and equipment for the development of therapeutic and biologically active substances from plants and the production and utilisation of cells and enzymes for improved carbohydrate conversion.

9. Non-conventional energy research includes energy conservation in buildings, in industry, and training in instrumentation and measurement.

10. Cooperation on Energy Cogeneration to result in reduction of ASEAN dependence on oil for energy requirement and the reduction in the environmental load from the energy and the waste sector. Publication on the Biomass Technology is now available in the EC upon request.

11. Cooperation on the development of living Marine Research to assess fish stocks shared by two or more countries in ASEAN and to identify sources and effects of various pollutants critical for sustaining living marine resources.

In June 2000, a group of scientists from US, Scotland, Sweden, and the Philippines reported that fish farming, promoted as a smart way to feed the world's surging population, has a disastrous impact on the environment and on stocks of wild fish.

Agriculture is leading to the collapse of fishstocks. While fish and shellfish farms are known to provide cheap food, shellfish are scooped from the oceans and ground into meal to feed penned fish. Fish farms destroy habitat in fragile tropical areas, encourage the spread of fish diseases and cause pollution in the form of fish effluent and decomposed uneaten food. Escaping penned fish have interbred with the wild population and could transfer weak genes which could lead to the decline of the fish population.[20]

A UNESCO Report in 1992 states that science and technology (S & T) have had great impact on reducing the burden of physical work and improving social welfare. S & T structures have been affected by world trends for globalisation such as the need for technological innovation in response to production systems. While it is impossible to construct a society with social justice and harmony based on general scarcity, there is also ample proof which shows that, overall, materials produce or ensure conditions of social well-being and equilibrium. To reorganise the national and international economy it is essential to distribute costs and benefits with respect to environmental impact and the integration of the "backward" regions with the highly industrialised.

S and T can contribute to these ends but people who will use S and T will be moved by interests, passions, faith or ideologies. So solutions of problems will never be purely scientific and technological but solutions should reflect a complex blend of historical, contextual, social, economic, scientific and technological factors.[21]

4) Environment

State of Environment in ASEAN

Environmental problems include conserving resources and protecting the environment.

One of the most important environmental problems in Southeast Asia is the decreasing forest cover or deforestation which is by per capita term about 45 square metres per person per year. Deforestation results from commercial logging, conversion of forests to industrial and residential uses, and fuel wood gathering, and leads to soil erosion which is increased by intensive and improper soil cultivation practices. Most serious land degradation in ASEAN is in 25 per cent of the land area.

Another is the dying seas which in Southeast Asia are the natural habitat of 2,500 species of fish and invertebrates, providing 11 per cent of the world's supply of marine products and livelihood for the region's fishermen. In this century, many of the fishing areas are over fished and being destroyed by discharges from land and sea sources including oil spills. Many mangrove areas which are spawning grounds for fish and aquatic life have been converted to brackish water prawn farms and building areas. Overpumping of ground of water for irrigation, industrial, and drinking purposes has led to land subsidence. This also results in flooding. Ground water is now also polluted by human and factory waste disposal.

Increasing energy consumption is the result of urbanisation and industrialisation. High energy use results also in air pollution.

ASEAN member states have taken some measures to protect their natural resources and environment. Indonesia banned log export in 1985, Thailand did so in 1989. The Philippines has a selective log ban. However all in all, the implementation of the laws is the main problem.

ASEAN states have also set aside protected areas at an average of 4.5 per cent of the total land area.[22]

ASEAN cooperation in environment started in 1977 when the ASEAN Sub-Regional Environment Programme (ASEP) was established. The programme stated the extent of regional cooperation, the priority areas, and the projects/activities on environment. The Committee on Science and Technology (COST) recommended that the first meeting of the ASEAN Experts Group in the Environment (AEGE) be held in Jakarta in December 1978.[23]

ASEAN Actions for the Protection of the Environment[24]

1. The Manila Declaration of 1981 defined the broad objective of cooperation to protect the ASEAN environment and sustainability of its natural resources, to eradicate poverty, and to raise the quality of life.

2. The Bangkok Declaration of 1984 established more guidelines, even while noting the progress of the ASEAN Environment Programme. The new guidelines were environmental management, nature conservation, marine management, urban environment, information systems, and involvement of NGO's and international cooperation.

3. The Bangkok Declaration also declared a number of sites and reserves in the respective countries as ASEAN National Heritage Parks and Nature Reserves. These are in Brunei Darussalam, Indonesia, Malaysia, the Philippines, and Thailand.

4. Agreement on the Conservation of Nature and Natural Resources (1985) in Kuala Lumpur.

5. Jakarta Resolution on Sustainable Development (1987) to integrate environmental concerns in national development plans and processes.

6. In 1989, the AEGE was upgraded to the ASEAN Senior Officials on the Environment (ASOEN). It set out six working groups, namely, Nature Conservation, ASEAN Seas and Marine

Environment, Transboundary Pollution, Environmental Management, Environmental Economics, Environmental Information, Public Awareness and Education.

7. Kuala Lumpur Accord on Environment and Development (1990).

8. Singapore Resolution on Information Exchange in 1992 for harmonisation of environmental quality standards.

9. The Sixth ASEAN Ministerial Meeting on the Environment held in Bandar Seri Bagawan, Brunei on 25-26 April 1994 adopted the ASEAN Strategic Plan of Action on the Environment (ASPEN) and also approved, among others, a set of ASEAN Harmonized Environmental Quality Standards for Ambient Air Quality and River Water Quality.[25]

10. At the Informal ASEAN Ministerial Meeting on the Environment held in Kuching, Malaysia on 21 October 1994 the Ministers discussed the problem of transboundary pollution and agreed that ASEAN should collaborate actively to manage natural resources and control transboundary pollution within ASEAN, to develop regional early warning and response systems, and to improve the capacity of member countries in these areas. In 1995, in Kuala Lumpur an ASEAN Meeting on the Management of Transboundary Pollution adopted the ASEAN Cooperation Plan in Transboundary Pollution, covering three programme areas, namely, transboundary atmosphere pollution, transboundary movement of hazardous wastes, and transboundary shipborne pollution.[26]

11. At the Ninth Meeting of the ASOEN on 23-25 September 1999, in Singapore, the working groups were restructured to three, to be more issue-oriented than project-oriented, while maintaining the existing ASOEN Haze Technical Task Force (HTTF).

The Restructured ASOEN Working Groups are:

1. Working Group on Nature Conservation and Biodiversity (chaired by the Philippines);

2. Working Group on Coastal and Marine Environment (chaired by Thailand);

3. Working Group on Multilateral Environmental Agreements (chaired by Malaysia).[27]

Projects

Some of the projects that have been implemented under ASEP are the following:[28]

1. Development of a test model for environmental assessment statements;
2. Quantification of Environment Parameters;
3. Soil erosion control;
4. Pollution control technology;
5. National survey of existing monitoring capabilities;
6. Inter-Oceania regional workshop on higher environmental education;
7. Action Plan on Environmental Education and Training;
8. Preparation of environmental country profiles;
9. Comparative Study of Environmental Law in ASEAN countries;
10. ASEAN Waterbirds and Wetlands;
11. Integrated Hydrological Technology for Water Resources;
12. Environmental Education Materials for Primary and Secondary Schools;
13. Impact of Human Activities on the Productivity of Mangrove Ecosystems;
14. Urban Parks Development and Greenery;
15. Impact Study on Coal-Fired Power Plants;
16. Technology Transfer on the Treatment of Effluents from Palm Oil and Rubber Industries;
17. Anti-Pollution Control and Management in Fine Gas Desulphurisation and Denitrification;
18. Application of Meteorological Data in Air Pollution;
19. Cooperative Action Plan for Oil Pollution Combat in South China Sea;
20. Seminar on Toxic and Hazardous Wastes.

In 1998-1999, seven projects were completed, eight were on-going, and 24 projects pending.

In 1999, there were eight on-going ASEAN projects, namely:[29]

1. Management Plan for ASEAN Heritage Parks and Reserves;
2. Management of Transfrontier Parks and Protected Areas in the ASEAN Region;
3. ASEAN Regional Centre for Biodiversity Conservation;

4. Regional Technical Assistance (RETA) to Strengthen the Capacity of ASEAN to Prevent and Mitigate Transboundary Atmosphere Pollution;
5. ASEAN Cooperation on the Management and Control of Transboundary Movements of Hazardous Wastes within the ASEAN Region;
6. Booklet on ASEAN Achievements and Future Directions in Pollution Control;
7. Waste Water Treatment Technology Transfer;
8. ASEAN Environmental Education Action Plan.

Rio Declaration, Agenda 21
The Rio Declaration on Environment and Development published in Rio de Janeiro in June 1992 addressed the critical environmental problems. While there had been no common strategy yet for sustainable development, the Rio Declaration came up with Agenda 21 to provide certain general guidelines for the international and national communities.

For ASEAN, Agenda 21 has guidelines for regional and sub-regional organisations in Asia and the Pacific, such as strengthening implemental capacities and integrating environmental matters into development programmes.

Even before Agenda 21, ASEAN had already issued declarations and resolutions for intensive cooperation in environmental efforts for protection and sustainable development.[30]

The following are short descriptions of some on-going projects.[31]

1. **Regional Haze**: In late 1997 up to early 1998, a haze disaster occurred in Southeast Asia due to the forest fires in Indonesia. This caused the ASEAN member countries to collaborate closely to prevent, monitor, and mitigate the trans-boundary haze pollution problem. The ASEAN Haze Technical Committee (HTTF), supported by the Regional Technical Assistance (RETA) in strengthening ASEAN's Capacity to Prevent and Mitigate Transboundary Atmospheric Pollution have helped to implement the Regional Haze Action Plan (RHAP). Its three components and coordinators are: preventive measures (Malaysia), monitoring measures (Singapore) and strengthening fire-fighting capabilities

(Indonesia). RETA is funded by the Asian Development Bank and implemented by the ASEAN Secretariat. There are major donor organisations that support RHAP. The RETA Work Plan will emphasise the operationalisation of the RHAP.

In 1999, the ASEAN Ministerial Meeting on Haze (AMMH) met three times to provide overall direction to the HTTP. The Sixth AMMH on 16 April 1999 (Bandar Seri Begawan) adopted the policy on zero-burning and its promotion of action among plantation owners and timber concessionaires. The AMMH also agreed to use the presumptive clause in the law against open burning and to enforce strictly zero-burning regulations. A Coordination and Support Unit (CSU) in the ASEAN Secretariat will later take over the core functions of RETA including a study of funding resources.

2. **Nature Conservation**: The Hanoi Plan of Action mandated the formulation and adoption of an ASEAN Protocol on Access to Generic Resources. A workshop in the Philippines in December 1998 drafted the ASEAN framework agreement.

    The ASEAN Regional Centre of Biodiversity Conservation (ARCBC) which is an ASOEN flagship project funded by the European Union is now operational. A network of National Biodiversity Reference Units (NBRUs) will be assisted by the ARCBC in the ASEAN states, in data management and exchange, in providing needed hardware to NBRUs, train their staff, offer grants for research and training on matters related to biodiversity conservation, and bring EU institutions into partnership with ASEAN counterparts.

3. **Water Conservation**: The Second ASEAN Informal Summit in Kuala Lumpur in December 1997 decided to have a Consultative Working Group Meeting on ASEAN Cooperation on Water Conservation. The meeting recommended the establishment of an ASEAN Network of Water Resources Agencies (ANWRA) to promote ASEAN cooperation in ensuring the conservation and sustainability of water resources and the systematic transfer of knowledge and technology. The ANWRA is a working-level body under the ASOEN to help realise an ASEAN regional water conservation programme contained in the Hanoi Plan of Action.

4. **ASEAN Seas and Marine Environment**: The Coastal Zone Environmental and Resources Management Project (CZERMP)

was completed in June 1998 except the activities in Vietnam which were to continue up to June 1999. One of three working groups will oversee the ASEAN cooperation in the protection of coastal and marine environment. It will focus on the promotion of regional policies and activities for the prevention and control of marine pollution and on the management of ASEAN coastal zones as generally identified in the Hanoi Plan of Action. The CZERMP is supported by Australia under Phase III of the ASEAN-Australia Economic Cooperation Programme.

5. **Transboundary Pollution**: The ASEAN Working Group on Transboundary Pollution (AWGTP) is strengthening the exchange of information among national focal points of the Basel Convention on the Control of Transboundary Movements of Hazardous Waste and their Disposal. The AWGTP will develop a mechanism to expedite the approval process on the transshipment of hazardous waste from one member country to another. An ASEAN Experts Group Meeting on Nuclear Safety and Waste Management recommended the establishment of a sub-committee experts group in Manila in August 1998 on nuclear safety and waste management within the ASEAN institutional framework to look at the specific and common interest of the ASEAN Member Countries and lead to a better and safer environment in the region.

6. **Environmental Management**: An ASEAN Workshop on Long-Term Environmental Goals for Ambient Air and River Water Quality was held in Sydney in 19-22 July 1998, with funding from Australia. The workshop aimed to push the implementation of the Framework to Achieve the Long-Term Environmental Goals for Ambient Air and River Water Quality for ASEAN countries as stated in the workshop and to develop air quality legislation and monitoring and reporting measures as indicated in the ASEAN Regional Haze Action Plan. It also recommended steps to achieve ASEAN's harmonised environmental air and river quality standards by 2010.

7. **Environmental Economics** has to do with Environmental and Natural Resources Accounting (ENRA). The project was completed in 1998 with Indonesia, Malaysia, the Philippines and Thailand collaborating on the study. A pilot project using ENRA tools for a specific resource such as forestry or water may be undertaken.

8. **Multilateral Environmental Agreements** are commitments of ASEAN to share in international cooperation for the protection and enhancement of the environment. The ASEAN Working Group on Multilateral Environmental Agreements (AWGMEA) has been established by ASOEN to enhance cooperation among the Member Countries in multilateral agreements on environment and to reach a common ASEAN approach wherever appropriate in the negotiation and implementation of these agreements.

5) Drugs and Narcotics Control

State of Drug Abuse and Illicit Trafficking[32]

At the Third Meeting of the ASEAN Heads of Government at Manila in December 1987, Prime Minister of Malaysia Mahathir Mohamad said in his opening statement that drug abuse and illicit trafficking is recognised by ASEAN as a menace which needs the concerted efforts of the international community to eradicate. ASEAN resolve on this matter has been an example to all countries countering this terrible scourge to mankind. He urged ASEAN to remain steadfast in the fight against the drug menace.

Drug abuse and trafficking seriously threaten people's health and society's moral and social fabric. Under the influence of drugs, the AIDS virus has spread around the world. The results are incalculable.

Illicit trading and consumption of drugs are done underground and defy reliable estimates. ASEAN is particularly sensitive to this drug problem because the "Golden Triangle" constituted by some parts of Myanmar, Laos, and Thailand are all within the ASEAN region.

Each ASEAN member state has a government agency which is responsible for formulating drug policies and implementing them to address the problem. The extent of the drug problem is unknown, the causes of the problem are also difficult to say because the extent is not known; so also are the outcome of efforts to eradicate the problem.

Illicit trafficking in drugs by producers, sellers, and users involves two or more countries; it is transnational and would require international cooperation.

For itself, ASEAN exerted efforts to combat drug abuse as early as 1972 with the ASEAN Experts Group Meeting. ASEAN Legal Experts on Narcotics met in September 1973. Even at the highest levels, ASEAN has supported the regional effort to combat drug abuse.

In 1976 the Bali Declaration named cooperation to prevent and eradicate drug abuse as one of the elements in ASEAN cooperation. In June 1976, ASEAN Foreign Ministers signed a Declaration of Principles to Combat Drug Abuse which calls on each member country to increase vigilance and take preventive and penal measures, stop cultivation of opium poppy and other drug sources, cooperate on drug research and education and improve national legislations against drug abuse. ASEAN Drug Experts in 1976 held their first meeting under the ASEAN Permanent Committee on Socio-cultural activities. Experts meet every year.

The Sixth ASEAN Summit and the Hanoi Plan of Action in 1998 called on member countries to implement the ASEAN Work Programme to Operationalise the ASEAN Plan of Action on Drug Abuse Control by 2004, and to develop and implement high profile flagship programmes on drug abuse control such as preventive education programme for youth, treatment, and rehabilitation.[33]

In July 1998, member countries issued a Joint Declaration for a Drug-Free ASEAN by year 2020. The Declaration embodied 14 specific measures to reduce demand and supply, and eradicate illicit drug production, processing, trafficking and use in ASEAN by year 2020. The Declaration encourages linkages among regional institutional mechanisms, such as the ASEAN Senior Officials on Drug Matters (ASOD), the ASEAN Chiefs of National Police (ASEANAPOL), and the ASEAN Ministerial Meeting on Transnational Crime.

Earlier in December 1997, ASEAN Member Countries adopted an "ASEAN Declaration on Transnational Crime", in accordance with the fact that illicit drug trade is transnational in nature. An ASEAN Plan of Action to Combat Transnational Crime is considering the establishment of an ASEAN Centre on Transnational Crime.

A Regional Conference on Drug Abuse Among the Youth was held in Hanoi in November 1998 and endorsed the "Appeal to the Youth in the ASEAN Region for a Drug-Free Life". In 1999, the 21st Meeting of the ASEAN Senior Officials on Drugs (ASOD) in Jakarta discussed the implementation of the HPA and the Joint Declaration for a Drug-Free ASEAN and the international cooperation in the field of drugs and narcotics. The ASOD decided to invite as observers in future ASOD meetings in Papua, New Guinea, representatives from United Nations Drug Control Programme, Interpol, the Colombo Plan, ASEAN-NGOs for the Prevention of Drug and Substance Abuse, and the Foreign Anti-Narcotics Community. Funding is still a problem for the projects.

ASEAN has three high-profile projects on Drug Abuse. These are 1) Enhancement of Community-based Drug Prevention Activities; 2) Youth Empowerment Against Drug and Substance Abuse; and 3) Training in Intelligence Operations Management and Supervision.

The ASEAN-EU Three Year Plan of Action in Preventive Drug Education has improved country capacities to develop community-based drug prevention programmes. The plan is focused on several components among which are 1) drug information; 2) parent-youth movement; 3) integrated multi-pronged prevention programmes to involve media, community, and parents; and 4) prevention and control programmes and increasing awareness.

Together with combating drug abuse and illicit trafficking in drugs, ASEAN is also exerting efforts in Preventive Education and Information which include drug education for teachers and researchers. Efforts are also along law enforcement which include cooperative activities on training of enforcement agencies in trends, modus operandi and route of narcotics trafficking. Treatment and Rehabilitation includes provision for laboratory facilities for early detection and social reintegration of drug users.

There are four training centers based in ASEAN Member Countries to add to the above efforts. These are:

1) ASEAN Training Centre for Narcotics Law Enforcement (Bangkok);
2) ASEAN Training Centre for Preventive Drug Education (Manila);
3) ASEAN Training Centre for Treatment and Rehabilitation (Kuala Lumpur); and
4) ASEAN Training Centre for the Detection of Drugs in Body Fluids (Singapore).[34]

Projects on Drug Abuse and Trafficking Prevention[35]
Some of the completed and on-going projects on drug matters are:

1. Training for Narcotics Detection and Investigation, to train narcotics handlers on the work. Funded by New Zealand. Completed.
2. Workshops on Drug Law Enforcement to Strengthen Capabilities of ASEAN Countries in Narcotics Law Enforcement with New Methods. Completed with USA funding, 1980-1985.

3. Workshops and Training Cources, funded by the UNDP, 1987-1992, completed.
4. Training of Narcodog Handling Instructions for Enforcement in Narcotics Detection, 1998. Completed, under European Community Funding.
5. Training of Native Dogs for Narcotics Detection Handlers. Completed, under UNDP funding.
6. Study on the Use of Preventive Detention Law in Malaysia and Singapore. Completed in 1994.
7. Study on the Implementation of Conspiracy Investigation and the Confiscation of Illegally Acquired Drugs of Drug Traffickers, 1998. Completed with USA funding.
8. Training Courses for Drug Rehabilitation Professionals, 1986-1988. Completed with UNDP funding.
9. Study on the Compulsory Treatment and Rehabilitation Systems in Malaysia and Singapore, 1985. Completed.
10. Development of an ASEAN Parent-Youth Movement in Drug Abuse Prevention, 1987. Completed.
11. ASEAN Research and Training Centre for the Detection of Drug Abuse in Body Fluids, 1990-1992, European Community Funding.

6) Culture and Information

ASEAN leaders, from the beginning of ASEAN, have hoped to develop an ASEAN collective consciousness and identity among the peoples of Southeast Asia to supplement their national consciousness and identities so that they could all identify with ASEAN as their community.

ASEAN is in a region of more than 500 million people which shows great diversities in culture. The peoples in this region, before, during and after they had established their states, had been under the influences of their geographical conditions; the continued exchanges of peoples and commerce with the North and the Middle East, Africa, and Pacific Islands; the historical legacies from centuries of political, economic, and educational experiences from the Americans, Dutch, British, French, and Spanish colonisers; intermarriages; and from their own indigenous ways of life. Within each state, there are ethnic, linguistic, religious, food and other habits, and other differences or diversities.

Among the factors that have contributed to these divergences in culture, geography has possibly the greatest influence. In the earliest historical times, people lived along coastal and river waterways. Even the scope of authority of kings was limited to geographical areas because there were no vehicles in those days to enable people to traverse mountains and lands. Elephants and horses were the means of travel, besides walking. Therefore local communities developed their own lifestyles. However, the sea lanes were great transport routes so the Chinese, Indians, Arabians, and even early Europeans arrived on the shores, so to speak, with their own trading goods which reflected their ways of life, dresses, languages, and religions, altogether bringing with them their own cultures. It is a certainty that those cultural aspects did not remain pure where they landed for they were also syncretised with the local cultures. There were intermarriages, constant use of commercial languages, curiosity, and willingness to try what was new and so there was development of culture, from simple to complex and from local to foreign orientation.

But geography was also a unifying factor because most of the peoples in Southeast Asia came from the Austronesian stock which accounted for great similarities in languages except where dialects made the languages unintelligible to one another. The root of the languages is basically Melayu or Melanesian. As the sea-going people came and went, Sanskrit, Chinese, Arab, and Indian words and phrases brought more similarities for more mutuality in understanding and for the growing political institutions to support the new styles of political authority.

In modern times, the colonisers brought new cultures, new political, economic, educational, religious, and food styles. So heavy were these overlay that they caused the peoples in the Southeast Asian states to place their affinity more with the Western colonial powers than with their neighbours who were culturally their bond kins.

History affirms all the problems brought about by these multidiversities.

Thus ASEAN aims to bring the peoples of Southeast Asia together and stand in unity as a community where bonds are more than trade and aid. It is the culture that brings identity and strength to peoples.[36]

Contemporary literature on social progress and "cultural development" in Southeast Asia has brought out academic and professional views of what constituted "social" and "cultural" as against what could be the operational and functional matters. For example, one scholar brought out the idea that cultural changes as results of modernisation and Westernisation are to be met through adaptation of traditional cultural values and norms to the new social and cultural milieu. Cultural development may refer to cultural change which is no longer considered as a natural gradual process but as something that requires active cultural engineering.[37] Since modernisation is an important concern of all ASEAN countries for nation-building, cultural development may then be thought of as bringing about national identity and national integration, the first necessitating a deep study into the "roots" or the revival of cultural heritage of a country. On national integration, one has to look at the composition of the population, the ethnic groups and their positive or negative potential for nation-building. Can a national consciousness be developed among ethnic groups or can there be a "national culture"? Will a national culture lead to a regional identity? Patya Saihoo says that a regional treaty is usually for political and economic interests which may not always be sustained by the consciousness of "common ties of race and culture" but in fact mostly by mutually satisfactory benefits in political and economic matters.[38]

The Bangkok Declaration of 1967 aims to accelerate cultural development and promote collaboration in the cultural field among others. The Cameron Highlands Agreement of 1969 identified some mass media and cultural activities for ASEAN cooperation. These are 1) broadcasts of regular programmes "to reflect the aims, purposes, and activities of ASEAN"; 2) organisation of film festivals; exchange of film artists and joint film productions; and 3) seminars and other activities on mass media. Cultural cooperation would mean the exchange of artists in the visual and performing arts, joint research in the arts and literature, and cultural festivals. In its first ten years, ASEAN had promoted an ASEAN Journal in 1971, established a National Depository for ASEAN Publications in each member country in 1972, promoted the understanding of the traditional dances and music in 1973 in the ASEAN countries, and had the First Summer Field School of Archaeology in the same year. There were travelling exhibits of Radio-Television Artists Programmes in 1975, Art and Photography, ASEAN Film Festivals held yearly, and ASEAN Literary Awards in fiction, non-fiction, drama, and poetry, all promoting mutual appreciation and understanding of ASEAN cultures.[39] The Bali Declaration of 1976 defined some ways by which the objectives can be achieved such as by 1) introduction of the study of ASEAN, its member states and their national languages as part of the curriculum of schools; 2) support of ASEAN scholars, writers, artists, and mass media representatives to enable them to foster a sense of regional identity and fellowship; and 3) promotion of Southeast Asian studies through closer collaboration among national institutions.

All these are successful and are on-going.

Commitment to ASEAN cooperation begins from the mind. The concept of ASEAN should be particularly strong among the people who play leadership roles in the political, military, media, business, and academic fields. There is therefore a need for cooperation in education at all levels in ASEAN states to create a regional orientation. There have been activities for education exchange before ASEAN, sponsored by United Nations agencies, intergovernmental agencies such as the SEAMEO, ASAIHL, RIHED in Singapore, and SEACEN, and educational centres such as the Asian Institute of Technology in Bangkok, Asian Institute of Management in Manila, and others.

Education is necessary to enhance the learning process by cooperative activities with academic mobility such as travelling, lectureship, fellowships, student scholarships and visitorships, conferences and exhibitions, and an ASEAN Education Cooperative Fund.[40]

Promoting ASEAN Awareness and Identity

ASEAN documents have consistently expressed the objective of developing regional identity and awareness of one another's culture to promote collaboration in the cultural field. This would bring about greater understanding among them, sympathy and care for one another, and real cooperation in all other fields, altogether leading to peace, progress, and stability in the region. It is easy to see that the strength from the unity in ASEAN will support peoples' activities to make them enjoy their own security, and will make them devise ways to resist pressures from the international environment that will once again break the peoples apart and cause them to become easy prey to any of the external countries that are competing for power, international politics being the mode of modern times. Unity gives strength for survival and security, defined here as enjoyment of one's own values.

ASEAN cooperation on culture and information is done through the Committee on Culture and Information (COCI) which was established in 1978. COCI prepares programmes of action to implement the needed projects and manage the ASEAN Cultural Fund and to look for external funding for the project.[41]

COCI identified its priorities for 1994 to 1997, all of which should produce a prosperous and peaceful community of Southeast Asian Nations (based on the Bangkok Declaration of 1967). COCI will ensure excellence in all aspects of cooperation in culture and information, create greater awareness of ASEAN through COCI projects; develop cultural source materials from each member country for translation and replication for the teaching of ASEAN; preserve and revitalise ASEAN cultural heritage against the onslaught of modernisation and natural disasters, and adopt common themes for its projects, following the major concerns of ASEAN cooperation. The themes are environment, cultural heritage, women, children/youth, drugs and AIDS, and social and economic collaboration.

Some projects that have been completed or are on-going are the following:[42]

1. Publication of a series of books entitled *Anthology of ASEAN Literature*, a compilation of literary works from each member country;
2. Resource material for drama presentation on Forms of Courtesy among ASEAN countries; Joint ASEAN Oral History Project to Interview Senior ASEAN Statesmen; and Exchange of ASEAN Archivists;
3. ASEAN Sculpture Symposium and ASEAN Youth Painting Workshop; Travelling Exhibitions of Paintings, Photography and Children's Art; ASEAN Architecture Symposium and Exhibitions; and Workshops on script development for films and TV;
4. ASEAN Dance Festival; ASEAN Festival of Children's Chorus, ASEAN Festival of Songs and Dances held annually;
5. For 1998-1999, the COCI Projects were:
    a. Publication on ASEAN traditional festivals;
    b. Workshop on Standardisation of Archaeological Conservation and Restoration Procedures;
    c. Planning Disaster Management for ASEAN Museums and Heritage Institutions;
    d. Compilation of ASEAN Traditional Children's Songs, Dance, Games, and Story Telling;

e. ASEAN Youth Friendship Camp for the Study of Cultural Heritage held in Thailand in March, 1999; ASEAN Performing Arts Tour Across ASEAN of the *Ramayana*, the great traditional Asian epic premiered in 1998 in Hanoi and Ho Chin Minh City, and to be followed by a tour around the region;

f. Conference of journalists and editors on Economic Trends and Development of ASEAN Countries by 35 journalists from ASEAN in Jakarta in April 1999;

g. Formulation of Communication Plans for ASEAN Vision 2020;

h. Projects with Dialogue Partners: Australia, Regional ASEAN Policy and Strategy for Cultural Heritage; Japan, ASEAN-Japan Multinational Cultural Mission; and Study Tour of Korean Libraries by Korean and ASEAN Senior Librarians in November 1998;

i. Expansion of the ASEANWEB and setting up the ASEAN Satellite Channel;

j. ASEAN TV News Exchange: This is a regular weekly exchange of audio and video news materials among ASEAN national television networks;

k. Special Projects:
    1) Expansion of the ASEANWEB by putting up homepages for culture and information on the ASEANWEB;
    2) Strengthening Public Information and Public Relations Thrusts in promoting ASEAN to provide basic news and information on ASEAN regional cooperation through workshops of secretariat officers in 1998 and production of three booklets on the thrust;
    3) ASEAN Satellite Channel with the Singapore International Media (SIM) as network coordinator.

The Hanoi Plan of Action (HPA 1998) reiterated the need to make peoples of the region aware of ASEAN programmes to help instill in them a sense of regional identity, confidence, and cooperation. COCI will align its work programmes to the HPA to implement the HPA in the next three to six years.

ENDNOTES

1   David Mitrany, "Functional Approach to World Organization", *International Affairs*, XXIV (July 1948). p.359.

2   David Mitrany, *A Working Peace System* (Chicago: Quadrangle books, 1966). p. 97.

3   Ernst Haas, *The Uniting of Europe* (Stanford: Stanford University Press, 1958).

4   http://www.aseansec.org/history/asn_fnc2.htm, 9/28/99, p. 1.

5   This section is taken from the ASEAN Annual Report 1998-1999, Jakarta: ASEAN Secretariat, pp. 56-57.

6   All data here is taken from *From Strength to Strength, ASEAN Functional Cooperation: Retrospect and Prospect* (Jakarta: The ASEAN Secretariat, 1993), pp. 73-75.

7   The data presented here is from http://www.aseansec.org/history/asn_fnc2.htm, 9/28/99. p. 4.

8   Association of Southeast Asian Nations Annual Report 1998-1999, p. 59.

9   UN, "The World's Women, Trends, and Statistics, 1970-1990".

10 Association of Southeast Asian Nations Annual Report 1998-1999, Jakarta, p.60.

11 *Ibid*, pp. 61-62.

12 *Ibid*, pp. 62-63

13 *Ibid.*, pp. 63-65.

14 *Ibid.*, pp. 65-66.

15 http://www.aseansec.org/history/asn_fnc2.htm, 9/28/99, p. 2.

16 Annual report 1998-1999, *op. cit.*, pp. 68-69.

17 *Ibid.*, pp. 70-74.

18 *Ibid.*, pp. 72-75.

19 *From Strength to Strength, op. cit.*

20 *Ibid*, Research by a team from Stanford University, SEAFDEC Philippines, the University Sterling of Scotland, Beyer Institute of Sweden, and the World Wide Fund of Nature and Environmental Defence.

21 *Ibid.*

22 *From Strength to Strength, op. cit.*

23 http://www/aseansec.org/history/asn_fnc2.htm, 9/28/99. p.2.

24 *From Strength to Strength, op. cit.*

25 http://www/aseansec.org/history/asn_fnc2.htm, 9/28/99. p. 3.

26 *Ibid.*

27 Association of Southeast Nations Annual Report 1998-1999, Jakarta: ASEAN Secretariat, p. 75.

28 Data from *From Strength to Strength, op. cit.*, pp. 33-50.

29 Association of Southeast Asian Nations Annual Report 1998-1999, *op. cit.*, p. 76.

30   Taken from *From Strength to Strength*, *op. cit.*

31   Association of Southeast Asian Nations Annual Report 1998-1999, *op. cit.*, p. 76.

32   *From Strength to Strength*, *op. cit.*, pp. 87-89.

33   This updated information is taken from the Association of Southeast Asian Nations Annual Report 1998-1999, Jakarta: ASEAN Secretariat, *op. cit.*, pp. 81-83.

34   http://www/aseansec.org/history/asn_fnc2.htm, p. 5.

35   *From Strength to Strength*, *op. cit.*, pp. 265-273.

36   *From Strength to Strength*, *op. cit.*, pp. 51-62.

37   Sharon Siddique, "Cultural Development: An ASEAN Overview" in K.S. Sandhu, S. Siddique, *et al.*, *The ASEAN Reader* (Singapore: ISEAS), 1992, pp. 133-135.

38   Patya Saihoo, "Problems in Cultural Development" in *The ASEAN Reader*, *ibid.*, p. 136.

39   Lau Teik Soon, "Cultural Cooperation Between the ASEAN States" in *ibid.*, pp. 141-144.

40   Ungku A. Aziz, "Cooperation on Education in ASEAN", in *ibid.*, pp. 167-174.

41   http://www.aseansec.org/history/asn_fnc2.htm,9/28/99, pp. 3-4.

42   Association of Southeast Asian Nations Annual Report 1998-1999,, *op. cit.*, pp. 83-90. Sharon Siddique, "Cultural Development: An ASEAN Overview" in K.S. Sandhu, S. Siddique, *et al.*, *The ASEAN Reader* (Singapore: ISEAS), 1992, pp. 133-135.

6

Economic Cooperation in ASEAN

FUNDAMENTAL PRINCIPLES

The ASEAN Declaration of 1967, while providing for the aims of economic growth, social progress, and cultural development of the region, also mentioned as one of its purposes a more effective collaboration "for the greater utilization of their agriculture and industries; the expansion of their trade, including the study of the problems of international commodity trade; the improvement of transport and communications facilities; and the raising of the living standards of their people".[1]

While the ASEAN Declaration provided for cooperation and did not mention the integration, ASEAN officials have avoided mention of the idea. This is evidence of their faithfulness to the original principles that ASEAN ensures the sovereignty of each member state and that the association is a loose, flexible community of states for cooperation.

BASIC POLICIES

The declared aims for economic development of the ASEAN Declaration were operationalised by the ASEAN Summit Meetings.

The First ASEAN Summit held in Bali in 1976 called for intensifying cooperation in economic and social development and for taking cooperative action in national and regional development programmes, using as much as possible the resources available in the ASEAN region to broaden the complementarity of their respective economies.

The Second ASEAN Summit held in Kuala Lumpur in 1977 stressed that efforts should be intensified and the pace of economic cooperation accelerated with greater vigour; that the efforts of the private sector to implement the industrial complementation schemes and projects and industrial development in the region be increased; and that measures be taken to stimulate the flow of technology, know-how, and private investment among the member countries.

The Third ASEAN Summit held in Manila in 1987 emphasised that ASEAN regionalism based on political, economic, and cultural cohesion is more vital than ever for the future of Southeast Asia. Member states should strengthen intra-ASEAN economic cooperation to realise the region's potential in trade and development, increase ASEAN's efficacy in combating protectionism and countering its effects, and promote an environment for the private sector to have an increasing role in economic development and intra-ASEAN cooperation.

The Fourth Summit held in Singapore in 1992 reiterated the efforts to enhance intra-ASEAN cooperation and to adopt new economic measures as contained in the Framework Agreement on Enhancing ASEAN Economic Cooperation. The focus was on sustaining ASEAN growth and development for stability and prosperity in the region.

The Fifth Summit held in Bangkok in 1995 focused on the theme "Greater ASEAN Economic Cooperation" and decided on the acceleration of the commitments under the ASEAN Free Trade Area (AFTA), expansion of economic cooperation in new sectors to include services and intellectual property, and new ASEAN Industrial Cooperation Schemes (AICO), and proposed to create an ASEAN Investment Area (AIA). AICO will replace the Brand-to-Brand Complementation (BBC) and the ASEAN Industrial Joint Venture (AIJV) Schemes. The summit looked at how ASEAN could participate in the development of the Mekong Basin and agreed to implement the plans of action on Infrastructure Development, Transport and Communication, Energy, and Small and Medium Enterprises (SME).

The First Informal Summit held in Jakarta on 30 November 1996 requested the ministers to develop the ASEAN Vision 2020, considering that AFTA would have been fully implemented for almost two decades. The leaders also endorsed the Basic Framework of the ASEAN – Mekong Basin Development Cooperation hoping also to promote the interconnection between the economies of ASEAN and the non-ASEAN Mekong Riparian states. The Economic Ministers were also to develop ASEAN cooperation on the facilitation of goods in transit.

COOPERATION IN INDUSTRIAL DEVELOPMENT[2]

Industrial cooperation schemes (IC) based on the principles of resource pooling and market sharing have been introduced to facilitate effective exploitation of economies of scale and the region's complementary location advantages. The following are the IC schemes:

a. The ASEAN Industrial Projects (AIP 1976), such as the ASEAN-Acheh Fertilizer and the ASEAN – Bintulu Fertilizer Plants aimed to establish large scale regional projects to meet the basic needs of the region and ensure efficient use of the region's resources.

b. The ASEAN Industrial Complementation Scheme (AIC 1981) and the Brand-to-Brand Complementation Scheme (BBC 1988). These involved the automotive sector where the various companies operating in the region could produce and exchange automotive parts and components. Automotive brand owners could have horizontal specialisation of the products, exploit economies of scale, and allow exchange of approved automotive parts and components for specific brand models.

c. The ASEAN Industrial Joint Venture (AIJV 1983) was revised in 1987 to encourage greater investment into and within the region and increase industrial production through resource pooling and market sharing activities. Both AIC and AIJV Schemes would get tax reductions.

d. The basic agreement on the ASEAN Industrial Cooperation Scheme (AICO 1997) replaced the BBC and AIJV Schemes because of the increased industrial development of the region and the gradual tariff liberalisation of the Common Effective Preferential Tariff Scheme (CEPT), the main mechanism towards the ASEAN Free Trade Area (AFTA 1992). The AICO Scheme became operational on 1 November 1997. It aims to promote joint manufacturing activities of companies operating in ASEAN. The private sector is actively participating in this. Products under the AICO Scheme will be granted 0-5 per cent preferential tariff rate which is equivalent to the final CEPT rate.

COOPERATION IN THE ASEAN
FREE TRADE AREA (AFTA 1992)[3]

The Fourth ASEAN Summit in 1992 decided to establish AFTA by year 2008. In 1994 the member states agreed to accelerate the time frame from 15 years to ten years. In 1998 at the Sixth ASEAN Summit, the original six members will implement AFTA by 2002 when all items in the Inclusion List will have tariffs of 0-5 per cent with some flexibility.

AFTA is planned to enhance ASEAN's position as a competitive production base to service the global market. This can be achieved through increased intra-ASEAN trade, greater specialisation, economies of scale, and increased foreign direct investments which should be attracted to a new single ASEAN market. The newer members of ASEAN shall maximise their tariff lines, between 0-5 per cent by 2003 for Vietnam, and 2005 for Laos and Myanmar, and expand the number of tariff lines in the 0 per cent category by 2006 for Vietnam and 2008 for Laos and Myanmar.

The main mechanism to realise AFTA is the Common Effective Preferential Tariff Scheme (CEPT 1993). It covers manufactured and agricultural products. This is the most comprehensive ASEAN trading arrangement. More than 90 per cent of the total tariff lines in ASEAN are now included in the CEPT Scheme, representing more than 81 per cent of intra-ASEAN trade values. More products are being transferred from the Temporary Exclusion and the Sensitive Lists to the Inclusion List.

The CEPT Scheme requires reduction of tariffs for all products in the Inclusion list, elimination of quantitative restrictions, and abolition of other non-tariff barriers. By year 2003 all CEPT rates of tariffs for products in the Inclusion List should be at 2.63 per cent. To hasten AFTA's realisation, other measures are also used, for example:

1. harmonisation of customs matters (tariff nomenclature, customs valuation systems, customs procedures and a Green Lane System to expedite clearance of CEPT products).
2. harmonisation of product standards for intra-ASEAN trade.

Intra-ASEAN exports have increased from US$ 42.77 billion to $68.83 billion between 1993 and 1995, an increase of 30.46 per cent per annum, and higher by 2 per cent than the average 20 per cent growth of total ASEAN exports. In 1995, 59 per cent of intra-ASEAN exports consisted of machinery and electrical appliances. Other products are petroleum, base metals, chemicals, and plastics.

AFTA is establishing linkages with other regional groupings such as the Common Economic Relations (CER) between Australia and New Zealand, the North American Free Trade Agreement (NAFTA), the Mercado Comun del Sur (MERCOSUR), the European Free Trade Association (EFTA), the Southern African Development Cooperation (SADC), the South Pacific forum, Gulf Cooperation Council, South Asian Association for Regional Cooperation (SAARC) and others.

COOPERATION IN FINANCE AND BANKING[4]

ASEAN finance cooperation has been strengthened by the First ASEAN Finance Ministers Meeting (AFMM) on 1 March 1997 in Phuket, Thailand. Finance cooperation will support the AFTA, AICO, and AIA. Two documents signed in the AFMM will strengthen finance activities.

First is the Ministerial Understanding (MU) on Finance Cooperation which provides a framework for enhanced cooperation in banking, financial and capital markets development, customs matters, insurance matters, taxation, monetary policy cooperation, and human resource development in the area of finance. Second is the ASEAN Agreement on Customs which will expedite the realisation of AFTA and which stipulates joint efforts in anti-smuggling and customs control activities, mutual technical assistance, customs modernisation, and upgrading customs skills for present and future challenges. A new ASEAN Senior Finance Officials Meeting (ASFOM) will assist the AFM. Other finance-related bodies such as insurance regulators, capital market, tax, and central bank authorities need to cooperate with the finance sub-sectors.

The ASEAN Surveillance Process (ASP) is seen to strengthen ASEAN finance cooperation. ASEAN member countries also reached a consensus in 1999 to present a common ASEAN position in reforming the international financial structure. Consultations with China, Japan, and the Republic of Korea have led to exchange of views in monitoring short-term capital flows and international financial reforms.

COMMON ASEAN POSITION IN THE REFORM OF THE INTERNATIONAL FINANCIAL ARCHITECTURE[5]

(i) The global effort to resolve the current crisis must recognise the diverse circumstances and priorities of individual economies at different stages of development. Any proposed solution must therefore be sufficiently flexible to accommodate these differences.

(ii) In view of the global nature of today's financial markets, the reform of the international financial architecture must involve the participation of all countries, including the emerging economies.

(iii) ASEAN shall adopt a more proactive role at various international and regional fora to ensure that its interests and priorities are given due consideration in any proposal to reform the international financial architecture.

(iv) While the purpose of any international reform is to enhance efficiency and stability in financial markets and to promote global economic activity, such efforts must not lose sight of the overriding objective of improving living standards. Due priority must, therefore, be accorded to measures to protect the poor and most vulnerable segments of society.

(v) Measures to strengthen the international financial architecture would need to include a review of the roles of the international financial institutions (IFIs), as well as the international regulatory bodies, in order to enhance their capacity and capability to contain and resolve crises.

(vi) Appropriate mechanisms are needed to enhance greater private sector participation in crisis management and resolution.

(vii) Standards of transparency and disclosure must be applied equally to the public and private sectors. In particular, large market participants, such as highly leveraged institutions which have systemic significance, should be subject to regular and timely transparency and disclosure requirements.

(viii) The dissemination of necessary information will help investors to make better decisions and not rely solely on the information of rating agencies. Given the important role that credit rating agencies play in the international financial markets, there should be greater transparency in the rating process.

(ix)   There must be closer and more coordinated monitoring of short-term capital flows. In particular, there should be global agreement on the disclosure requirements for such flows and closer collaboration and information sharing among national and international regulators.

(x)   To complement the ASEAN Surveillance Process, ASEAN shall explore options to strengthen regional support activities.

(xi)   An orderly and well-sequenced approach to capital account liberalisation in tandem with the degree of development of the domestic financial sector and supervisory regime should be supported.

(xii) Sound, consistent, and credible macroeconomic policies are fundamental to the sustainability of any exchange rate regime. There is no single exchange rate regime that is suitable for all countries and countries have a right to choose their own exchange rate regime based on their national objectives and priorities.

COOPERATION IN INVESTMENT

This should achieve a bold regional arrangement for investment known as the ASEAN Investment Area (AIA). This AIA should help ASEAN attract more foreign Direct Investment (FDI). Towards this goal, ASEAN has institutionalised some investment bodies to handle an increasing level of regional investment matters.[6]

Some important areas of investment cooperation have been achieved since December 1995. Among these are:

1.   A Plan of Action on Cooperation and Promotion of FDI and Intra-ASEAN Investment;

2.   A Work Programme on Cooperation and Promotion of FDI;

3.   The Protocol Improving the 1987 ASEAN Agreement for the Promotion and Protection of Investments;

4.   Joint Annual Training Workshops for ASEAN Investment Policy Making Officials;

5.   A Comprehensive Survey on the Promotion of FDI;

6.   A High-Level Roundtable for the Formulation of Strategic Plans on Cooperation and Promotion of FDI in ASEAN; and

7.   An Experts Seminar on the Promotion of FDI in the Context of the ASEAN Investment Area.

AIA aims to promote the inflow of direct investment from ASEAN and non-ASEAN sources by making ASEAN a competitive, open, and liberal investment area.[7] Under the AIA, ASEAN shall:

1. Implement coordinated ASEAN investment cooperation and facilitation programmes;
2. Implement coordinated promotion programmes and investment awareness activities;
3. Open immediately all industries, except those specified in the Temporary Exclusion List (TEL) and Sensitive List (SL), to ASEAN investors by 2010 and to all investors by 2020;
4. Grant immediately national treatment, except those specified in the TEL and SL, to ASEAN investors by 2010 and to all investors by 2020;
5. Involve the private sector actively in the AIA development process;
6. Promote freer flow of capital, skilled labour and professionals, and technology among the member countries;
7. Provide transparency of investment policies, rules, procedures and administrative processes; and
8. Develop a more streamlined and simplified investment process.

COOPERATION IN FOOD, AGRICULTURE, AND FORESTRY

To improve the competitiveness of ASEAN agriculture and forestry products, a Ministerial Understanding on ASEAN Cooperation in Food, Agriculture, and Forestry has provided a framework for sectoral cooperation in these areas. The ASEAN Food Security reserve will be reviewed for a more dynamic food security arrangement to enhance intra-ASEAN trade and promote food production under the principle of comparative advantage. An ASEAN food security information system will enable member countries to effectively forecast, plan, and manage their supplies and use of basic food and help investors to invest in food production. Food security also involves handling of Halal food for Muslims, control on the use of additives, the use of irradiation as a quarantine treatment for traded fresh fruits and vegetables, and quality assurance systems for ASEAN fruits, this last being a project with Australia. ASEAN has general guidelines for Halal food and additives and has endorsed the Model Protocol for the Use of Irradiation as a quarantine treatment for fresh fruits and vegetables.

ASEAN countries have completed a comprehensive pest list for mango and rice and is preparing a pest list for coconut, ginger, potato, groundnut, beach pepper, and orange, for the harmonisation process. ASEAN is also selecting pesticides for future harmonisation. ASEAN countries are also looking at the harmonisation of livestock sanitary measures to promote intra-ASEAN trade in livestock and livestock products, including vaccines. Thailand wants to build a research centre in Chiang Mai province for ASEAN-Mekong Basin Fisheries Development Cooperation. Singapore has trained participants from Myanmar in fisheries post-harvest technology. ASEAN and the Southeast Asia Fisheries Development Centre (SEAFDEC, Philippines) will collaborate on sustainable fisheries development in Southeast Asia. ASEAN has also taken collective stands on agriculture and forest products.[8]

COOPERATION IN MINERALS

This was approved by the Fifth ASEAN Summit to promote trade and investment in industrial minerals. Member countries need to exchange information on policy, regulation, and legislation to attract investments. A Director of Research and Development and Training Centres will be available in the region.

COOPERATION IN ENERGY

ASEAN will become a net oil importing region with the new century. Collective action is being taken to ensure greater security and sustainability of energy supply through diversification, development, and conservation of resources, efficient use of energy, and wide application of environmentally sound technologies. The Agreement on ASEAN Energy Cooperation of 1986 provides for vigorous implementation of the Medium Term Programme of Action on Energy Cooperation(1995-1999) in electricity, oil and gas, coal, new and renewable sources of energy, energy efficiency and conservation, and energy policy and planning. There is also an ASEAN emergency petroleum-sharing scheme in place. Cooperative efforts will focus on regional interconnecting arrangements for electricity and natural gas through the ASEAN Power Grid and Trans-ASEAN Gas Pipeline Projects. Research and training will be centralised in the ASEAN Centre for Energy. The ASEAN Centre for Energy (ACE) was established in Jakarta on 4 January 1999 to accelerate the integration of energy strategies in ASEAN by providing information, state-of-the-art technology, and expertise to ensure that energy development policies and programmes are in harmony with economic growth and environmental sustainability of the ASEAN region.

ASEAN is also looking at financing for regional energy development and studies in petroleum transactions and on electricity interconnections.

COOPERATION IN TRANSPORT AND COMMUNICATIONS

ASEAN has an Integrated Implementation Programme involving 45 projects and activities in multimodal transport, interconnectivity in telecommunications, harmonisation of road transport laws, rules and regulations, airspace management, maritime safety and pollution, human resources, and air services liberalisation. Feasibility studies are being made on the Singapore-Kunming (China) Rail Link Project, Facilitation of Goods in Transit, improved infrastructure and communications for an integrated trans-ASEAN transportation network, information highways, multimedia corridors in ASEAN, open sky policy, and a regional shipping policy.

COOPERATION IN TOURISM

ASEAN tourism has strong growth potentials and has given significant gains to the regional economy. The aim of cooperation in tourism is to develop ASEAN as a single tourist destination product with world class attractions, standards and facilities, better intra-ASEAN travel, and freer trade in tourism. In line with the Hanoi Plan of Action, ASEAN Tourism Ministers implemented the Visit ASEAN Millenium Year (VAY) Programme in the year 2002. All member countries cooperated with equal financial contributions to develop and market the branding and image positioning of VAY 2002. The Ministers also are working for increased tourism investments.[9]

POSITIONING COOPERATION IN SERVICES

This is a new area of economic cooperation. The ASEAN Framework Agreement on Services (1995) provides for negotiations to produce commitments on increased market access and national treatment from member countries in the seven priority services of air transport, business services, construction, financial services, maritime transport, telecommunications, and tourism.

COOPERATION IN INTELLECTUAL PROPERTY

ASEAN needs to continuously upgrade its technological competitiveness to sustain high economic growth. ASEAN has to strengthen its intellectual property (IP) legislations, administration, and enforcement. The Framework Agreement in Intellectual Property Cooperation (Bangkok 1995) is aimed at increasing the confidence of owners of technology that their ideas and technology are protected well in the region by enforcement, protection, administration, legislation and public awareness of IP.

PRIVATE SECTOR

ASEAN recognises the role of the private sector for the success of various economic cooperation programmes. Regarded as the engine of growth, the private sector under the ASEAN Chambers of Commerce and Industry (ASEAN-CCI) maintains linkages with Senior Economic Officials and ASEAN Economic Ministers regularly. An ASEAN-CCI secretariat is in Jakarta for better linkages between the policy-making bodies and the private sector.

THE SIXTH ASEAN SUMMIT

This was held in Hanoi on 15-16 December 1998.[10] Its theme was "Unity and Cooperation for an ASEAN of Peace, Stability, and Equitable Development". For this, ASEAN leaders adopted the Hanoi Declaration which outlined ASEAN's policy directions and priorities in the context of the existing regional situation. The summit issued a "Statement on Bold Measures" which provided specific regional and national measures to enhance investment in ASEAN economies particularly for the next two years.

The Sixth Summit adopted the Hanoi Plan of Action (HPA 1998) towards the realisation of ASEAN Vision 2020 which was adopted by the ASEAN leaders in December 1997. The HPA aims to:

1. Strengthen macroeconomic and financial cooperation;
2. Enhance greater economic integration;
3. Promote science and technology development;
4. Promote social development and meet the social impact of the economic crisis;
5. Promote human resource development;
6. Protect the environment and promote sustainable development;
7. Enhance ASEAN's role as an effective force of peace, justice, and moderation in the Asia-Pacific region and in the world;
8. Strengthen regional peace and security;
9. Promote ASEAN awareness and its standing in the international community;
10. Improve ASEAN's structures and mechanisms;
11. Follow up cooperation between Southeast Asia and Northeast Asia into the 21st century within the framework of ASEAN + 3.

To encourage Pacific Settlement of Disputes, the HPA directed the drafting of rules of procedure for the High Council as provided for by the TAC (1976). The ASEAN leaders reaffirmed their determination to strengthen ties with other countries.

IMPROVED REGIONAL ECONOMY

In 1999, the economic situation in ASEAN had improved considerably since the financial crisis of 1997. Although the pace of recovery had been uneven, depending on the reforms of each member state, there were forecasts for economic growth. According to the Annual Report of the ASEAN Secretariat for 1998-1999, the positive indicators that are now visible are:

1. Return of stability in the foreign exchange markets;
2. Rising current accounts surplus and reserves;
3. Decline in interest rates;
4. Easing of inflationary measures;
5. Recovery in stock markets;

6. Improvement in consumer sentiment;
7. Levelling off in the contraction of industrial production.

However, new social, political, and economic problems in Indonesia, the Philippines and perhaps Malaysia as well as in Europe and the US may show downturn of the indicators. There are other factors that may also affect the recovery such as rising protectionism, exchange rate misalignment of major world currencies, and uncertainty of external financial flows. In 2003, the continued transboundary spread of the Severe Acute Respiratory Syndrome (SARS) in the world brought many social and economic activities to very low levels due to the fear of contamination and death.

The ASEAN member countries adopted certain policies to alleviate the financial crisis such as reviving domestic demand and economic activity, easing monetary and fiscal policies, and increasing fiscal spending to cushion the impact of the financial crisis on the poor and other vulnerable parts of societies.

ASEAN finance cooperation is being strengthened by the ASEAN Surveillance Process (ASP 1998) which is intended to prevent future crisis through early warning systems and regional economic surveillance activities. The ASP will function through a peer review process and exchange of views and information among ASEAN Financial Ministers in macroeconomic and finance matters. ASP's work is supported by several institutions such as the ASEAN Finance Ministers fora, Central Bank officials, ASEAN Secretariat, and a Support Unit.[11]

At the ASEAN-Japan Summit in Kuala Lumpur on 16 December 1997, the leaders agreed to establish a new body within the existing AEM-MITI (Ministry of International Trade and Industry). The new body at the ministerial level is now named AEM-MITI Economic and Industrial Cooperation Committee (AMEICC). It will enhance industrial cooperation and assist economic recovery in the region by studying the areas where ASEAN lost its competitiveness and see how these areas could regain it, study demand trends, supply structures, and strengthen centres of excellence for more engineers, technical personnel, and managers. It will also provide development assistance to new member countries of ASEAN.

In the matter of reform of the International Financial Architecture, ASEAN has declared its common position that any global effort to reform finance must recognise the diverse circumstances and priorities of individual economies at different stages of development. Any proposed reform should involve all countries, including emerging economies, must be flexible, transparent to all participants, must have close coordination of short-term capital flows, a well-sequenced approach to capital account liberalisation, and freedom to adopt appropriate exchange rate regimes.[12]

ASEAN has also implemented to a certain extent the greater use of ASEAN currencies for trade settlement. A bilateral payments arrangement (BPA) by which the balance of trade transactions between any two member states could be settled by the currency of one of the two is now in use. At present Malaysia and the Philippines have concluded a BPA, while arrangements between Malaysia and Thailand and Malaysia and Indonesia are being discussed.

Intra-ASEAN trade will be facilitated by the Framework Agreement on the Facilitation of Goods in Transit (Hanoi December 1998). By this, member countries are granted the right of transit transport for goods and vehicles across the territory of one or more members from point of origin to final destination and the transit transport will not be subject to any unnecessary delays or restrictions such as customs duties, taxes and other charges and examination by customs officials en route, for drivers and vehicles too.

ASEAN's economic cooperation includes open investment areas for its member countries, Joint Investment Promotion events like seminars and fairs, support by harmonised data collection, and investment privileges as contained in the Statement on Bold Measures (Hanoi 1998) which includes a minimum three-year corporate income tax exemption or a minimum 30 per cent corporate investment tax allowance, 100 per cent equity ownership, duty-free imports of capital goods, domestic market access, minimum industrial land leasehold of 30 years, employment of foreign personnel, and speedy customs clearance. Investment privileges were extended to all investors, ASEAN and non-ASEAN, within the promotion period for applications from manufacturing investors, ending in December 2000.[13]

PROJECTS IN ECONOMIC COOPERATION

As has been said earlier, economic cooperation in ASEAN was the last to develop because of structural difficulties which made the shift from trade with colonial masters to intra-ASEAN trade very slow.

In 1976, 1977 and 1987, during the first three Summit Meetings, many economic arrangements were made through direct government arrangements and through influencing trade directions by altering the tariff structures of privately traded goods. Since 1992, ASEAN developed new economic measures for expanded regional and international cooperation.

Below are summaries of some of the current economic cooperation activities aside from the Preferential Trading Arrangements, CEPT, AFTA, AIJV, and Industrial Cooperation:

1. A Food Security Reserve System that provides an emergency rice reserve. On oil and rice supply crisis, the principle to be observed is the principle of first refusal. No net exporter can sell to new buyers unless ASEAN members who need the supply express a first refusal (First ASEAN Summit 1976). This is now being updated to relate to intra-ASEAN trade and food production on the principle of comparative advantage.
2. Joint programmes for the eradication of foot and mouth disease.
3. Training institute for agriculture.
4. ASEAN Swap Arrangement that provides US $299 million in standby credit for members with balance of payment problems.
5. Tourism.
6. Rural Development and Poverty Eradication.
7. Agriculture and Forest Products; Forestry Protection.
8. Preservation of Environment.
9. Consultation with Chambers of Commerce.
10. Harmonisation of Maximum Residue Limits on Pesticides.
11. Fisheries Postharvest Technology.
12. Harmonisation of Regulations for Agricultural Products Derived from Biotechnology; Food Irradiation.
13. International Standardisation and Quality.
14. Regulations on Cosmetics.
15. Banking, Insurance Regulations.
16. Central Banks Cooperation.
17. Consumer Electronics Industry.
18. Energy Cooperation, Efficiency and Conservation.
19. Transport Safety, Pollution, Traffic and Regulation.
20. Communication, Electronics and Commerce.
21. Foreign Investments.

22. Development and support of growth areas which are intended to reduce the gap in levels of socio-economic development in the region. Present growth areas are the Brunei-Indonesia-Malaysia-Philippines East Asia Growth Area (BIMP-EAGA), Indonesia-Malaysia-Singapore Growth Triangle (IMS-GT), Indonesia-Malaysia-Thailand Growth Triangle (IMT-GT), and the inter-states areas along the West-East Corridor (WEC) of the Mekong Basin in Vietnam, Laos, Cambodia, North Eastern Thailand within the ASEAN Mekong Basin Development Cooperation Scheme, and the Cambodia-Laos-Vietnam Development Triangle.

THE SEVENTH ASEAN SUMMIT

The Seventh ASEAN Summit on 5-6 November 2001 in Bandar Seri Begawan focussed on efforts for economic reforms, integration and cooperation in the region. These included ASEAN's commitment to accelerate its economic integration through the development of the Roadmap for the Integration of ASEAN (RIA) which is seen to produce coherence and cohesiveness to respond to the challenges of the economic diversity of the expanded ASEAN. The RIA will help to bridge the development gap in ASEAN, strengthen AFTA, accelerate the ASEAN Investment Area (AIA), integrate measures in the APEC, and implement bilateral free trade agreements consistent with the goals of the Doha (Qatar) Development Agenda. The WTO Ministerial Meeting in Doha emphasised the importance of development in the trade agenda because of the difficult time for the multilateral trading system. ASEAN will work closely with its economic partners in negotiations at the WTO towards achieving greater market access for products and services of developing economies.

THE EIGHTH ASEAN SUMMIT[14]

The Chairman of the Eighth ASEAN Summit in Phnom Penh on 3-5 November 2002 summarised the highlights of the summit.

At the opening of the ASEAN Summit, the Chair outlined the Phnom Penh Agenda, Towards a Community of Southeast Asian Nations. It had four themes: (1) Collaboration with the Greater Mekong Sub-region Programme to accelerate ASEAN integration; (2) ASEAN as a single tourist destination; (3) ASEAN solidarity for peace and security especially in the fight against terrorism; and (4) bold steps in sustainable natural resource management, including ratification of the Kyoto Protocol by all ASEAN members.

Addressing the latest transnational problem of terrorist attacks which had slowed down economic activities internationally, the Eighth ASEAN Summit adopted the Declaration on Terrorism which condemned the recent heinous acts of terrorism. Malaysia's Prime Minister Mahathir Mohamad said that the September attacks had "changed the world. The world today is almost like a world at war" because of terrorist strikes and the fear they ignite. Singapore's Prime Minister Goh Chok Tong said Southeast Asia presented "a new set of soft targets" for international terrorism. Indonesian Prime Minister Megawati Sukarnoputri said, "terrorism can strike anywhere. It does not relate to a particular religion, race, or country". Cambodian Prime Minister Hun Sen said "we cannot allow the evil of terrorism to prevail". The Declaration binds the ASEAN leaders to build on the specific measures outlined in the ASEAN Declaration on Joint Action to Counter Terrorism which was adopted in Brunei Darussalam in November 2001. The ASEAN countries agreed to intensify their efforts to prevent, counter and suppress the activities of terrorist groups in the region, using practical cooperative measures among them and with the international community.

ASEAN states continue to increase their efforts against terrorism. These include Thailand's accession to the Agreement in Information Exchange and Establishment of Communication Procedures between Indonesia, Malaysia, the Philippines and Cambodia, the arrest of persons plotting to commit acts of terrorism, and the implementation of the Work Plan adopted by the Special ASEAN Ministerial Meeting on Terrorism in Kuala Lumpur in May 2002. ASEAN Leaders called on the international community to support ASEAN's efforts to combat terrorism, avoid indiscriminate advice to their citizens to refrain from visiting or dealing with ASEAN countries, in response to rumours of possible terrorist attacks, which advisories could only achieve the objectives of the terrorists, and to restore business confidence in the region.

With its deep concern on the Middle East crisis, the ASEAN Summit asked the international community to formulate a peaceful solution to end the violence in Israel. ASEAN expressed support for the

United Nation's efforts to eliminate all weapons of mass destruction in Iraq and for the UN and UNSC to decide on appropriate enforcement action in the Iraqi situation.

The Eighth Summit also adopted the ASEAN Work Programme which addresses transnational issues such as diseases and trafficking of humans, drugs and weapons, which issues require international cooperation and unified action.

The strategy of ASEAN for sustained economic development in a condition of rapid globalisation is the Initiative for ASEAN Integration (IAI) to strengthen national and regional competitiveness. ASEAN needs to cooperate with its partners through enhanced trade and investment links, and bold unified strategies for growth.

On faster ASEAN integration, the Eighth Summit recommended schemes on tariffs, such as the ASEAN Integration System of Preferences to allow Cambodia, the Lao People's Democratic Republic, Myanmar and Vietnam to gain tariff-free access to the more developed markets by 2003, seven years ahead of the target of 2010. Harmonisation of product standards, streamlining of customs procedures, strengthening of transport links, increasing the use of information and communication technology, and liberalising investment within ASEAN are deemed important for economic integration. On the missing link in the Singapore-Kunming Railway Link (SKRL), Malaysia offered to help Cambodia build it.

The ASEAN Leaders reaffirmed their enhanced partnership with China, Japan, and the Republic of Korea and their support for the IAI Work Plan and projects to accelerate the integration of ASEAN's new members. The leaders also acknowledged the expansion of the ASEAN + 3 process to include regional political and security issues. The three countries have been helping integration through their own efforts, which could later lead to an East Asia Free Trade Area.

The Eighth Summit signed the ASEAN Tourism Agreement giving a new high priority on tourism development and making the ASEAN region a single tourist destination. The aim is to have a free flow of tourism services before 2020.

COOPERATION OR INTEGRATION FOR ASEAN?

Economists are at variance about whether ASEAN is leading towards integration (which was not stated in the Bangkok Declaration of 1967)

174

or will remain in the cooperation level. However, ASEAN has adopted the Initiative for ASEAN Integration (IAI) to strengthen national and regional competitiveness in the face of rapid globalisation. The ASEAN Vision 2020 has affirmed the goal of economic integration.[15]

Mohamed Ariff's study argues that regional economic integration might do more harm than good if it makes ASEAN inward-looking. Moreover, the textbook models for customs union, common market, and economic unions would not necessarily be good for ASEAN. Its member states are heterogeneous in size, production structures, natural resources, population, and other factors. Florian Alburo states that the theoretical argument for regional integration is improving welfare.[16] ASEAN economies which are homogeneous indicate that integration benefits may not accrue uniformly across countries. If integration leads to trade diversion from efficient sources to an inefficient source, under a non-discriminatory situation, then resource misallocation takes place and may not create more trade. Then integration will not be welfare-improving. On another point, ASEAN's projects may not pass a stringent market test and may not be competitive at world market prices even if ASEAN goes for integration.

Economic cooperation in ASEAN still has much space for growth. Economists strongly suggest a continuation of trade and investment liberalisation policies but allowing market forces to influence individual economies, closer government-private sector cooperation, and concentration on collective goods which cannot be produced by individual ASEAN states. ASEAN should develop itself into a strong bloc to negotiate with other international organisations and internationalise ASEAN economies although ASEAN must safeguard its principles for free trade because global economic interdependence leads also to greater conflicts.

The expansive concerns of ASEAN economic cooperation reflect the magnitude of the problems in the world today, produced both by underdevelopment and by advances in science and technology. It is ASEAN's wisdom that makes it attend to the problems simultaneously.

Through Dialogue relations, ASEAN has linked up with the industrial world for access to their markets, to buy time for regional development, for protection from sudden shifts in global structure, for access to new business opportunities, to gain experiences in multilateral negotiations, for trade and economic concessions through ASEAN collective lobbying, to strengthen political relations with Dialogue

Partners, and to boost ASEAN standing. On the other hand, Dialogue Partners have access to an enlarged ASEAN market. But more than economic matters, ASEAN Dialogue Partners' cooperation is now covering nearly all the functional matters and transnational problems to achieve peace and shared prosperity.

ENDNOTES

1   The ASEAN Declaration, Bangkok, 8 August 1967. Data in the paragraphs is taken from website http://www.aseansec.org/history/asn_eco2.htm. (9/28/99, pp. 1-2.)

2   *Ibid.*, p. 3.

3   *Ibid.*, pp. 2-3.

4   *Ibid.*, pp. 3-4. See also Association of Southeast Asian Nations Annual Report 1998-1999, ASEAN Secretariat, p. 14.

5   Document on the Common ASEAN Position on the Reform of the International Financial Architecture as adopted at the Special ASEAN Finance Ministers' Meeting in Manila on 30 April 1999. From ASEAN Annual Report 1998-1999, Jakarta: Central Secretariat, pp. 16-17.

6   http://www.aseansec.org/history/asn_eco2.htm. *Ibid.*, p.4.

7   ASEAN Annual Report 1998-1999, *op. cit.*, pp. 30-31.

8   *Ibid.*, pp. 49-52.

9   *Ibid.*, p. 45.

10 ASEAN Annual Report 1998-1999, ASEAN Secretariat, pp. 10-11.

11 *Ibid.*, p. 15.

12 Adopted at the Special ASEAN Finance Ministers Meeting in Manila on 30 April 1999, *op. cit.*

13 Annual Report 1998-1999, op. cit., p. 32.

14 Press statement by the Chairman of the Eighth ASEAN Summit, the Sixth ASEAN + 3 Summit and the ASEAN + China Summit, 4 November 2002, Phnom Penh.

15 Mohamed Ariff, "The Changing Role of ASEAN in the Coming Decade" in K.S. Sandhu, Sharon Siddique, *et. al.* (eds.), *The ASEAN Reader* (Singapore: ISEAS 1992), p. 212.

16 Florian Alburo, "The ASEAN Summit and ASEAN Economic Cooperation" in *the ASEAN Reader, ibid.*, p. 203.

7

ASEAN External Relations

From its earliest successes in relating to countries that had wished to develop cooperation with ASEAN as a group, perceiving that it is better to deal with a group that represents a total population of about 500 million, a total area of 4.4 million square kilometres, a combined gross domestic product of $735 billion, and total trade of $720 billion, ASEAN in year 2000 had 11 Full Dialogue Partners and one Sectoral Dialogue Partner. ASEAN and its Dialogue Partners have joint cooperative activities supported by regular exchanges of views on areas of mutual interest.

ASEAN COOPERATION AND DIALOGUE RELATIONS[1]

ASEAN's commitment to develop its external relations was enunciated at the First Meeting of the ASEAN Heads of Government in 1976 which "expressed ASEAN's readiness to develop fruitful relations and mutually beneficial cooperation with other countries in the region". The Second Summit in 1977 also reiterated that economic cooperation with third countries or group of countries be further intensified and expanded.

The first group of countries which ASEAN's external relations centered on were the major trading partners of ASEAN. ASEAN formally established full dialogue relations with Australia, Japan, New Zealand and the UNDP in 1976; the United States (US) in 1977; the European Union (EU) in 1980; Canada in 1981; Republic of Korea in 1991; India which was a Sectoral Dialogue Partner in 1995; and China and Russia which began consultative relations with ASEAN in 1991 and were accorded Dialogue status in 1996. Pakistan also established Sectoral relations with ASEAN in 1997.

ASEAN's dialogue relations have promoted trade and investment, facilitated the transfer of technology and know-how and improved access of ASEAN products into the markets of its dialogue partners. It has also served as an avenue for ASEAN to engage in dialogue on regional and global issues with some of the most important countries of the world and to secure development and technical assistance.

Economic cooperation has become the most important area of cooperation of ASEAN's relations with its Dialogue Partners, in particular trade and investment. Apart from these, ASEAN's economic cooperation with its Dialogue Partners extend to industrial development, transfer of technology, energy, communications, transport, and tourism.

ASEAN's development cooperation with Dialogue Partners is increasingly being linked to the economic interests of both sides and many of the development cooperation programmes and projects are now designed to enhance this objective. Moreover, the nature of development cooperation has also changed with the emphasis being on partnership and shared thematic programming instead of project-specific financing. The main areas of development cooperation are in the fields of science and technology, human resource development, environment, social and cultural development, and narcotics control.

ASEAN's development cooperation stems from both its collective national efforts and positive responses from its Dialogue Partners. Recognising the critical importance of prudent aid management to maximise the benefits of external assistance, the 22nd AMM agreed to the formation of an ASEAN Cooperation Unit (ACU). This Unit, since established in a restructured Secretariat, is responsible for all aspects of project appraisal and funding management, in close cooperation with Dialogue Partners.

Apart from Dialogue relations with its existing Dialogue Partners, the Fourth ASEAN Summit of 1992 agreed that, as a part of an increasingly interdependent world, ASEAN should "intensify cooperative relationships with interested non-dialogue countries and international organization". At the Fifth ASEAN Summit this was again emphasised when the ASEAN Heads of Government called ASEAN to "remain outward looking and deepen its external relations with its partners in a globally interdependent world". In this regard, ties are being forged with other sub-regional groupings such as the South Pacific Forum, Economic Cooperation Organization, Gulf Cooperation Council, South Asian Association for Regional Cooperation, South African Development Cooperation, MERCOSUR and other organisations in Central and South America through the development of concrete and action oriented activities.

ASEAN – AUSTRALIA

The ASEAN–Australia Economic Cooperation Programme (AAECP), established in 1974, is the cornerstone of ASEAN–Australia relations. Building on its previous successes, the AAECP Phase III through the Project Steam activities, continues with its commitment towards enhancing trade and investment opportunities between ASEAN and Australia. Science and technology and human resource development are the two themes of the AAECP. The Linkages Stream acts as a major facilitator for networking between ASEAN and Australian private sectors.

ASEAN – CANADA

Although a Dialogue relationship was already in process in 1977, ASEAN–Canada relations were formalised in 1981 through the setting up of the ASEAN–Canada Joint Cooperation Committee (JCC). The Joint Planning and Monitoring Committee (JPMC) was set up in 1994 to oversee various projects at the planning and implementation level. Canada has provided technical assistance to ASEAN for projects on science and technology, human resources development, information and culture, and women in development with a very strong emphasis on science and technology. Greater impetus is being given to the expansion of trade and investments between ASEAN and Canada.

ASEAN – PEOPLE'S REPUBLIC OF CHINA

In September 1993, the Secretary-General of ASEAN led a delegation to Beijing for exploratory talks with senior Chinese officials on ways and means of developing the ASEAN–China relationship. Two Joint Committees on Economic and Trade and Cooperation, and on Cooperation in Science and Technology were set up as a result of an exchange of letters between the Secretary-General of ASEAN and the Minister of Foreign Affairs of China during the 27th AMM in Bangkok in July 1994. ASEAN and China held their first political consultation at Senior Officials (SOM) level in Hangzhou in April 1995. The second and third consultations were held in Bukittinggi, Indonesia, in June 1996 and in Huangshan, China, in April 1997. In 1996, at the 29th AMM in Jakarta, the Vice Premier and Minister of Foreign Affairs of China attended the AMM/PMC as a Dialogue

Partner for the first time. ASEAN and China convened the first meeting of their Joint Cooperation Committee in Beijing in February 1997. At the meeting it was agreed that all existing mechanisms, including the two Joint Committees and the SOM Political Consultation, would become an integral part of the ASEAN–China Dialogue. An ASEAN-China Cooperation Fund was set up with a contribution of US$700,000 from China. ASEAN Ambassadors in Beijing have formed their Committee in Beijing and the ASEAN-CCI and its Chinese counterpart have formed the ASEAN–China Joint Business Council. ASEAN–China consultations include the code of conduct for the South China Sea and accession to the Protocol by China to the SEANWFZ Treaty.

ASEAN – EUROPEAN UNION

The European Union (EU) is ASEAN's oldest Dialogue Partner. Relations with EU began informally in 1972 and were formalised in 1980 through the ASEAN–EC Cooperation Agreement. ASEAN–EU relations cover wide-ranging areas which include trade, business and investment, standards and conformance, intellectual property rights, science and technology, environment, human resource development, narcotics control, and institutional linkages. Enhanced ASEAN–EU cooperation include measures to promote trade and investment flows, industrial complementation, greater involvement of EU financial institutions in ASEAN projects and access to European technology and know-how. Regular meetings are held between ASEAN and EU Foreign Ministers and senior officials from the two sides to set the directions and pace for ASEAN–EU relations and to oversee the cooperation in the various fields. An offshoot of the ASEAN–EU relations is the Asia–Europe Meeting (ASEM) which held its inaugural summit in Bangkok in March 1996 and its first Foreign Ministers Meeting in Singapore in February 1997.

ASEAN – INDIA

In early 1993, ASEAN and India started their Sectoral Dialogue in the areas of trade, investment, tourism, and science and technology. An ASEAN–India Fund was set up to finance joint studies and other cooperation activities. By 1997, India's contribution to the Fund exceeded

US$660,000. At the Fifth ASEAN Summit in Bangkok in December 1995, a decision was reached to accord India full Dialogue Partner status. ASEAN and India have since set up their Joint Cooperation committee and convened the first meeting of the JCC in New Delhi in November 1996. The two sides agreed to expand their areas of cooperation to include, among others, human resources development and people-to-people contacts. ASEAN and India have also agreed to start their political dialogue at Senior Officials (SOM) level.

ASEAN – JAPAN

ASEAN–Japan relations began in 1973 and were institutionalised in 1977. Through the mechanism of the ASEAN–Japan Forum, the two sides discussed a wide-range of issues of common interest, including trade, commodities, investment, transfer of technology, cultural cooperation and development cooperation. Japan has provided funds for the establishment of the ASEAN Cultural Fund which in 1997 grew to more than US$40 million, the Japan–ASEAN Exchange Programme, and the Inter-ASEAN Technical Exchange Programme. ASEAN welcomed Prime Minister Ryutaro Hashimoto's initiative in calling for a "broader and deeper partnership" between ASEAN and Japan. At their 15th Forum Meeting in Tokyo in May 1997, ASEAN and Japan agreed that the Forum Meeting be strengthened to play the key role in their Dialogue and to convene a meeting of the Forum once every year before the ASEAN Post Ministerial Conferences. The two sides also agreed to create a multinational cultural mission comprising experts from ASEAN Member Countries and Japan to make recommendations for future cultural exchanges and cooperation. With regard to cooperation of the private sector, the ASEAN Promotion Centre in Tokyo has played an important role in promoting trade, investment, and tourism.

ASEAN – NEW ZEALAND

ASEAN–New Zealand's early activities began in 1975. ASEAN–New Zealand development cooperation activities are spearheaded by the ASEAN–New Zealand Economic Cooperation Programme (ANZECP) which has a long-term objective of achieving sustainable development benefits for ASEAN countries and facilitating linkages between New

Zealand and ASEAN. The ANZECP incorporates the now completed Inter-institutional Linkages Programme (IILP) which emphasised people-to-people contact; the ASEAN–New Zealand Cooperation in Science and Technology which centres around material science and biotechnology; the Trade and Investment Promotion Programme (TIPP) which emphasises fostering sustainable commercial and economic links, particularly missions to New Zealand by the ASEAN business community; and the ASEAN–New Zealand Energy Development Programme, which aims at advancing commercial viability in natural gas utilisation in transport within ASEAN through its Natural Gas Utilization in Transport (NGUT).

ASEAN – REPUBLIC OF KOREA

The Republic of Korea (ROK) became a Dialogue Partner of ASEAN in July 1991. Cooperation between ASEAN and ROK covers trade, investment, tourism, science and technology, human resource development, and development cooperation. Future areas of cooperation will include youth, media, and culture. The ASEAN–ROK Special Cooperation Fund was established under the Dialogue to finance technical and development cooperation activities. So far, 41 projects have been successfully implemented. An ASEAN–ROK Forum for the 21st Century has also been inaugurated in 1997 to recommend measures for the improvement of ASEAN–ROK relations for the next century.

ASEAN – RUSSIA

The Russian Federation became a full Dialogue Partner of ASEAN in July 1996. Prior to this, the Russian Federation began attending the AMM/PMC as a consultative partner in 1991. On 3 October 1996, the ASEAN Committee in Moscow was established by the Heads of the ASEAN Missions in Moscow. In January 1997, ASEAN and Russia adopted the Rules of Procedure for the ASEAN–Russia Joint Cooperation Committee (JCC) and the Terms of Reference for the ASEAN–Russia Joint Science and Technology Committee (JSTC). The inaugural meeting of the Joint Cooperation Committee was held in Moscow in June 1997.

ASEAN – UNITED STATES

Formalised in 1977, the ASEAN–US Dialogue promotes active participation of the private sector in advancing cooperation. Through the ASEAN Private Investment and Trade Opportunities (PITO) project, development cooperation, trade and investments cooperation are being strengthened. The US has also provided assistance on technology transfer, human resources development, environment, science and technology, and narcotics control. The Dialogue meeting is also a forum to discuss international, regional, political, and security issues.

ASEAN – UNDP

ASEAN–UNDP cooperation dates back to the 1970s, with the "Kansu Report" (1972), which formed the basis for establishing subsequent ASEAN–UNDP sub-regional programmes. Since then UNDP has become the largest single multilateral aid organisation and the only non-government Dialogue Partner of ASEAN. The ASEAN–UNDP Sub-regional Programme for the Fifth Cycle (1992-1996) or ASP-5, provided technical assistance in five sub-programme areas i.e., 1) Human Development with elements such as the socio-economic changes and their effect on people; distributive justice for the disadvantaged and vulnerable social groups; community-based drug and AIDS intervention activities, and ASEAN Universities; 2) Capacity building which provides assistance to enhance ASEAN institutional arrangements; management systems and procedures for ASEAN cooperation programme including upgrading of the skills and knowledge of the ASEAN Secretariat's professional and support staff; 3) Liberalisation of Trade and Investment which assists in the standardisation and simplification of intra-ASEAN trade transactions; enhances the efficiency and effectiveness in implementing the CEPT (Common Effective Preferential Tariff) Scheme; develops strategies and plans to strengthen selected industries and promote investments; 4) Trade and Environment to familiarise on the linkages between trade and environment issues, ASEAN policy towards external trade-related environmental policies and the preparation of six national research studies on environment; 5) Science and Technology which provided assistance for the operationalisation of the 1994 ASEAN Plan of Action on Science and Technology, ASEAN S & T Indicators and Information System, Public and Private Collaboration in Regional

Science and Technology and in Technology and Environment. The total allocation of ASP–5 is US$5.8 million. Steps are being carried out for the preparation of the ASEAN-UNDP sub-regional programme for the Sixth Cycle (ASP-6).

ASEAN – PAKISTAN

ASEAN–Pakistan Sectoral Dialogue was formally established in June 1997 through an exchange of letters between the Secretary-General of ASEAN and the Minister for Foreign Affairs of Pakistan. The Sectoral Dialogue will cover trade, investment, industry, science and technology, tourism, drugs and narcotics, and human resource development. An ASEAN–Pakistan Joint Sectoral Cooperation Committee (APJSCC) will be set up to explore and develop, cooperation in the sectors agreed upon. The Committee will be chaired by the Secretary-General of ASEAN and the Minister for Foreign Affairs of Pakistan. The inaugural meeting of the APJSCC was to be convened in Islamabad in November 1997.

MUTUAL BENEFITS FROM DIALOGUE RELATIONS

Through Dialogue relations, ASEAN has linked up with the industrial world for access to their markets, to buy time for regional development, for protection from sudden shifts in global structure, for access to new business opportunities, to gain experiences in multilateral negotiations, for trade and economic concessions through ASEAN collective lobbying, to strengthen political relations with Dialogue Partners, and to boost ASEAN standing. On the other hand, Dialogue Partners have access to an enlarged ASEAN market.[2]

ASEAN has developed extensive relations with its Dialogue Partners and international organisations which have benefited both sides of the relationship. For its part, ASEAN has "developed a united perception of the many regional and international economic issues, such as protectionism that affect it as a group".[3] ASEAN member states have enhanced their efforts in managing the regional financial and economic crisis which started in 1997. ASEAN has sustained the momentum of cooperative activities through its external relations.[4]

ASEAN +3 AND ASEAN + 1 SUMMIT[5]

A new development in ASEAN's external relations is the ASEAN + 3 Process and ASEAN + 1 Summitry between the ASEAN Heads of State and Government and their counterparts from China, Japan, and the Republic of Korea (ROK). This new process was inaugurated in Kuala Lumpur in December 1997.

After its inauguration, ASEAN leaders met again with the leaders of China, Japan, and the ROK in Hanoi at the Sixth ASEAN Summit in December 1998. There the participants found the process useful and they agreed to convene the summits annually.

On China's proposal, a meeting of Vice Finance Ministers and Deputy Governors of Central Banks was held within the framework of the ASEAN + 3 in Hanoi on 18 March 1999. The meeting looked at the international financial architecture, particularly on the need to involve emerging economies in the process of restructuring. They agreed to maintain close cooperation on the issues.

Japan proposed that ASEAN + 3 Senior Officials meet to discuss the follow-up and implementation of initiatives of the ASEAN + 3 Summit meeting and to prepare an indicative agenda of the next summit meeting.

The ROK proposed at the ASEAN + 3 Summit in Hanoi that a Vision Group of eminent persons from ASEAN and Northeast Asian countries on East Asian Cooperation be formed to explore ways to expand cooperation in all sectors and in all levels among the countries of East Asia. The Vision Group will formulate a common vision reflecting the rapidly changing regional and global environment and offering the direction for future cooperation among the countries of East Asia.

At the same Hanoi Summit, Singapore proposed the creation of an East Asia – Latin American Forum. It will aim to enhance trade and investment ties between the two regions. Depending on the level of interest, Singapore suggested a ministerial meeting in the year 2000 in one of the countries in South America and a Summit in 2001 in one of the ASEAN countries. [6]

THE ASEAN + 1 MEETINGS [7]

From the press statement by the Chairman of the ASEAN-single country summits, the following highlights show the increasing relations of ASEAN in the region.

COOPERATION BETWEEN ASEAN AND JAPAN

Prime Minster Junichiro Koizumi of Japan affirmed full support for the implementation of the Initiative for ASEAN Integration (IAI) by financing IAI projects under both bilateral and multilateral mechanisms. Japan is also intensifying support for the ASEAN Solidarity Fund and the Japan–ASEAN General Exchange Fund. During the ASEAN–Japan Exchange Year in 2003, cooperation will be intensified and will include other areas such as politics, economics and industry, security, education, science and technology, and culture, all to further build partnership for Japan's call of "acting together and advancing together". Japan has already established an economic partnership agreement with Singapore and is discussing similar arrangements with the Philippines, Thailand, and Vietnam, to spur renewed growth across ASEAN. Future cooperation will be further discussed at the ASEAN-Japan Commemorative Summit on 11-12 December 2003, which celebrates the 30th anniversary of ASEAN–Japan Dialogue Relations.

COOPERATION BETWEEN ASEAN
AND THE REPUBLIC OF KOREA

Prime Minister Kim Suk-Soo of the Republic of Korea expressed full support for ASEAN's anti-terrorism efforts. The Republic of Korea has expanded its cooperation with ASEAN on agriculture, trade and investment, human resource development, tourism, and advanced informational technology training programmes. The Republic of Korea has made significant contributions to the ASEAN–Republic of Korea Special Cooperation Fund which focuses on the newer ASEAN members. The Republic of Korea wants to improve transport networks in ASEAN and the sustainable development of the areas along the Mekong River. The Final Report of the East Asia Study Group will be implemented for closer economic partnership and lead to the formation of an East Asia Free Trade Area over the long-term and will consider the Work Plan under the IAI.

ASEAN and the ROK expressed concern about the nuclear weapons of the DPRK and wished to have a non-nuclear Korean peninsula.

ASEAN-INDIA COOPERATION

On the first ASEAN-India Summit held in the Eighth ASEAN Summit, Prime Minister Shri Atal Bihari Vajpayee of India supported ASEAN's stand on nuclear non-proliferation and encouraged the development of intra-ASEAN and Asian trade which could lead to a free trade area within ten years. India is willing to extend special and differential treatment to the newer members and support the entry to the WTO of Cambodia, Lao People's Democratic Republic and Vietnam.

ASEAN leaders and the Prime Minister of India agreed to cooperate on the eradication of terrorism, transnational crime, strategic, political, economic partnership, and people exchange. The leaders affirmed the principles of the UN Charter, the Treaty of Amity and Cooperation in Southeast Asia (TAC), the Five Principles of Coexistence and of international law to govern the relations. India expressed willingness to accede to the TAC and to consider participation in the ASEAN–Mekong Basin Development Cooperation and the Greater Mekong Sub-region.

ASEAN AND THE NEW PARTNERSHIP FOR AFRICA'S DEVELOPMENT

President Thabo Mbeki of South Africa explained the origins and aspirations of the New Partnership for Africa's Development (NEPAD), a programme that expresses Africa's renaissance towards peace, stability, and rapid socio-economic growth. NEPAD will be implemented by the African Union. President Mbeki recalled Asia-Africa cooperation in the Bandung Conference in 1955 and the Non-Aligned Movement. He also supported ASEAN's anti-terrorism efforts, South-South cooperation and the promotion of nuclear weapon-free regimes. The African Union wants to have cooperation with ASEAN which in turn agreed to promote stronger ties with Africa.

ASEAN AND THE UNITED NATIONS

The Fifth ASEAN Summit held in Bangkok in 1995 agreed that ASEAN shall explore ways and means to enhance cooperation with the United Nations to promote peace and stability in the region. ASEAN shall also work towards making the UN a more equitable, effective, and relevant body for promoting peace and prosperity in the region and globally in the post-Cold War era. ASEAN shall focus its attention on making the membership of the Security Council more reflective of the prevailing balance among nations; enhancing the capacity and effectiveness of the world body to carry out its peace-making, peace-building, peace-keeping, and preventive diplomacy function and to strengthening the work of the UN in the social and economic fields.[8] On 11-12 September 1998, the ASEAN Secretariat and UNESCO held a regional symposium which adopted a Statement on Peace in Southeast Asia on the Eve of the Third Millennium. The statement called on all countries to mobilise all concerned institutions and key social actors to foster a culture of peace. The year 2000 was proclaimed International Year for the Culture of Peace by the United Nations General Assembly.

ASEAN DEVELOPMENT COOPERATION FORUM

The ASEAN Development Cooperation Forum was organised by the ASEAN Secretariat on 6-7 May 1999. In this forum the Secretariat briefs the Dialogue Partners and other interested organisations on the immediate and mid-term priorities of ASEAN as outlined by the Hanoi Plan of Action (HPA). The Secretariat sought the Forum participants' assistance in realising the HPA through concrete cooperation activities to implement development cooperation programmes in the priority areas of economic recovery and greater economic integration in light of the financial crisis, environment, and human development conditions.[9]

ASEAN-EUROPE MEETING (ASEM)

The Asia-Europe Meeting (ASEM) is an offshoot of the ASEAN-European Union (EU) relations. The EU is ASEAN's oldest Dialogue Partner. Relations with the EU began informally in 1972 and were formalised in 1980 through the ASEAN-EC cooperation agreement. ASEM held its inaugural Summit in March 1996 and its first Foreign Ministers meeting in Singapore in February 1997.[10] Subsequently, ASEM had to cancel some meetings because of the objection of European countries to the participation of Myanmar. European countries have a policy not to deal with Myanmar for as long as its human rights record remains as it is. ASEAN supports Myanmar's participation because it is a member of ASEAN. A new arrangement has to be found for this problem. In January 2001, officials from the European Union were able to visit Aung San Suu Kyi in Rangoon. She expressed to them a desire to have a dialogue with the officers of the State Peace and Development Council.

ASEAN – NON-DIALOGUE COUNTRIES AND INTERNATIONAL ORGANISATIONS

The Fourth ASEAN Summit of 1992 agreed that as a part of an increasingly interdependent world, ASEAN should intensify cooperative relationship with interested non-dialogue countries and international organisations. At the Fifth Summit, this was emphasised when the ASEAN Heads of Government called ASEAN to "remain outward-looking and deepen its external relations with its partners in a globally interdependent world".

ASEAN has acted on these policies by establishing ties with other sub-regional groupings such as the South Pacific Forum, Economic Cooperation Organization, Gulf Cooperation Council, South Asian Association for Regional Cooperation, South African Development Cooperation, Mercado Comun del Sur (MERCOSUR) and other organisations in Central and South America through the development of concrete and action-oriented activities.[11]

1. Economic Cooperation Organization (ECO)

The Secretary-General of ASEAN met with the Secretary-General of the Economic Cooperation Organization (ECO) in Kathmandu, Nepal, on 27 October 1998. This was a follow-up to the Fouth ASEAN-ECO Foreign Ministers Meeting in New York on 1 October 1998. The bilateral meeting in Nepal was a result of the Fourth Consultative Meeting among the Executive Heads of sub-regional organisations and ESCAP.

The two Secretaries-General agreed to organise a workshop on trade and investment opportunities and electronic commerce in the ECO and ASEAN regions at the ECO headquarters in Teheran in late 1999.

The two sides also agreed to encourage and support their respective Chambers of Commerce to establish direct contact as soon as possible and to provide them with relevant information.[12]

2. South Asian Association for Regional Cooperation (SAARC)

The Foreign Minister of Singapore and Chairman of the ASEAN Standing Committee and the Foreign Minister of Sri Lanka and Chairman of the SAARC Council of Ministers met in New York on 25 September 1998. They were joined by other SAARC Foreign Ministers, ASEAN and SAARC officials and the Secretaries-General of ASEAN and SAARC. It was agreed that ASEAN–SAARC Foreign Ministers would meet annually in New York to coordinate their positions on WTO matters through their representatives in Geneva. ASEAN agreed to share with SAARC its experience on economic cooperation, particularly in setting up the ASEAN Free Trade Area (AFTA). [13]

3. Gulf Cooperation Council

At the initiative of the ASEAN Ambassadors and Chiefs of Missions in Riyadh, the ASEAN Standing Committee agreed in February 1999 to establish an ASEAN Riyadh Committee.[14]

4. Rio Group

The Foreign Ministers of ASEAN and the Rio group met in New York on 21 September 1998 to exchange views on issues before the United Nations General Assembly.[15]

5. South Pacific Forum

The Secretaries-General of ASEAN and the South Pacific Forum met in Kuala Lumpur in November 1998. Forum members were keen to learn from the ASEAN experience in taking collective actions to complement national efforts of its members to cope with the impact of the financial crisis and bring about recovery.[16]

6. Asian Development Bank (ADB)

ASEAN and the ADB cooperated actively in a regional technical assistance programme worth about US$ 1 million to enhance ASEAN's capability to combat forest fires and cope with transboundary haze. A

new programme will assist the ASEAN Surveillance Process which will
be an early warning system to help safeguard against the recurrence of
the crisis.[17]

7. Hans Seidel Foundation

ASEAN and the Hans Seidel Foundation have agreed to develop an
ASEAN Environmental Education Action Plan. The foundation has also
assisted the ASEAN Secretariat's training programmes for new members
of ASEAN in the implementation of the ASEAN Free Trade Area (AFTA)
and the liberalisation of trade and services.[18]

OTHER REGIONAL COOPERATION GROUPS IN THE ASIA-PACIFIC REGION

Some scholars perceive a rapidly emerging division of labour in the Asia-
Pacific region to which ASEAN countries' economic growth and political
legitimacy would be increasingly tied. This is because of the decline of
US hegemonic power and the rise of multi-polarity and the increasing
trend towards economic groupings. ASEAN has to evaluate the costs
and benefits of ASEAN's participation in the regional economic groupings
and their effects on ASEAN's unity, its collective bargaining power, and
leverage with economic groupings.[19]

The Asia-Pacific Economic Cooperation (APEC) is an
intergovernmental forum which was launched in Australia in 1989.
From the beginning, ASEAN was wary about APEC's domination of
the economic issues in the Asia-Pacific region because of the disparities
in the national capabilities of ASEAN member states to derive benefits
from joint cooperation and regional development which therefore
could lead to asymmetrical relations between ASEAN and the other
APEC economies. But rising economic interdependence between
ASEAN and Asia-Pacific economies and the outward orientation
strategy influenced ASEAN to participate in a wider forum on
economic cooperation. ASEAN therefore has insisted that APEC
should be an informal arrangement and should not be institutionalised.
ASEAN's identity and cohesion should be preserved; APEC's process
should be based on the principles of equality, equity, and mutual
benefit; APEC should not be an inward-looking trading bloc but must
strengthen multilateral economic systems; APEC should be a forum

for consultation and constructive discussions of economic issues through dialogue rather than through unilateral or bilateral measures; APEC must develop the individual and collective capability of the participants and articulate them in multilateral forums; and must have a gradual and pragmatic approach which may be recommended towards institutionalisation.[20]

APEC could be an effective forum for promoting ASEAN interests such as by counter-balancing the inward-looking tendency of the European Community and could be the channel for Japan and NIE's capital flows to develop the Asia-Pacific region instead of being diverted to Eastern Europe.

Fortunately, Malaysia has led ASEAN countries to resist some undesirable tendencies of the US and other large economies in APEC.

In the year 2000, some economic analyses projected the idea that APEC may be losing its importance in the light of the world-wide financial and economic crisis, of the inability of the larger economies to help the more battered developing economies, and the tendency towards protectionism of the larger economies.

APEC has now 24 members, namely, the US, Canada, Australia, New Zealand, Japan, Republic of Korea, People's Republic of China, Taiwan, HongKong, Mexico, Peru, Chile, Papua New-Guinea, Russia, and the ASEAN Ten.

EAST ASIAN ECONOMIC CAUCUS (EAEC)[21]

Another group is the East Asian Economic Caucus (EAEC), originally East Asian Economic Group (EAEG) which was suggested by Malaysian Prime Minister Dr. Mahathir Mohamad when GATT failed in the meeting at Brussels. He suggested that Malaysia should lead in setting up an East Asian Economic Group (EAEG) to counter the single market concept of the European Community and the North American Free Trade Area (NAFTA with Canada, US, and Mexico) by having members only from East Asia. Mahathir wanted Japan to lead the group to anchor Japan to East Asia which is Japan's natural area rather than go to Europe or the US. Mahathir also wanted China to face the rise of trading blocs such as EC, a reunited Germany, East European countries joining the EC, NAFTA, and Latin American blocs.

The EAEG should preserve the free trading system in Asia because the trading blocs would kill free trade. EAEG would include ASEAN,

192

Hong Kong, China, Republic of Korea, and Japan to speak in one voice. EAEG would become a forum to interact with EC and the US. EAEC could fend off ASEAN's premature membership in the Organization for Economic Cooperative and Development (OECD). EAEC would not be a trading bloc but just a small alliance to strengthen ASEAN's voice in APEC and G-7 (now 33 members). However, the idea drew various reactions especially from Japan which, as the supposed leading member, has argued that EAEC is against the APEC philosophy and that it had left out the US, Canada, and Australia. The US objected to EAEC because it could not help bring about trade liberalisation and that EAEC could not succeed without the US. But ASEAN states like Singapore said that the EAEC is another platform for ASEAN to interact with other countries like the US and EC and did not imply to discard the strong traditional trade ties.

By this time, in spite of opposition to it, EAEC is now within the framework of APEC.

PACIFIC ECONOMIC COOPERATION CONFERENCE (PECC)

The Pacific Economic Cooperation Conference (PECC) was born out of Japan's continued attempts to set up a Pacific Community which was assiduously opposed by Southeast Asian states because of their traumatic experiences during the Japanese Occupation in the Pacific area. Malaysian officials commented that a community could not simply be so just because of the presence of trade and investment among rich and the poor states, but rather requires more in terms of bonding, valuing, and doing more things together than trading alone. Moreover, the authors for a Pacific Community came from the same institution that conceived and set up the infamous wartime Greater Southeast Asia Co-Prosperity Sphere where the resources of the Southeast Asian states were taken by Japan to sustain its war machine and economy.

Aware that such bitter thoughts remained among Southeast Asians, Japan asked Australian leaders to initiate the forming of the PECC. At the start, Southeast Asian leaders were distrustful of the new presentation especially because it came soon after determined efforts by Japan to set up the Pacific Community and because at the time, Australia's economic orientation was towards Europe, not Asia.

In time, the distrust was overcome and replaced by friendship because of Japan's sincere and positive efforts over the years in providing ASEAN with assistance and advice as well as cooperation in ASEAN initiatives.

The PECC was set up in September 1980 in Canberra. By 1990, the members were the six ASEAN states, Australia, New Zealand, Canada, the United States, China, Japan, Republic of Korea, and Taiwan. In 1991, four members were admitted, namely Hong Kong, Chile, Peru, and Mexico. In 1992, Russia became a member.[22]

PECC is composed of government officials, businessmen, and academics, all in their private capacities. PECC has task forces and working groups, covering such activities as agriculture and fisheries, minerals and energy, trade, transportation, telecommunication, tourism, science and technology, human resource development, and economic forecasting.

PECC has a close relationship with APEC which has utilised the expertise and resource of the former, including studies for mutual use.

It is likely that if a tighter East Asian economic grouping develops closer relations with ASEAN economies there would be a more substantial network of investments and trade, ASEAN states will become production bases for exports to American and European markets. But in this situation, trade conflicts may occur and these may be focused on ASEAN states. Another undesirable occurrence is that ASEAN states will continue to be "hewers of wood and carriers of water" for the industrialised Northeast economies.

Thus ASEAN's direction is obviously to develop its own strength from its own policies and collective interests even as it maintains its forum relations with developed states. The objective is to see that a balance exists between ASEAN and other partners in their relationships.

ENDNOTES

1   This portion is a reprint of ASEAN Cooperation and Dialogue Relations, http://www.aseansec.org/history/asn_ext3.htm, 9/28/99 pp. 1-4 to preserve accuracy of the data.

2   B. A. Hamzah, "Dialogue Partners" in K. S. Sandhu and Sharon Siddique (eds.), *The ASEAN Reader* (Singapore: ISEAS, 1992), p. 69.

3   John Wong, "The ASEAN Model of Regional Cooperation" in the *ASEAN Reader, ibid.*, p. 228.

4   Association of Southeast Asian Nations Annual Report 1998-1999, Jakarta: ASEAN Secretariat, p. 91.

5   *Ibid.*, pp. 91-92.

6   *Ibid.*, pp. 91-92.

7   Press statement by the Chairman of the ASEAN-Japan Summit, the ASEAN-Republic of Korea Summit, the First ASEAN-India Summit and the South African President's Briefing, 5 November 2002, Phnom Penh.

8   http://www.aseansec.org/history/an_pol2.htm, pp. 1-2.

9   Association of Southeast Asian Nations Annual Report 1998-1999, *op. cit.*, pp. 92-93.

10 http://www.aseansec.org/history/asn_ext3.htm, p. 1.

11 *Ibid.*, p. 1.

12 Annual Report 1998-1999, *op. cit.*, p. 110.

13 *Ibid.*, p. 110.

14 *Ibid.*, pp. 110-111.

15 *Ibid.*, p. 111.

16 *Ibid.*, p. 111.

17 *Ibid.*, p. 111.

18 *Ibid.*, p. 111.

19 Tan Kong Yam, Toh Mun Heng, and Linda Low, "ASEAN and Pacific Economic Cooperation" in Sandhu and Siddique, (eds.), *The ASEAN Reader*, *op. cit.*, p. 313.

20 *Ibid.*, p. 314.

21 *Ibid.*, pp. 315-318.

22 *Ibid.*, pp. 318-319.

CHAPTER **8**

Security in ASEAN

The ASEAN Declaration of 1967 stated that the countries of Southeast Asia share a primary responsibility for strengthening the economic and social stability of the region and for ensuring their peaceful and progressive national development. Toward this end, the countries of Southeast Asia are determined to ensure their stability and security from external interference in any form or manifestation in order to preserve their national identities in accordance with the ideals and aspirations of their peoples.

Since 1967, one of the most important preoccupations of the states in the region has been security. From the developments in the region and the responses of ASEAN leaders to those problems all through the years, it may be seen that security is not perceived in the military sense but in the fulfillment of the ASEAN objectives of peace, progress and social stability, economic growth, and cultural development, all of which are to be obtained through cooperation.

In 1976, at the first ASEAN Heads of Government Meeting (First ASEAN Summit) the Heads of Government offered a definition of security. Indonesian President Suharto said that security is "inward-looking", the establishment of an orderly, peaceful, and stable condition within each individual territory. Prime Minister Hussein Onn of Malaysia said, "If we can progress in economic cooperation we would have made substantial contributions towards the maintenance of our respective national security and regional security...In the final analysis our security depends on our ability to provide the goods of life for our people and to build societies which are just and fair to all".

Scholars have likewise contributed to the strength of this idea of security which is not in terms of military. An Indonesian scholar, Daued Jusuf wrote, "national security lies not in military alliance or under the military umbrella of any great power but in self-reliance deriving from domestic factors such as economic and social development, political stability, and the sense of nationalism".[1]

A more specific explanation from ASEAN leaders that ASEAN is not going to be a military organisation in spite of the military threats to member states was made in 1984 by Indonesian Foreign Minister Mochtar Kusuma Atmadja when he declared that military alliance was "not in the cards" and that ASEAN was not changing its original philosophy of promoting economic, cultural, and social cooperation for the mutual benefit of its members.[2]

EARLY THOUGHTS ON SECURITY IN ASEAN

Literature on the concept of security in ASEAN reflects many misperceptions about it. This is in spite of "one of the great truisms of the character of ASEAN that its avowed desire is to remain as a prime example of regional cooperation in Southeast Asia without being in the least suspected of serving the covert security needs of either the individual member countries or its own collectively".[3] Since ASEAN was established at the time when the region was in the midst of great power rivalries involving military actions and military alliances, such as the SEATO of 1954, the Anglo-Malayan Agreement (AMDA of 1957), the Five-Power Defence Agreements (FPDA of 1971), and the Soviet-Vietnamese Treaty of Friendship and Cooperation of 1978, and of domestic insurgencies, analysts tended to impute military content to ASEAN security.

It would be interesting to see the views of analysts on security. J.L.S. Girling, writing on "Regional Security in Southeast Asia", referred to the security movements or associations in the region and the emergence of ASEAN as a force for protection of the region but which has so far avoided an explicit defence commitment. He noted that in spite of some attempts by South Vietnam President Thieu to induce states like Vietnam, Cambodia, Laos, and Thailand to get into a joint anti-communist fight to shorten the Vietnam War, Laotian Prime Minister Prince Souvanna Phouma and the Thai Foreign Minister rejected any plan for military action. Laos opted for negotiated settlements with the Pathet Lao for it not to get further involved in the Vietnam conflict, while Thai leaders, considering domestic insurgencies and the reaction of the United States, found a formal pact irrelevant because the US was providing the major military support for South Vietnam, Laos, and Thailand itself. Anyway SEATO failed to give the expected military support to Laos which was a Protocol State. SEATO showed great fissures internally because of the different interests of the member states. France withdrew as its act of disapproval to American intervention in Vietnam; Pakistan withdrew because it could not use SEATO in its conflict with India.[4] Finally on 30 June 1977, Thailand and the Philippines agreed to put an end to their membership in SEATO because the new appropriate strategy for peace in Southeast Asia was political accommodation. This move also announced that the ASEAN member states were determined to express and follow their own goals and actions without external interference.

Sheldon Simon asks the question "if superpower détente translates into a reduction of forward deployed forces in Southeast Asia during the 1990s, are the ASEAN states considering an alternative security posture?" His views of security lie primarily on defence arrangements such as what the alternatives should be. He envisions other forms of military cooperation within ASEAN. Among these alternatives are an ASEAN-wide maritime defence including trilateral exercises for Malaysia, Indonesia, and Singapore.[5] Another innovative security arrangement is a Thai-Chinese arms stockpile. While Indonesia could be the region's primary maritime power, Thailand believes more in a relationship with China to balance off Vietnam. Malaysia, Singapore, and Indonesia can be buffers against China.

Jusuf Wanandi of the Centre for Strategic and International Studies at Jakarta, writing in 1990, says that ASEAN has to begin to prepare for the possibility that US withdrawal from the Western Pacific, however remote, will create a vacuum which might be filled up by another great power. He proposed that ASEAN needs to enhance cooperation in the defence field and might consider a more formal defence arrangement with the countries of Southwest Pacific (Australia, New Zealand, and Papua New Guinea), and seek cooperation with Japan in technology and equipment transfer to assist ASEAN in safeguarding the Sea Lanes of Communication (SLOC) in Southeast Asia.

Although cooperation among the armed forces of the ASEAN countries in the defence field has been undertaken for some time now, bilaterally or trilaterally, these are undertaken outside the framework of ASEAN, in accordance with the ASEAN Concord of 1976. The possibility of transforming this "web of bilateral defence relations" into a multilateral framework for cooperation needs to consider many things like common perceptions of threats which have been elusive because the perceptions of threats proceeded from different interests, and a common interpretation of ZOPFAN based on national and regional resilience, which is based on economic and national development and which should therefore be given highest priority in ASEAN countries.[6]

Michael Leifer argues that ASEAN is a security organisation in spite of giving priority to economic, social, and cultural progress because it is concerned with the changes in the balance of power in the region and had expressed a common perception of threat which was subversion but he also observed that ASEAN does not have the structure of an alliance. However, ASEAN has already adopted the Kuala Lumpur Declaration of 1971 for a ZOPFAN which provides for security without extra-regional involvements and for meeting the ideological challenge through political solidarity, harmonisation of policy, and economic cooperation. The ASEAN governments seek to promote mutual security by consultation and cooperation and conflict avoidance. There are limitations on ASEAN being a security organisation such as the absence of a common threat in an external form.

The above-presented views of security in terms of defence or military written from the 1970s to as late as 1990 were prevalent when the Soviet Union was still in power, when the Indochinese states were still pawns of either the Soviet Union or China in their competition for power, and when great power involvement was feared in the ASEAN region. Many of those writers however acknowledged the emphasis given by ASEAN to economic, social, cultural, and political development as the most effective form of security although ASEAN "avoids security decisions", meaning defence or military decisions to meet the military threats from the great powers through their pawn states in Southeast Asia. Up to 1990, the policies of China, Vietnam, Laos, and Cambodia were not yet known in so far as military plans were concerned although the ASEAN states had already extended their hand of friendship to them by 1976 and had used confidence-building measures (CBMs) to encourage positive relations.

One of the earliest concepts of ASEAN for security was the Zone of Peace, Freedom, and Neutrality (ZOPFAN) of 1971.

Bilveer Singh analysed ZOPFAN for security by starting the discussion with the earliest devices for security since the Treaty of Westphalia (1648). Those measures were building national power, joining alliances, having a policy of neutrality, and maintaining armed neutrality, all of which should protect the sovereignty of states. In

Southeast Asia the attempts to produce security were the Southeast Asia Treaty Organization (SEATO 1954), neutralisation of Laos by the Geneva Powers in 1954 and 1962 and non-alignment of Cambodia (1954). ASEAN produced the ZOPFAN in 1971 for regional security and the means for it were neutrality and non-military.[8]

Singh saw ASEAN as a regional security order brought about by the mutuality of interests of the members to pursue common goals "that will prevent certain outcomes with regard to security issues". This security order in SEA has been established through a mixture of policies, such as conflict avoidance, self-restraint, and in addition, mutual restraint, accommodation, regular consultation, the firm rejection of the idea to make ASEAN a military pact which can provoke counter-alliances and misunderstanding, ASEAN Spirit, ASEAN Way, low-key behaviour, confidence-building measures, consensus-building, and continuous dialogue.[9]

The Declaration for ZOPFAN firmly states the merits of regional cooperation, relaxation of international tensions, achieving lasting peace in Southeast Asia, nuclear-free zones, and peaceful and progressive national development. ASEAN member states are determined to secure the recognition of and respect for Southeast Asia as a Zone of Peace, Freedom, and Neutrality, free from any form of interference by outside powers, and to broaden the areas of cooperation for strength, solidarity, and closer relationship. ZOPFAN later included the concept of national and regional resilience as proposed by Indonesia. National Resilience also known as the Suharto Doctrine embodies the national experience of Indonesia for national security through self-help and self-reliance to repel Great Power inter-penetration in the region. National resilience emphasises the non-military aspects of security.[10] Indonesia's comprehensive security consists of political, economic, sociocultural, and military components which are all interrelated. Indonesia rejects the idea that security is military power. In Malaysia, Prime Minister Tun Abdul Razak in 1975 named security as the preservation of the people's way of life. In 1976 Prime Minister Hussein Onn said that ZOPFAN was to preserve the national identity, integrity and stability of each state to enable it to pursue national development. In 1983 Indonesia and Malaysia proposed the Southeast Asia Nuclear Weapon-Free Zone (SEANWFZ) which then became part of ZOPFAN. In 1995 the Treaty on the SEANWFZ was signed by the ten Heads of Government of ASEAN.

CHANGES IN WORLD CONDITIONS

Changes in world conditions were reflected in Southeast Asia. For example, President Mikhail Gorbachev of the Soviet Union in 1986 at Krasnoyarsk announced his *glasnost* and *perestroika* policies, a New Asia policy, and rapprochement with the People's Republic of China. Vietnam followed suit with its *doi moi* or reformation. Vietnam would no longer be the hegemon over Laos and Cambodia which would now be separated from Vietnam because Soviet support would not be forthcoming anymore. Vietnam had to withdraw its troops from Laos and Cambodia.

When the Soviet Union collapsed in 1991, Vietnam became isolated from socialist camp partners in East Europe but it still had its traditional threat from the north, China, at its door. Vietnam adopted a pragmatic foreign policy of friendship with ASEAN states and later with ASEAN itself. Vietnam also restored relations with China. Meanwhile Vietnam adopted a socialist market economy and Laos used the new Economic Mechanism with its reliance on the market system and foreign investments.

As for Cambodia, ASEAN took an active policy to encourage self-determination for the Cambodians, from "cocktail party talks", to the Kuantan Initiative, to the formation of the Coalition Government for Democratic Kampuchea (CGDK), Jakarta Informal Meetings I and II, to the Paris Peace Talks of 1991 and the entry of the UN Transitional Authority in Cambodia (UNTAC), and elections for the Royal Government of Cambodia in 1993.

The remaining country in Southeast Asia that did not have any ASEAN engagement was Myanmar where the record of the State Law and Order Restoration Council was not acceptable to many sectors. ASEAN from the beginning aimed to bring in all Southeast Asian states to its membership. ASEAN used confidence-building measures (CBM) and constructive engagement with Myanmar. Since 1997, the State Peace and Development Council (SPDC) which was formerly the SLORC has tried to achieve a new direction in its regional relations, such as strengthening Yangon-New Delhi relations to offset the strong Chinese influence in Myanmar, and the care the SPDC showed in making statements on the September 2002 crash in New York as well as on the Afghanistan problem in order to prevent religious groups clashes in Myanmar. By 1999 Vietnam, Laos, Myanmar, and Cambodia completed the ASEAN Ten by first acceding to the TAC which is the Code of Conduct in Southeast Asia, committing themselves to ASEAN's principles of good neighbourliness, cooperation, self-denial, mutual restraint, non-interference in the domestic affairs of the other states, and the rule of law. By 2000, the four states were being socialised into the ASEAN Way and the ASEAN Spirit.

On record, by year 2000, ASEAN resolved all the issues and political threats to security in the region through peaceful means, using Asian solutions to Asian problems and all engagements for peace, without having had to use military means.

However, by 2003, new threats to the region had developed, namely, terrorism, transnational crimes, trafficking in drugs and money and of humans and environmental degradation. The latest transnational problem in 2003 was the devastating spread of the Severe Acute Respiratory Syndrome (SARS) virus. It has caused great fear, loss of investments, decreased travels, reduced exports and imports, and decreased confidence among government, churches, and people because the virus continued to spread without any countermeasures in sight. In the ASEAN Summit Meeting in April 2003 on SARS, ASEAN and China agreed on some measures to contain the spread of SARS such as proper pre-departure health screening for travellers at the point of origin, standardised measures for proper health screening, public information and education to promote awareness, cooperation among front-line enforcement agencies, and early warning system on emerging infectious diseases. Singapore recommended the ASEAN Containment Information Network for the states to share essential information and best practices taken from their experiences in dealing with SARS.

On these, ASEAN has expanded the scope of its political, economic, and functional cooperation to strengthen the capability of each member state as well as the social safety nets, and cooperating with its Dialogue Partners up to the level of summit meetings for wise decisions.

EXPANDING ASEAN VIEWS OF SECURITY

ASEAN has moved onwards to achieve security which has now been accepted to mean as the enjoyment of the ASEAN values of peace, economic, social and cultural development, cooperation, political stability, and regional stability and progress.

The Treaty of Amity and Cooperation in Southeast Asia (TAC 1976) was amended on 25 July 1998 in Manila to enable non-Southeast Asian countries to accede to the TAC. By 1999 seven countries in ASEAN had ratified the Second Protocol. ASEAN has also invited all the ASEAN Dialogue Partners to accede to the TAC.

To encourage the Pacific Settlement of Dispute, which is in the TAC, the Hanoi Plan of Action (HPA 1998) directed the drafting of rules of procedures for the High Council which was provided for in the TAC (1976).

The ASEAN Senior Officials Working Group on ZOPFAN and SEANWFZ are consulting with the Nuclear Weapon States to get their support for the Treaty on the SEANWFZ by signing its Protocol. The major subjects of consultation remain to be the zone of application of the Treaty and the provision concerning negative security assurances. The other point is the basic undertakings of the Treaty States and their implications for port visit of foreign ships and aircraft, as a concern of Nuclear Weapon States.

In 1994, ASEAN took a pre-emptive move in the Asia-Pacific Region as its initiative on security matters. By establishing the ASEAN Regional Forum (ARF), ASEAN has assumed the primary role for security in the region. Its basic philosophy was expressed by Thai Prime Minister Anand Panyarachun at the 1992 Singapore Summit which was that ASEAN believed it was time to handle the question of security themselves. "We have to rely on inner strength and reduce dependency on outside powers", he said.

The political environment showed threats to ASEAN's security. The nuclear weapons production of North Korea and the rise of APEC which was perceived to evolve into a security association could set back ASEAN's role and control of Southeast Asian matters on security. ASEAN's pre-emptive move was its comprehensive engagement to include the other states of the region in such a forum. The ASEAN Regional Forum (ARF) as established does not institutionalise what is desired but must accommodate the agenda that is in every member's mind.[11]

Author M. Antolik explains that constructive engagement contributes to regional security by bringing about conflicted nations in friendly consultations. Together with preventive diplomacy, constructive engagement implies that states with differences and conflicts of interests are also committed to consultations and will follow agreed-upon rules and norms. A Singaporean ambassador has said that the Asian preference is for the step-by-step, non-institutional approach. The norms are the ASEAN Way of mutual-restraint and low-key behaviour. The rules are non-use of force, non-interference in each other's domestic affairs, and mutual respect.[12]

The earliest views of security in ARF are contained in the Chairman's Statement in the First Meeting on the ARF at Bangkok on 25 July 1994. ASEAN Heads of Government "proclaimed their interest to intensify ASEAN's external dialogues on political and security matters as a means of building cooperative ties with states in the Asia-Pacific Region". ARF is a high-level consultative forum to foster the habit of constructive dialogue. It will study the comprehensive concept of security including its economic and social aspects as well as internationally recognised norms and principles for international and regional political and security cooperation for possible contributions to ARF's security cooperation.

ARF endorses the principles of the TAC as a unique diplomatic instrument for regional confidence-building, preventive diplomacy, and political cooperation. ARF needs a predictable and constructive pattern of relationship and stronger political and security cooperation to ensure a lasting peace stability, and prosperity for the region and its peoples. The means include confidence and security-building measures, nuclear non-proliferation, peacekeeping cooperation, exchanges of non-classified military information, preventive diplomacy and new approaches to conflict: ARF has added economic, social, and human components to security issues such as effects of globalisation and transnational crimes.

During the year 1998-1999, several meetings were held on confidence building measures (Honolulu and Bangkok), disaster relief (Moscow), comprehensive security and cooperation in the Asia Pacific (Vladivostok), and on preventive diplomacy (Bangkok).

At the intra-ASEAN level the Special Meeting of ASEAN Senior Officials (Special SOM) consisting of foreign ministry and defence officials of ASEAN member countries, areas of political and security cooperation, to include confidence-building measures, security cooperation programmes, promotion of ASEAN security concepts and coordination of ASEAN's position on security-related international instruments are discussed.

ASEAN Senior Officials also periodically consult non-governmental ASEAN Institutes of Strategic and International Studies (ASEAN-ISIS) and other non-governmental institutions or persons acting in their personal capacity to contribute to ARF's purposes through the "Track Two" process.

To advance the ARF process and to maintain ASEAN's position as ARF's driving force, ASEAN is reviewing its progress, such as on organisational matters, implementation of projects, additional participation in the ARF, subjects for discussion, the role of ASEAN, the pace and future direction of ARF, and the move towards preventive diplomacy.[13] Meanwhile the ASEAN Secretariat should provide technical and secretarial support, monitor ARF activities, and keep all ARF documents. In 1999, ARF had ten ASEAN member countries, ten Dialogue Partners and Papua New Guinea as Special Observer, Mongolia, and the Democratic People's Republic of Korea. In 1995, the ARF adopted four criteria for participation:

1. Commitment to the key goals of ARF and to all the decisions before admission;
2. Relevance of the applicant state to the peace and security of the region;
3. Gradual expansion of membership for manageability;
4. Consultation with ARF and all other participants to get consensus.

THE NINTH MEETING OF THE ARF[14]

The Ninth Meeting of the ASEAN Regional Forum (ARF) on 31 July 2002 at Bandar Seri Begawan identified the ARF as the main cooperative security forum in the Asia Pacific Region. The meeting showed the versatility and determination of ARF members in addressing regional security concerns while, at the same time, keeping in mind the goals of preserving regional peace and stability. The Foreign Ministers of ASEAN emphasised ASEAN's role as the primary driving force of the ARF while recognising the contributions of all ARF participants to move the ARF process forward at a pace comfortable to all, and always based on decision-making by consensus and on non-interference into one another's internal affairs. The Ninth Meeting considered the adoption of the "Paper on Concept and Principles of Preventive Diplomacy (CPD)" by the Eighth ARF in July 2001 as a major achievement in the evolution of the ARF.

The ARF faced the new and broader challenges of the times, to start with the terrorist acts of 11 September 2001 in the United States which placed on alert the whole security environment. It supported the collective and concerted global campaign against terrorism and reaffirmed the principles in the UN Security Council Resolution on the Prevention and Suppression of Terrorist Acts and issued a Statement on Measures Against Terrorist Financing. On the need to support capacity building of participants to counter terrorism, especially in areas such as legal assistance, financial measures, and practical law enforcement cooperation, further collaboration is needed. The ministers remained committed to strengthen bilateral, regional and international cooperation in combating terrorism comprehensively to make the region a safer place for all.

The Ninth ARF also considered security measures for areas with heightened tensions. In the incidents between North and South Korea, the ARF stressed the need for the easing of tensions, the use of confidence building measures (CBMs), and reconciliation and cooperation, full implementation of the 1994 Project of the Korean Peninsula Energy Development Organization and the Code of Conduct in the South China Sea as ASEAN's new approach to work closely with China in the spirit of self-restraint and with a view to peaceful settlement of disputes in the South China in conformity with international law. The ministers also encouraged ASEAN and Russia to continue their work on the draft Pacific Concord. The ministers also welcomed the idea of an East Asian partnership which could contribute to regional peace, stability and prosperity.

The other concerns of the ARF in 2002 were the territorial integrity and national unity of Indonesia, the reconstruction and development of newly independent Democratic Republic of East Timor (DRET), the national reconciliation process in Myanmar, the easing of tension between India and Pakistan, the security challenges in Bougainville, Fiji, Solomon Islands and other Pacific island governments, and the formation of the Transitional Government of Afghanistan.

The ARF still projects the principles of the Treaty of Amity and Cooperation in Southeast Asia (TAC 1976) as the basis for the promotion of cooperation and amity in Southeast Asia and between ASEAN and ARF participants. ASEAN is in continuing consultations with nuclear weapon states for the latter to sign the Protocol on the SEANWFZ and supports Mongolia's nuclear-free status.

The terrorist attacks of 11 September 2001 brought to the fore the need to prevent the proliferation of weapons of mass destruction and their means of delivery. ARF called on all its participants to implement the UN Programme of Action to Prevent, Combat, and Eradicate Illicit Trade in Small Arms and Light Weapons. ARF Ministers called on states to accede to the Nuclear Non-Proliferation Treaty (NPT) which remains as the cornerstone of the nuclear non-proliferation regime and step up efforts to strengthen the Biological and Toxin Weapons Convention (BTWC).

Measures against terrorist financing include implementation of UN SCR 1373 to stop such financing, freeze without delay the assets of terrorists and their associates, and exchange of financial intelligence.

The Ministers reaffirmed that the ARF is the effective forum for political and security dialogues and cooperation in the changing security situation in the Asia-Pacific region. The ARF process is evolving from confidence-building to preventive diplomacy and elaboration of approaches to conflicts. While the CBMs promote trust, understanding, and cooperation among ARF participants, PD would now include ARF's role against terrorism.

ASEAN AND CHINA IN THE FIELD OF NON-TRADITIONAL SECURITY ISSUES

ASEAN and China also issued the Joint Declaration on Cooperation in the Field of Non-Traditional Security Issues during the Eighth ASEAN Summit Meeting.[15] The Heads of State/Government of the ASEAN member states and of the People's Republic of China, recalling the Statement of the Heads of State/Government of ASEAN states and of China in 1997 which provided for cooperation and dialogue in all fields, for mutual understanding and mutual trust, expressed their deep concern over the serious nature of non-traditional security issues such as trafficking in illegal drugs, people smuggling, trafficking in women and children, sea piracy, terrorism, arms smuggling, money laundering, international economic crime and cyber crime, all of which pose new challenges to regional and international peace and stability.

These non-traditional security issues have been subjects of action by ASEAN in 1997, with China in 2001, and by ASEAN in 2002. Cooperation on these issues shall be based on the Five Principles of Peaceful Coexistence, the UN Charter, the TAC, and other norms of international law, and using an integrated approach to address the issues.

ASEAN and China agreed to deepen the existing multilateral and bilateral cooperation by strengthening exchanges of information, personnel, training for enhancing capacity building, practical cooperation, and joint research. ASEAN and China will use existing mechanisms such as various levels of ASEAN meetings and working groups and formulating action plans.

The leaders of ASEAN member countries and the People's Republic of China are calling on other regions and countries to cooperate with ASEAN and China on these non-traditional security issues.

DEEPENING COOPERATION BETWEEN ASEAN AND CHINA[16]

During the ASEAN-China Summit, ASEAN leaders acknowledged the growing role of China in regional and world affairs. Premier Zhu Rongji of China outlined China's vision for strengthened ties with ASEAN, especially the goal of establishing an ASEAN-China Free Trade Area within the next decade.

The ASEAN and Chinese leaders signed the Framework Agreement on ASEAN-China Economic Cooperation which will usher in the establishment of the free trade area by 2010 for the older ASEAN members, and 2015 for the newer members with flexibility on sensitive commodities. This free trade area will be the world's biggest, having 1.7 billion people and trade worth US$1.2 trillion. As early as next year, there will be tariff cuts in selected farm products under an "early harvest package" to include live animals, meat, fish, dairy products, live trees, vegetables, fruits and nuts. This means that ASEAN nations will benefit earlier than China because ASEAN nations will have greater market access to China ahead of its access to ASEAN.

China granted special and preferential tariff treatment to Cambodia, the Lao People's Democratic Republic and Myanmar. China also reduced the debt obligations of the less-developed ASEAN members and launched an information-technology training programme. ASEAN invited China to participate in the sub-regional development cooperation arrangements concerning the growth areas such as the Greater Mekong Sub-region (GMS), the BIMP-EAGA, and the Malaysia-Indonesia-Singapore growth triangle.

ASEAN STRATEGIES FOR SECURITY

Since 1967, ASEAN has viewed security together with stability and progress as a value to be ensured or preserved from external interference in any form or manifestation. Malaysian and Indonesian leaders equated security with progress in economic cooperation and as depending on their ability to provide the goods of life for the people, and as the self-reliance that derives from domestic factors such as economic and social development, political stability, and a sense of nationalism. The leaders also said that security does not lie in military alliances nor was military alliance "in the cards" because ASEAN was committed to the earliest-stated goals of peace and development in all fields through economic, social, cultural, and political cooperation for the mutual benefit of its members.

Because of these commitments to the goals of ASEAN cooperation which the leaders have been reiterating, security in ASEAN was never equated with military solutions for the great problems that faced ASEAN since 1967.

Analysts of international and regional developments which were mostly producing issues and conflicts equated security with military means or military power to solve the problems. Some of the problems were the rise to power of communist parties in Vietnam, Laos, and Cambodia; the support of the Soviet Union and China to whichever pawn state in Southeast Asia, the ever-presence of US military power to prevent China or the Soviet Union from gaining more influence in the region, for each such gain is loss to US predominance in the region, and the ramifications on the domestic affairs of the ASEAN states of those conflicts and on the regional peace. Analysts wrote about the "security environment" mentioning military flash points such as territorial disputes and ideological conflicts and therewith gave security a military or defence connotation.

On the other hand, if as in 1967 ASEAN leaders said that security should be ensured, then it is something good or valued. So a security environment should rather include political, economic, social, and cultural conditions which are desirable as they are the positive aspects of security which should be ensured or preserved. Then there will also be a negative or undesirable environment which should include problems such as drug abuse, refugees, poverty, kidnapping, AIDS/ HIV, human rights violations, and military and political threats, all of

209

which threaten the enjoyment of what are desired, valued, or to be ensured such as security. The problems herewith enumerated are threats to security.

With all wisdom, since 1967, ASEAN has met the problems or threats in the domestic and from the external environment with strategies that were never military in nature, but with political, diplomatic, economic, and functional cooperation.

ASEAN supported the Arabs in the conflict with Israel in 1973 in order to protect the Muslim population in Southeast Asia. ASEAN became active in the Non-Aligned Movement and in the Organization of Islamic Conference. ZOPFAN in 1971 which was enriched with national and regional resilience and the SEANWFZ are strategies for peace freedom, and neutrality. ASEAN successfully brought into membership Vietnam, Laos, Myanmar, and Cambodia which had earlier acceded to the TAC as their code of conduct. ASEAN used Asian solutions for Asian problems, bilateral summitry, low-key diplomacy, confidence building measures, constructive engagement, comprehensive engagement, preventive diplomacy, continuous dialogues, *mushawarah*, consensus-minus-X, ASEAN Way, not naming the enemy, assistance in disasters, economic cooperation through AFTA, APEC, growth triangles, and cooperation with sub-regional groups and ASEM, and now the ARF for security cooperation.

In the 35th ASEAN Ministerial Meeting at Bandar Seri Begawan, 27-30 July 2002, the ministers stressed the importance of maintaining the territorial integrity, sovereignty, and unity of states. In this context ASEAN needs to address threats and challenges posed by issues such as separatism and terrorism. ASEAN maintains informal open and frank dialogues through its mechanisms of Leaders' Summit and Ministerial Meetings and reviews and assesses developments with its friends and partners.

All these strategies are to produce a positive environment in Southeast Asia which are to help achieve the stated goals of ASEAN and to eliminate or transform to positive factors the threats to security, that is to say, the conditions in the environment which prevent or threaten the enjoyment of peace, development, economic, social and political progress, altogether security itself.

If security is clearly understood at this point as an ASEAN good or value to be ensured or preserved and enjoyed then it is a goal and not a strategy for something else. For example, the presence of food sufficiency is called food security, the accessibility of social goods to people is social security, political stability is security, altogether they are under the concept comprehensive security because of the number and variety of values to be preserved. Comprehensive security is now being used by Indonesia, Malaysia, and Japan. It includes military capability which is a desired factor to protect the state.

Certainly ASEAN states are modernising their armed forces to fulfil the inherent obligation of every state to provide for the defence of its sovereignty, territorial integrity, and well-being of the people. However, military cooperation for increasing military capability is outside the framework of ASEAN as stated in the First Summit.

Political security may be differentiated from defence security (existence of or access to military capability for defence). ASEAN leaders do not always view defence as military in nature. For example, "collective political defence" as explained by Thai Foreign Minister Thanat Khoman meant the ability of ASEAN states to derive political and psychological strength from their cooperation. Moreover, Malaysia sees diplomacy as its main defence instrument. The Indonesians espouse non-alignment and national resilience as their defence for national independence.

ASEAN has rejected the idea of the use of military to defend or ensure security. Defence is a strategy to produce security by meeting with force threats that come in any form. Defence comes in the form of what is practicable and appropriate to the threat. On the other hand, the popular view of defence is the use of military. More commonly but mistakenly, security as a goal to be ensured is seen as the possession of military itself. So the goal, objective or something to be valued which is security becomes also the means for defence itself or the strategy. Finally, security (military) is the means to ensure security. This is not correct logic.

Philippine Strategist General Jose T. Almonte said that ASEAN culture is one of "security with and not against others, and prosperity with and not at the expense of others". Almonte advocates raising the sights of ASEAN to a higher level to embrace the Asia-Pacific region. The long term objective is to replace security arrangements based on the military balance of power with cooperative security based on mutual benefit, all for "A Pacific Peace".

A NEW SECURITY FRAMEWORK

One security framework that accommodates the deep feelings of ASEAN leaders for a community of peace, prosperity, and security (which is to be ensured) and for other desired goals, and their views that security is the provision of the goods of life for the people is described below.[17]

Security is the feeling that accompanies the actual, perceived, or sustained satisfaction of values or the reasonable expectation of their realisation. Values are what we have a constant preference for and their satisfaction produces a feeling of security. Security is experienced differently under different conditions such as status quo, change, isolation, and interdependence. ASEAN wants to ensure or preserve security in a condition of interdependence through cooperation defined as working together for common goals.

The indicators for security in interdependence are:

1. A belief that an increase in benefit to one will be a benefit to all.
2. A feeling that the resources of any member will be mutually shared in their use or that a member's needs for such resources will be accommodated.
3. A belief that if a member state needs some changes due to pressures impinging on it, that state will not be left alone to absorb the consequences of such pressures.
4. A growing feeling among the member states that as cooperation leads to achievement of goals, the limiting boundaries among them such as tariffs, and bureaucratic attitudes and procedures, will be altered or set aside to facilitate the transfer of resources leading to an increase in the quantity or quality of values or goals.
5. A growing belief that if a situation or event threatens any member state, its individual capacity to meet such a threat will be increased by the aggregate capability of all the units.

There are objective conditions in the environment that are productive of greater enjoyment or satisfaction of values. Therefore a state designs strategies such as alliances, cooperation with others, agreements, friendship, exchanges, and others, to increase the positive conditions in the environment that will increase the quantity and quality of values to be satisfied, or finally to say, increase security.

There are also conditions that tend to threaten or reduce the satisfaction of values. They are called threats to security. The states or association will devise strategies to neutralise, eliminate or transform such threat conditions. One of the strategies is the use of military power singly or in alliances. The others are isolation, distancing, and reduction of values, transferring the imminent threat to the environment, such as to other countries, and transforming the threat conditions into advantageous conditions such as from enemies to friends or arms race to peace race by constructive engagement or as the Thais say "from battlefield to market place". This new perspective of security has accommodated the statements on security of ASEAN leaders since 1967.

ENDNOTES

1   "Regionalism in Southeast Asia", Proceedings of a Conference, 1975.

2   *Kompas Daily*, July 23 1984, and *Asia Research Bulletin*, Vol.14, no.3, August 1984, p.1196 as quoted by J.Soedjati Djiwandono in May 1997.

3   Chandran Jeshurun, "Introduction to Defense and Security," in K.S. Sandhu and S. Siddique (eds.), *The ASEAN Reader* (Singapore: ISEAS, 1992), p.367.

4   J.L.S. Girling, "Regional Security in Southeast Asia", in *The ASEAN Reader, ibid*, pp. 369-370.

5   Mochtar Kusuma Atmadja shares the idea of a three-power defence cooperation among Indonesia, Malaysia, and Singapore. He thinks that an ASEAN military capability with the armed forces of Indonesia, Malaysia, and Singapore can be the nucleus of what he calls a three-power defence cooperation. *The ASEAN Reader, ibid.*, pp.415-416.

6   Jusuf Wanadi, "ASEAN Security Cooperation in the Post-Cold War Era", *The ASEAN Reader, ibid.*, pp. 417-418

7   Michael Leifer, "Is ASEAN a Security Organization?", in *ibid*, pp. 379-381.

8   Bilveer Singh, *ZOPFAN and the New Security Order in the Asia-Pacific Region*, Malaysia: Pelanduk Publication (CM) SDN Bhd., 1992, p.7.

9   Pushpa Thambipillai, "Negotiating Styles" in *The ASEAN Reader, op.cit.*, pp. 72-75.

10 General Soedibyo, "Changing Super Power Policies (Questions for ASEAN)" Roundtable Conference in Manila, undated but possibly 1992.

11 Michael Antolik, "The ASEAN Regional Forum: The Spirit of Constructive Engagement" in *Contemporary Southeast Asia* (Singapore: ISEAS, Vol.16 no.2 September 1994) pp.124-128.

12 *Ibid.*

13 Association of Southeast Asian Nations Annual Report 1998-1999, Jakarta: ASEAN Secretariat, pp. 9-10.

14 Chairman's Statement, the Ninth Meeting of the ASEAN Regional Forum (Bandar Seri Begawan, 31 July 2002).

15   Joint Declaration of ASEAN and China on Cooperation in the Field of Non-Traditional Security Issues, Phnom Penh, 04 November 2002.

16   Press statement by the Chairman of the Eighth ASEAN Summit, 04 November 2002, Phnom Penh.

17   Estrella D. Solidum, Teresita Saldivar-Sali and Roman Dubsky, *Security in a New Perspective*, first published in *Asian Perspectives*, Fall/Winter 1981, (Seoul: Institute of International Affairs, 1981) and reprinted in various journals elsewhere.

CHAPTER **9**

Conclusion

The continued vitality of ASEAN comes from its "political formula" which is the basis for its existence, intra-regional relations, external relations, the ASEAN mechanism and structures, and the direction of its life. The principles that have been adopted by ASEAN have provided the stability for the decisions of the leaders while the shared cultural values have sustained the moral foundation of ASEAN.

The history of ASEAN from its founding on 8 August 1967 to year 2003 would seem to tell its whole story but it really does not. A full appreciation of its unprecedented success would include an understanding of the efforts of the leaders of the states in Southeast Asia from 1947 to the present to get together to cooperate on projects and face the common problems that produced threats to their peoples. The decisions of ASEAN leaders have been based on the experiences, principles and goals of the earlier attempts at regional cooperation.

The ASEAN Declaration of 1967 established an Association for Regional Cooperation among the countries of Southeast Asia to be known as the Association of Southeast Asian Nations (ASEAN), although signed by only five states—Indonesia, Malaysia, the Philippines, Singapore, and Thailand. At that time, it was clear to the founders that the idea was to include all the states of Southeast Asia although it was evident that the rest of the states had no positive attitudes toward ASEAN. The aims of ASEAN were to promote regional peace, freedom and prosperity, through cooperation in the spirit of equality and partnership, and preserving their national identities. ASEAN would promote active collaboration and mutual assistance on matters of common interest in the economic, social, cultural, technical, and administrative fields, promote Southeast Asian studies, and maintain close and beneficial cooperation with international and regional organisations with similar purposes.

These aims of ASEAN can be traced to the earliest attempts to express the idea of regional cooperation that a number of Asian leaders had had for some time. At the Asian Relations Conference in 1947 at New Delhi, Indian Prime Minister Nehru stressed the

215

need for Asian unity and for regional cooperation. The conference agreed to promote Asian studies, greater cooperation, freedom for colonial areas, lifting the status of women in Asia, inter-Asian communication, and economic progress.

The New Delhi Conference of 1949 agreed to explore ways of promoting consultation and cooperation. The Baguio Conference of 1950 was an anti-communist conference but the discussions brought out many similarities among the delegates' vision, especially to improve the social and economic conditions of the people. SEATO of 1954 was anti-neutralist as much as anti-communist for such neutralist states would fall like dominoes to the communists if the U.S. did not maintain a military presence in the region.

The Asian-African Conference better known as the Bandung Conference of 1955 aimed to promote goodwill and cooperation among Asian and African nations to promote their common interests, to consider social, economic and cultural problems and national sovereignty. The Bandung Conference laid out the famous Ten Principles which included among others, mutual respect for sovereignty and territorial integrity, mutual non-interference in each other's internal affairs, peaceful coexistence, disarmament and prohibition of nuclear weapons, and respect for human rights. Later the Bandung Conference became the Non-Aligned Movement (NAM), now for economic development.

The first purely Southeast Asian states organisation was the Association of Southeast Asia (ASA 1961) composed of three states, Malaya, Thailand and the Philippines. The state leaders upheld the ideals of peace, freedom, social justice and economic well-being. ASA's projects were practical and useful, and included the promotion of Southeast Asian studies, exchange of youth and women leaders, cooperation on shipping, tourism and trade, and common positions in international bodies. The practical cooperation generated much goodwill, enabling the states to keep their problems at a very low key, use Asian solutions for Asian problems, encourage "give and take" of their resources, show self restraint in mutual consultation, and continue regional cooperation in the social, cultural, and economic fields. ASA's projects were taken over by ASEAN leaders in 1967 because MAPHILINDO of 1963 overtook ASA. MAPHILINDO prescribed *mushawarah* for consensus-making, Asian solutions for Asian problems, and trust to bring about unity.

MAPHILINDO of 1963 broke up before it could function because political problems were reducing the goodwill of the three states. Political and military matters should not be allowed during the period of learning cooperation. But MAPHILINDO had two big contributions to ASEAN's principles: *mushawarah* or consensus-making for all decisions and foreign military bases are temporary in nature.

From these early attempts at cooperation, ASEAN picked up principles and projects for cooperation, not only for the Bangkok Declaration but also for later Declarations which forthrightly declare the same principles and areas of concern.

ASEAN-5's earliest years were spent in learning cooperation and wisely avoided mention of political cooperation in the Bangkok Declaration, for community-building. All sectors of society must be brought in as members because it is the people for whom ASEAN aims to bring the blessings of cooperation. In the first few years the leaders were surprised to find that they were like one family with shared values. The spirit of good neighbourliness, community sentiments from cultural similarities, and common values to sustain cooperation built a strong sense of community. This shared behaviour was named ASEAN Way and the commitment to project the ASEAN name in all activities was called ASEAN Spirit. At the First Ministerial Meeting of ASEAN, their cooperation was one "among members of a great family" bound together by ties of friendship and goodwill in the spirit of equality and partnership. The foreign ministers "took counsel with one another in an atmosphere of informality and a real spirit of good neighbourliness". That first crucial year brought out the value of neighbourliness. "They had discarded their deplorable habit of going their own separate ways and turning their backs to one another" (Thanat Khoman). The leaders constantly invoked common values and the ASEAN Way provided stability and a high degree of predictability in their relationships. Even when there were differences of opinions, these were considered a healthy feeling, "that our minds remain active and our conceptions are developing prior to reaching a consensus" (President Suharto). The problems of adjustment and cooperation were a "necessary prelude to a new phase of consolidation". There is a unity of thought that ASEAN's end is peace and its means are peaceful.

Indeed the problems of the first few years of ASEAN were intra-ASEAN. The foreign ministers "made some gracious gesture", used the spirit of "give and take", avoided explicit references to what were objectionable to others, used bilateral meetings, or worked behind the scenes, and used "diplomatic informality" as Asian solutions to Asian problems. All those problems were resolved without the use of force.

By 1971, the conflict among the big powers had involved almost all the states of Southeast Asia. ASEAN adopted the Kuala Lumpur Declaration on the Zone of Peace, Freedom, and Neutrality (ZOPFAN, 1971) which stated that the original ASEAN member states are determined to exert efforts to secure the recognition of, and respect for, Southeast Asia as a Zone of Peace, Freedom, and Neutrality, free from any form of interference by outside Powers, to ensure the peace and stability necessary for their independence, economic and social well-being. The ZOPFAN invoked the validity of the principles of the Bandung Conference of 1955 by which states may coexist peacefully, and the Latin American and Lusaka declarations for a nuclear-free zone, for the desirable objective of neutralisation. Later ZOPFAN incorporated the Suharto Doctrine of national and regional resilience. So was the Southeast Asia Treaty of Amity and Cooperation (TAC) of 1976.

In 1983, ZOPFAN incorporated the principle of a Southeast Asia Nuclear Weapon-Free Zone. In 1985, the Treaty on the Southeast Asia Nuclear Weapon-Free Zone (SEANWFZ) was signed by the heads of the ten Southeast Asian countries although not all were members yet at the time.

After acquiring the shared behaviour of friendship and goodwill as "in a great family" ASEAN leaders and ministers were now prepared to go into political cooperation on a region-wide scale. In 1976, the First ASEAN Summit was held in Bali. The documents that they crafted and signed in Bali are of long-standing durability and wisdom. Based on the spirit and principles of the Charter of the United Nations, the Ten Principles of Bandung of 1955, the Declaration of ASEAN of 1967 and the Declaration on the ZOPFAN of 1971, the Treaty of Amity and Cooperation (TAC) in Southeast Asia of 1976 governs the relationships of the High Contracting Parties, with Indonesia, Malaysia, the Philippines, Singapore, and Thailand as signatories each of which ratified this treaty in accordance with the constitutional processes of each signatory state. The treaty is open for accession by other states in Southeast Asia. The TAC requires that the High Contracting Parties observe mutual respect, non-interference in the internal affairs of one another, renunciation of threat or the use of force, enhancement of national and regional resilience, use of peaceful means in settling disputes, and encouragement of effective cooperation in all fields and in all their relations.

There is a practice in ASEAN that any structure or mechanism will be set up only after the procedures have been found useful in their frequent use. It is in this sense that the TAC was formalised nine years after ASEAN was established. The processes of consultation, consensus, peaceful settlement of disputes, cooperation, and others had become habitual to the leaders because they were embedded in the cultures that they all shared, to the very pleasant surprise of the leaders in their first year of working together in ASEAN.

Thus the rest of the states in Southeast Asia which were critical of ASEAN acceded first to the TAC before becoming members of ASEAN. The partners of ASEAN are encouraged to accede to the TAC also. The TAC has become the Code of Conduct for every one dealing with ASEAN. In the same spirit, in formalising this Code of Conduct, ASEAN also formalised the principles and objectives of the UN Charter, the Bandung Conference, ASA, the MAPHILINDO, Bangkok Declaration of 1967, and ZOPFAN.

The TAC is an explicit statement of the goals of ASEAN which are to promote regional peace and stability, closest cooperation on the widest scale, and coordination of views, actions and policies by the signatories and by those who have acceded to it. A Protocol to the TAC enables non-Southeast Asian countries to accede to it.

All in all, it can be said that the principles and objectives of the TAC attracted Brunei, Vietnam, Laos, Myanmar and Cambodia to become members of ASEAN since the last four states had sat first as Observers before acceding to TAC and becoming members, and were also subjects of confidence building measures and constructive engagements. TAC served as guidelines for their relationships with other states and organisations outside the region. The Dialogue Partners especially respect the TAC.

The TAC in its time was "propitious for joint action to give effective expression to the ... desire of the peoples of Southeast Asia to ensure the conditions of peace and stability indispensable to their independence and their economic and social well-being".

In the same First ASEAN Summit (1976), the Declaration of ASEAN Concord provided the principles and framework for ASEAN cooperation in the political, security, economic, and functional fields.

ASEAN leaders discussed political matters "in the corridors of ASEAN" before 1976 because the Bangkok Declaration of 1967 did not provide for it. As the framers of the Bangkok Declaration had learned from the earlier attempts from 1947 to 1967 that political matters were "high politics" and risky for those learning cooperation for the first time, still, realistically speaking, most actions in the first ten years of ASEAN were political, such as settling intra-ASEAN disputes, making decisions at the highest levels which was at the level of the Foreign Ministers, and the Declaration of the ZOPFAN in 1971. The ASEAN Concord provided for cooperation in political matters. As for security cooperation, in the sense of military cooperation, security cooperation will continue "on a non-ASEAN basis".

In the first 14 years of ASEAN, there were certain matters that could not be handled at the structural level but which could have had far-reaching consequences. The Heads of Government met with one another informally to discuss the issues and make political decisions on them in bilateral summitry of which there were 96 in 14 years. In the order of importance by frequency of mention, the issues were 1) the need for mutual understanding and unity in all matters; 2) intra-ASEAN problems of secessionism, territorial claims and border problems; 3) foreign policies of non-alignment and neutralisation, and new policy shifts; 4) security problems including US military in Philippine bases, SEATO, military cooperation in ASEAN, bilateral military cooperation outside of ASEAN, ethnic insurgencies; 5) international developments; and 6) ASEAN organisation itself, summit meetings, restructuring of ASEAN.

In the 1970s, ASEAN had to face new international developments and increasing problems that were not substantively political in nature. The Second ASEAN Summit in 1977 (Kuala Lumpur) planned for cooperation in human resource development, women and youth development, disease and illiteracy, poverty, and abuse and traffic in drugs. The Third ASEAN Summit in 1987 (Manila) reiterated the importance of those problems as they threatened the social fabric. These areas were classified into "functional cooperation". The Fourth ASEAN Summit in 1992 (Singapore) included ASEAN studies in schools, student exchange programmes, efforts to curb the spread of AIDS, and promotion of sustainable development. The Fifth ASEAN Summit in 1995 (Bangkok) elevated functional cooperation to a higher plane, that of sharing prosperity. The theme was "shared prosperity through human development, technological competence, and social cohesiveness". What was functional was that which was not political, economic or security in nature. The leaders also committed themselves to greater economics cooperation, including on the Mekong Basin Development.

The Sixth ASEAN Summit in 1998 (Hanoi) resolved to safeguard the welfare of the poor and the disadvantaged. The summit adopted the Hanoi Plan of Action to implement plans on rural development, poverty eradication and social safety nets. The Seventh ASEAN Summit in 2001 (Bandar Seri Begawan) focused on efforts for economic reform, integration and cooperation in the region, particularly the Roadmap for the Integration of ASEAN (RIA) which should produce coherence and cohesion in the response to the challenges of the economic diversity and development gap of the expanded ASEAN. This was the time when globalisation began to hurt the lesser economies and ASEAN has had to work with its international economic partners to negotiate at the WTO for greater access for products and services of developing economies.

The Eighth ASEAN Summit in 2002 (Phnom Penh) faced greater international problems such as terrorism which made the world almost "like a world at war", the Middle East crisis, transnational issues like diseases and trafficking of human, drugs and weapons and security.

The scheduled summit in April 2003 addressed the latest threat to peoples all over the world. In the Asia-Pacific region, investments have been withdrawn, markets have collapsed, economic growth has been sized down and governments and churches have no answer yet to cope with the spreading virus of the still unknown Severe Acute Respiratory Syndrome (SARS). It is a transnational threat without a conflict.

The responses of ASEAN to the problems that it is facing include 1) enlarging of the capabilities and resources of ASEAN in all fields; 2) ASEAN mechanisms which include diplomacy of accommodation to meet intra-regional problems, and other engagements for peace; 3) formal process like the Hanoi Plan of Action (1998); 4) specific committees, boards, centres, units and working groups; 5) coordination with the private groups; 6) functional committees; 7) increased cooperation with the Dialogue Partners who have really been very cooperative with their ideas and technical, scientific, and financial support for ASEAN projects; 8) cooperation with non-Dialogue countries; 9) ASEAN +1, +3 Summits; 10) the ASEAN Regional Forum (ARF) as the main security forum in the Asian-Pacific region, using confidence building measures and preventive diplomacy; 11) the invariable use of consensus-making to arrive at all decisions and commitment to the often-stated principles; 12) effective outreach programmes through cultural cooperation, science and technology exchanges, heightened environmental awareness at the national, regional, and international levels, and others; and 13) specific Declarations for cooperation to transform troubled waters into harmonious areas, such as the Declaration on the Conduct of Parties in the South China Sea which prescribes cooperation and understanding among the claimant states pending a comprehensive and desirable settlement of the disputes, and the Joint Declaration of ASEAN and China on Cooperation in the Field of Non-Traditional Security Issues (Eighth ASEAN Summit 2002).

With the highest commitment to its goals of peace, freedom, stability, prosperity, rule of law, and security, unwavering observance of all the principles which it had adopted from its establishment, and constantly mindful of the need for newer and appropriate strategies and building blocks, to achieve the aspirations of the peoples, ASEAN has remained vibrant and relevant as the 21st century has begun. ASEAN has been able to respond and adapt to the changing conditions at the regional and international levels in coherent ways. ASEAN has engaged more friends and partners in all its cooperative endeavours, and within itself, the members have remained cohesive. The ideal of ASEAN toward which it is moving in the 21st century is summed up in its ASEAN Vision 2020 which is "a concert of Southeast Asian nations, outward-looking, living in peace, stability, and prosperity, bonded together in partnership in development, and in a community of caring societies".

The ASEAN Declaration

(Bangkok Declaration)
Bangkok, 8 August 1967

The Presidium Minister for Political Affairs/Minister for Foreign Affairs of Indonesia, the Deputy Prime Minister of Malaysia, the Secretary of Foreign Affairs of the Philippines, the Minister for Foreign Affairs of Singapore and the Minister of Foreign Affairs of Thailand:

MINDFUL of the existence of mutual interests and common problems among countries of South-East Asia and convinced of the need to strengthen further the existing bonds of regional solidarity and cooperation;

DESIRING to establish a firm foundation for common action to promote regional cooperation in South-East Asia in the spirit of equality and partnership and thereby contribute towards peace, progress and prosperity in the region;

CONSCIOUS that in an increasingly interdependent world, the cherished ideals of peace, freedom, social justice, and economic well-being are best attained by fostering good understanding, good neighbourliness, and meaningful cooperation among the countries of the region already bound together by ties of history and culture;

CONSIDERING that the countries of South-East Asia share a primary responsibility for strengthening the economic and social stability of the region and ensuring their peaceful and progressive national development, and that they are determined to ensure their stability and security from external interference in any form or manifestation in order to preserve their national identities in accordance with the ideals and aspirations of their peoples;

AFFIRMING that all foreign bases are temporary and remain only with the expressed concurrence of the countries concerned and are not intended to be used directly or indirectly to subvert the national independence and freedom of States in the area or prejudice the orderly processes of their national development;

DO HEREBY DECLARE:

FIRST, the establishment of an Association for Regional Cooperation among the countries of South-East Asia to be known as the Association of South-East Asian Nations (ASEAN).

SECOND, that the aims and purposes of the Association shall be:

1 To accelerate the economic growth, social progress, and cultural development in the region through joint endeavours in the spirit of equality and partnership in order to strengthen the foundation for a prosperous and peaceful community of South-East Asian Nations;

2 To promote regional peace and stability through abiding respect for justice and the rule of law in the relationship among countries of the region and adherence to the principles of the United Nations Charter;

3 To promote active collaboration and mutual assistance on matters of common interest in the economic, social, cultural, technical, scientific, and administrative fields;

4 To provide assistance to each other in the form of training and research facilities in the educational, professional, technical, and administrative spheres;

5 To collaborate more effectively for the greater utilization of their agriculture and industries, the expansion of their trade, including the study of the problems of international commodity trade, the improvement of their transportation and communications facilities and the raising of the living standards of their peoples;

6 To promote South-East Asian studies;

7 To maintain close and beneficial cooperation with existing international and regional organizations with similar aims and purposes, and explore all avenues for even closer cooperation among themselves.

THIRD, that to carry out these aims and purposes, the following machinery shall be established:

1 Annual Meeting of Foreign Ministers, which shall be by rotation and referred to as ASEAN Ministerial Meeting.

Special Meetings of Foreign Ministers may be convened as required.

2 A Standing Committee, under the chairmanship of the Foreign Minister of the host country or his representative and having as its members the accredited Ambassadors of the other member countries, to carry on the work of the Association in between Meetings of Foreign Ministers.

3 Ad-Hoc Committees and Permanent Committees of specialists and officials on specific subjects.

4 A National Secretariat in each member country to carry out the work of the Association on behalf of that country and to service the Annual or Special Meetings of Foreign Ministers, the Standing Committee and such other committees as may hereafter be established.

FOURTH, that the Association is open for participation to all States in the South-East Asian Region subscribing to the aforementioned aims, principles, and purposes.

FIFTH, that the Association represents the collective will of the nations of South-East Asia to bind themselves together in friendship and cooperation and, through joint efforts and sacrifices, secure for their peoples and for posterity the blessings of peace, freedom, and prosperity.

DONE in Bangkok on the Eighth Day of August in the Year One Thousand Nine Hundred and Sixty-Seven.

FOR THE REPUBLIC OF INDONESIA:	FOR THE REPUBLIC OF THE PHILIPPINES:	FOR THE REPUBLIC OF SINGAPORE:
ADAM MALIK Presidium Minister for Political Affairs Minister for Foreign Affairs	NARCISO RAMOS Secretary of Foreign Affairs	S. RAJARATNAM Minister of Foreign Affairs

FOR MALAYSIA:	FOR THE KINGDOM OF THAILAND:
TUN ABDUL RAZAK Minister of Defence and Minister of National Development	THANAT KHOMAN Minister of Foreign Affairs

Zone of Peace, Freedom and Neutrality Declaration

(Kuala Lumpur Declaration)
Malaysia, 27 November 1971

We, the Foreign Ministers of Indonesia, Malaysia, the Philippines, Singapore, and the Special Envoy of the National Executive Council of Thailand:

FIRMLY believing in the merits of regional cooperation which has drawn our countries to cooperate together in the economic, social, and cultural fields in the Association of South-East Asian Nations;

DESIROUS of bringing about a relaxation of international tension and of achieving a lasting peace in South-East Asia;

INSPIRED by the worthy aims and objectives of the United Nations, in particular by the principles of respect for the sovereignty and territorial integrity of all states, abstention from threat or use of force, peaceful settlement of international disputes, equal rights and self-determination, and non-interference in the affairs of States;

BELIEVING in the continuing validity of the "Declaration of the Promotion of World Peace and Cooperation" of the Bandung Conference of 1955 which, among others, enunciates the principles by which States may coexist peacefully;

RECOGNISING the right of every state, large or small to lead its national existence free from outside interference in its internal affairs as this interference will adversely affect its freedom, independence, and integrity;

DEDICATED to the maintenance of peace, freedom, and independence unimpaired;

BELIEVING in the need to meet present challenges and new developments by cooperating with all peace and freedom loving nations, both within and outside the region, in the furtherance of world peace, stability, and harmony;

COGNIZANT of the significant trend towards establishing nuclear-free zones, as in the "Treaty for Prohibition of Nuclear Weapons in Latin

America" and the Lusaka Declaration proclaiming Africa a nuclear-free zone, for the purpose of promoting world peace and security by reducing the areas of international conflicts and tension;

REITERATING our commitment to the principle in the Bangkok Declaration which established ASEAN in 1967, "that the countries of South-East Asia share a primary responsibility for strengthening the economic and social stability of the region and ensuring their peaceful and progressive national development, and that they are determined to ensure their stability and security from external interference in any form or manifestation in order to preserve their national identities in accordance with the ideals and aspirations of their peoples";

AGREEING that the neutralization of South East Asia is a desirable objective and that we should explore ways and means of bringing about its realization; and

CONVINCED that the time is propitious for joint action to give effective expression to the deeply felt desire of the peoples of South East Asia to ensure the conditions of peace and stability indispensable to their independence and their economic and social well-being.

DO HEREBY STATE:

1 That Indonesia, Malaysia, the Philippines, Singapore, and Thailand are determined to exert initially necessary efforts to secure the recognition of, and respect for, South-East Asia as a Zone of Peace, Freedom, and Neutrality, free from any form or manner of interference by outside Powers;

2 That South-East Asian countries should make concerted efforts to broaden the areas of cooperation which would contribute to their strength, solidarity, and closer relationship.

DONE at Kuala Lumpur on Saturday, the 27th of November 1971.

TREATY OF AMITY AND COOPERATION IN SOUTHEAST ASIA BALI, 24 FEBRUARY 1976

PREAMBLE

The High Contracting Parties:

CONSCIOUS of the existing ties of history, geography and culture, which have bound their peoples together;

ANXIOUS to promote regional peace and stability through abiding respect for justice and the rule of law and enhancing regional resilience in their relations;

DESIRING to enhance peace, friendship, and mutual cooperation on matters affecting Southeast Asia consistent with the spirit and principles of the Charter of the United Nations, the Ten Principles adopted by the Asian-African Conference in Bandung on 25 April 1955, the Declaration of the Association of Southeast Asian Nations signed in Bangkok on 8 August 1967, and the Declaration signed in Kuala Lumpur on 27 November 1971;

CONVINCED that the settlement of differences or disputes between their countries should be regulated by rational, effective, and sufficiently flexible procedures, avoiding negative attitudes which might endanger or hinder cooperation;

BELIEVING in the need for cooperation with all peace-loving nations, both within and outside Southeast Asia, in the furtherance of world peace, stability, and harmony;

SOLEMNLY AGREE to enter into a Treaty of Amity and Cooperation as follows:

CHAPTER I
Purpose and Principles
ARTICLE 1

The purpose of this Treaty is to promote perpetual peace, everlasting amity and cooperation among their peoples which would contribute to their strength, solidarity, and closer relationship.

ARTICLE 2

In their relations with one another, the High Contracting Parties shall be guided by the following fundamental principles:

a. Mutual respect for the i n d e p e n d e n c e, sovereignty, equality, territorial integrity, and national identity of all nations;

b. The right of every State to lead its national existence free from external interference, subversion or coercion;

c. Non-interference in the internal affairs of one another;

d. Settlement of differences or disputes by peaceful means;

e. Renunciation of the threat or use of force;

f. Effective cooperation among themselves.

CHAPTER II
Amity

ARTICLE 3

In pursuance of the purpose of this Treaty the High Contracting Parties shall endeavour to develop and strengthen the traditional, cultural and historical ties of friendship, good neighbourliness, and cooperation which bind them together and shall fulfill in good faith the obligations assumed under this Treaty. In order to promote closer understanding among them, the High Contracting Parties shall encourage and facilitate contact and intercourse among their peoples.

CHAPTER III
Cooperation

ARTICLE 4

The High Contracting Parties shall promote active cooperation in the economic, social, technical, scientific, and administrative fields as well as in matters of common ideals and aspiration of international peace and stability in the region and all other matters of common interest.

ARTICLE 5

Pursuant to Article 4 the High Contracting Parties shall exert their maximum efforts multilaterally as well as bilaterally on the basis of equality, non-discrimination, and mutual benefit.

ARTICLE 6

The High Contracting Parties shall collaborate for the acceleration of the economic growth in the region in order to strengthen the foundation for a prosperous and peaceful community of nations in Southeast Asia. To this end, they shall promote the greater utilization of their agriculture and industries, the expansion of their trade and the improvement of their economic infrastructure for the mutual benefit of their peoples. In this regard, they shall continue to explore all avenues for closer and beneficial cooperation with other States as well as international and regional organisations outside the region.

ARTICLE 7

The High Contracting Parties, in order to achieve social justice and to raise the standards of living of the peoples of the region, shall intensify economic cooperation. For this purpose, they shall adopt appropriate regional strategies for economic development and mutual assistance.

ARTICLE 8

The High Contracting Parties shall strive to achieve the closest cooperation on the widest scale and shall seek to provide assistance to one another in the form of training and research facilities in the social, cultural, technical, scientific, and administrative fields.

ARTICLE 9

The High Contracting Parties shall endeavour to foster cooperation in the furtherance of the cause of peace, harmony, and stability in the region. To this end, the High Contracting Parties shall maintain regular contacts and consultations with one another on international and regional matters with a view to coordinating their views, actions and policies.

ARTICLE 10

Each High Contracting Party shall not in any manner or form participate in any activity which shall constitute a threat to the political and economic stability, sovereignty, or territorial integrity of another High Contracting Party.

ARTICLE 11

The High Contracting Parties shall endeavour to strengthen their respective national resilience in their political, economic, socio-cultural as well as security fields in conformity with their respective ideals and aspirations, free from external interference as well as internal subversion activities in order to preserve their respective identities.

ARTICLE 12

The High Contracting Parties in their efforts to achieve regional prosperity and security, shall endeavour to cooperate in all fields for the promotion of regional resilience, based on the principles of self-confidence, self-reliance, mutual respect, cooperation, and solidarity which will constitute the foundation for a strong and viable community of nations in Southeast Asia.

CHAPTER IV
Pacific Settlement of Disputes

ARTICLE 13

The High Contracting Parties shall have the determination and good faith to prevent disputes from arising. In case of disputes on matters directly affecting them they shall refrain from threat or use of force and shall at all times settle such disputes among themselves through friendly negotiations.

ARTICLE 14

To settle disputes through regional processes, the High Contracting Parties shall constitute, as a continuing body, a High Council comprising a Representative at ministerial level from each of the High Contracting Parties to take cognizance of the existence of disputes or situations likely to disturb regional peace and harmony.

ARTICLE 15

In the event no solution is reached through direct negotiations, the High Council shall take cognizance of the dispute or the situation and shall recommend to the parties in dispute appropriate means of settlement such as good offices, mediation, inquiry or conciliation. The High Council may however offer its good offices, or upon agreement of the parties in dispute, constitute itself into a committee of mediation, inquiry or conciliation. When deemed necessary, the High Council shall recommend appropriate measures for the prevention of a deterioration of the dispute or the situation.

ARTICLE 16

The foregoing provision of this Chapter shall not apply to a dispute unless all the parties to the dispute agree to their application to that dispute. However, this shall not preclude the other High Contracting Parties not party to the dispute from offering all possible assistance to settle the said dispute. Parties to the dispute should be well disposed towards such offers of assistance.

ARTICLE 17

Nothing in this Treaty shall preclude recourse to the modes of peaceful settlement contained in Article 33 (1) of the Charter of the United Nations. The High Contracting Parties which are parties to a dispute should be encouraged to take initiatives to solve it by friendly negotiations before resorting to the other procedures provided for in the Charter of the United Nations.

CHAPTER V
General Provision

ARTICLE 18

This Treaty shall be signed by the Republic of Indonesia, Malaysia, the Republic of the Philippines, the Republic of Singapore, and the Kingdom of Thailand. It shall be ratified in accordance with the constitutional procedures of each signatory State.

It shall be open for accession by other States in Southeast Asia.

ARTICLE 19

This Treaty shall enter into force on the date of the fifth instrument of ratification with the Governments of the signatory State which are designated Depositories of this Treaty and of the instruments of ratification or accession.

ARTICLE 20

This Treaty is drawn up in the official languages of the High Contracting Parties, all of which are equally authoritative. There shall be an agreed common translation of the texts in the English language. Any divergent interpretation of the common text shall be settled by negotiation.

IN FAITH THEREOF the High Contracting Parties have signed the Treaty and have hereto affixed their Seals.

DONE at Denpasar, Bali, this twenty-fourth day of February in the year one thousand nine hundred and seventy-six.

For the Republic of Indonesia:

SOEHARTO
Prime Minister

For Malaysia:

DATUK HUSSEIN ONN
Prime Minister

For the Republic of Singapore:

LEE KUAN YEW
President

For the Republic of the Philippines:

FERDINAND E. MARCOS
President

For the Kingdom of Thailand:
KUKRIT PRAMOJ
Prime Minister

ASEAN Vision 2020

KUALA LUMPUR, 15 DECEMBER 1997

We, the Heads of State/Government of the Association of Southeast Asian Nations, gather today in Kuala Lumpur to reaffirm our commitment to the aims and purposes of the Association as set forth in the Bangkok Declaration of 8 August 1967, in particular to promote regional cooperation in Southeast Asia in the spirit of equality and partnership and thereby contribute towards peace, progress and prosperity in the region.

We in ASEAN have created a community of Southeast Asian nations at peace with one another and at peace with the world, rapidly achieving prosperity for our peoples and steadily improving their lives. Our rich diversity has provided the strength and inspiration to help one another foster a strong sense of community.

We are now a market of around 500 million people with a combined gross domestic product of US$600 billion. We have achieved considerable results in the economic field, such as high economic growth, stability and significant poverty alleviation over the past few years. Members have enjoyed substantial trade and investment flows from significant liberalisation measures.

We resolve to build upon these achievements.

Now, as we approach the 21st century, thirty years after the birth of ASEAN, we gather to chart a vision for ASEAN on the basis of today's realities and prospects in the decades leading to the Year 2020.

That vision is of ASEAN as a concert of Southeast Asian nations, outward-looking, living in peace, stability and prosperity, bonded together in partnership in dynamic development and in a community of caring societies.

A CONCERT OF SOUTHEAST ASIAN NATIONS

We envision the ASEAN region to be, in 2020, in full reality, a Zone of Peace, Freedom and Neutrality, as envisaged in the Kuala Lumpur Declaration of 1971.

ASEAN shall have, by the year 2020, established a peaceful and stable Southeast Asia where each nation is at peace with itself and where the causes for conflict have been eliminated, through abiding respect for justice and the rule of law and through the strengthening of national and regional resilience.

We envision a Southeast Asia where territorial and other disputes are resolved by peaceful means.

We envision the Treaty of Amity and Cooperation in Southeast Asia functioning fully as a binding code of conduct for out governments and peoples, to which other states with interests in the region adhere.

We envision a Southeast Asia free from nuclear weapons, with all the Nuclear Weapon States committed to the purposes of the Southeast Asia Nuclear Weapons Free Zone Treaty through their adherence to its Protocol. We also envision our region free from all other weapons of mass destruction.

We envision our rich human and natural resources contributing to our development and shared prosperity.

We envision the ASEAN Regional Forum as an established means for confidence-building and preventive diplomacy and for promoting conflict-resolution.

We envision a Southeast Asia where our mountains, rivers and seas no longer divide us but link us together in friendship, cooperation and commerce.

We see ASEAN as an effective force for peace, justice and moderation in the Asia-Pacific and in the world.

A PARTNERSHIP IN DYNAMIC DEVELOPMENT

We resolve to chart a new direction towards the year 2020, called ASEAN 2020: Partnership in Dynamic Development which will forge closer economic integration within ASEAN.

We reiterate our resolve to enhance ASEAN economic cooperation through economic development strategies, which are in line with the aspiration of our respective peoples, which put emphasis on sustainable and equitable growth, and enhance national as well as regional resilience.

We pledge to sustain ASEAN's high economic performance by building upon the foundation of our existing cooperation efforts, consolidating our achievements, expanding our collective efforts and enhancing mutual assistance.

We commit ourselves to moving towards closer cohesion and economic integration, narrowing the gap in the level of development among Member Countries, ensuring that the multilateral trading system remains fair and open, and achieving global competitiveness.

We will create a stable, prosperous and highly competitive ASEAN Economic Region in which there is a free flow of goods, services and investments, a freer flow of capital, equitable economic development and reduced poverty and socio-economic disparities.

We resolve, *inter-alia*, to undertake the following:

- maintain regional macroeconomic and financial stability by promoting closer consultations in macroeconomic and financial policies.

- advance economic integration and cooperation by undertaking the following general strategies: fully implement the ASEAN Free Trade Area and accelerate liberalisation of trade in services, realise the ASEAN Investment Area by 2010 and free flow of investments by 2020; intensify and expand sub-regional cooperation in existing and new sub-regional growth areas; further consolidate and expand extra-ASEAN regional linkages for mutual benefit, cooperate to strengthen the multilateral trading system, and reinforce the role of the business sector as the engine of growth.

- promote a modern and competitive small and medium enterprises (SME) sector in ASEAN which will contribute to the industrial development and efficiency of the region.

- accelerate the free flow of professional and other services in the region.

- promote financial sector liberalisation and closer cooperation in money and capital market, tax, insurance and customs matters as well as closer consultations in macroeconomic and financial policies.

- accelerate the development of science and technology including information technology by establishing a regional information technology network and centres of excellence for dissemination of and easy access to data and information.

– establish interconnecting arrangements in the field of energy and utilities for electricity, natural gas and water within ASEAN through the ASEAN Power Grid and a Trans-ASEAN Gas Pipeline and Water Pipeline, and promote cooperation in energy efficiency and conservation, as well as the development of new and renewable energy resources.

– enhance food security and international competitiveness of food, agricultural and forest products, to make ASEAN a leading producer of these products, and promote the forestry sector as a model in forest management, conservation and sustainable development.

– meet the ever increasing demand for improved infrastructure and communications by developing an integrated and harmonized trans-ASEAN transportation network and harnessing technology advances in telecommunications and information technology, especially in linking the planned information highways/multimedia corridors in ASEAN, promoting open sky policy, developing multi-modal transport, facilitating goods in transit and integrating telecommunications networks through greater interconnectivity, coordination of frequencies and mutual recognition of equipment-type approval procedures.

– enhance human resource development in all sectors of the economy through quality education, upgrading of skills and capabilities and training.

– work towards a world class standards and conformance system that will provide a harmonised system to facilitate the free flow of ASEAN trade while meeting health, safety and environmental needs.

– use the ASEAN Foundation as one of the instruments to address issues of unequal economic development, poverty and socioeconomic disparities.

– promote an ASEAN customs partnership for world class standards and excellence in efficiency, professionalism and service, and uniformity through harmonised procedures, to promote trade and investment and to protect the health and well-being of the ASEAN community.

– enhance intra-ASEAN trade and investment in the mineral sector and to contribute towards a technologically competent ASEAN through closer networking and sharing of information on mineral and geosciences as well as to enhance cooperation and partnership with Dialogue Partners to facilitate the development and transfer of technology in the mineral sector, particularly in the downstream research and the geosciences and to develop appropriate mechanism for these.

A COMMUNITY OF CARING SOCIETIES

We envision the entire Southeast Asia to be, by 2020, an ASEAN community conscious of its ties of history, aware of its cultural heritage and bound by a common regional identity.

We see vibrant and open ASEAN societies consistent with their respective national identities, where all people enjoy equitable access to opportunities for total human development regardless of gender, race, religion, language, or social and cultural background.

We envision a socially cohesive and caring ASEAN where hunger, malnutrition, deprivation and poverty are no longer basic problems, where strong families as the basic units of society tend to their members particularly the children, youth, women and elderly; and where the civil society is empowered and gives special attention to the disadvantaged, disabled and marginalised and where social justice and the rule of law reign.

We see well before 2020 a Southeast Asia free of illicit drugs, free of their production, processing, trafficking and use.

We envision a technologically competitive ASEAN competent in strategic and enabling technologies, with an adequate pool of technologically qualified and trained manpower, and strong networks of scientific and technological institutions and centres of excellence.

We envision a clean and green ASEAN with fully established mechanisms for sustainable development to ensure the protection of the region's environment, the sustainability of its natural resources, and the high quality of life of its peoples.

We envision the evolution in Southeast Asia of agreed rules of behaviour and cooperative measures to deal with problems that can be met only on a regional scale, including environmental pollution and degradation, drug trafficking, trafficking in women and children, and other transnational crimes.

We envision our nations being governed with the consent and greater participation of the people with its focus on the welfare and dignity of the human person and the good of the community.

We resolve to develop and strengthen ASEAN's institutions and mechanisms to enable ASEAN to realise the vision and respond to the challenges of the coming century. We also see the need for a strengthened ASEAN Secretariat with an enhanced role to support the realisation of our vision.

AN OUTWARD-LOOKING ASEAN

We see an outward-looking ASEAN playing a pivotal role in the international fora, and advancing ASEAN's common interests. We envision ASEAN having an intensified relationship with its Dialogue Partners and other regional organisations based on equal partnership and mutual respect.

CONCLUSION

We pledge to our peoples our determination and commitment in bringing this ASEAN Vision for the Year 2020 into reality.

List of Abbreviations*

A

ACE	ASEAN Centre for Energy
ACCSQ	ASEAN Consultative Committee on Standards and Quality
ACEDAC	ASEAN Centre for the Development of Agricultural Cooperatives
ACF	ASEAN Cultural Fund
ADB	Asian Development Bank
AEIC	ASEAN Earthquake Information Centre
AEM	ASEAN Economic Ministers' Meeting
AEMC	ASEAN-European Community Management Centre
AEMEC	ASEAN Minister's Meeting on Energy Cooperation
AEP	ASEAN Environmental Partnership
AERR	ASEAN Energy Rice Reserve
AFHB	ASEAN Food Handling Bureau
AFSRB	ASEAN Food Security Reserve Board
AFTA	ASEAN Free Trade Area
AHTN	ASEAN Harmonised Tariff Nomenclature
AICO	ASEAN Industrial Cooperation
AIFM	ASEAN Institute of Forest Management
AIJV	ASEAN Industrial Joint Venture
AJDF	ASEAN Japan Development Fund
ALMM	ASEAN Labour Ministers Meeting
AMCs	ASEAN Member Countries
AMEM	ASEAN Ministers on Energy
AMEICC	AEM-MITI Economic and Industrial Cooperation Committee
AMM	ASEAN Ministerial Meeting
AMME	ASEAN Ministerial Meeting on the Environment
AMMH	ASEAN Ministerial Meeting on Haze
AMRDPE	ASEAN Ministers on Rural Development and Poverty Eradication

AMRI	ASEAN Ministers Responsible for Information
ANDIN	ASEAN Natural Disasters Information Network
ANEX	ASEAN News Exchange
ANWRA	ASEAN Network of Water Resource Agencies
ANZERTA	ASEAN Australia-New Zealand Closer Economic Relation Trading Arrangement
APEC	Asia Pacific Economic Cooperation
ARCBC	ASEAN Regional Centre for Biodiversity Conservation
ARDCMR	ASEAN Regional Development Centre for Mineral Resources
ARF	ASEAN Regional Forum
ARYDEC	ASEAN Rural Youth Development Centre
ASA	Association of Southeast Asia
ASC	ASEAN Standing Committee
ASCH & N	ASEAN Sub-Committee on Health and Nutrition
ASCLA	ASEAN Sub-Committee on Labour Affairs
ASCOE	ASEAN Sub-Committee on Education
ASCU	ASEAN Surveillance Coordinating Unit
ASEAN ISIS	ASEAN Institutes of Strategic and International Studies
ASEANTA	ASEAN Tourism Association
ASF	ASEAN Science Fund
ASFOM	ASEAN Senior Finance Officials Meeting
ASNEM	ASEAN Network for Environment Management
ASOD	ASEAN Senior Officials on Drugs
ASOEN	ASEAN Senior Officials on the Environment
ASP	ASEAN Surveillance Process
ASP-5	ASEAN-UNDP Sub-Regional Programme Cycle Five
ASPEN	ASEAN Strategic Plan of Action on the Environment
ASTNET	ASEAN Science and Technology Information Network
ASTU	ASEAN Surveillance Technical Support Unit
ASW	ASEAN Sub-Committee on Women
ASY	ASEAN Sub-Committee on Youth
ATIC	ASEAN Tourism Information Centre
ATM	ASEAN Transport Ministers
AUN	ASEAN University Network

AUNQANET	ASEAN University Network Quality Assurance Network
AWGCM	ASEAN Working Group on Customs Matters
AWGCME	ASEAN Working Group on Coastal and Marine Environment
AWGEE	ASEAN Working Group on Environmental Economics
AWGEIPAE	ASEAN Working Group on Environmental Information, Public Awareness and Education
AWGMEA	ASEAN Working Group on Multilateral Environmental Agreements
AWP	ASEAN Women's Programme

B

BBC	Brand-to-Brand Complementation
BIMP-EAGA	Brunie Darussalam-Indonesia-Malaysia-Philippines East ASEAN Growth Area
BPA	Bilateral Payment Arrangements

C

CCI	Chamber of Commerce and Industry
CEPT	Common Effective Preferential Tariff Scheme
COCI	Committee on Culture and Information
COFAB	Committee on Finance and Banking
COFAF	Committee on Food and Agriculture
COIME	Committee on Industry, Minerals, and Energy
COSD	Committee on Social Development
COST	Committee on Science and Technology
COTAC	Committee on Transportation and Communication
COTT	Committee on Trade and Tourism
CPMS	Cooperative Programme on Marine Science
CTI	Committee on Trade and Investment (APEC)
CZERMS	Coastal Zone Environmental and Resources Management Project

D

| DOTS | Directly-Observed Treatment, Short Course |

E

EAEC	East Asia Economic Caucus
EC	European Community
EC-IIP	The European Community International Investment Partner
ECU	European Currency Union
ECAP	ASEAN-EC Patents and Trademarks Programme
EDP	Executive Development Programme
EE&C	Energy Efficiency and Conservation
EIP	Environmental Improvement Project
ELTO	English Language Training for Officials
ENRA	Environmental and Natural Resources Accounting
ESCAP	Economic and Social Commission for Asia and the Pacific

F

FAO	Food and Agriculture Organization
FANS	Future Air Navigation Systems
FASTW	Fourth ASEAN Science and Technology Week

G

GATT	General Agreement on Tariff and Trade
GMS	Greater Mekong Subregion
GMOs	Genetically Modified Organism
GRAs	Genetic Resource Areas
GSP	General System of Preference

H

HACCP	Hazard Analysis Critical Control Point
HPA	Hanoi Plan of Action
HRDM	Human Resource Development and Management
HS	Harmonized System
HTTF	Haze Technical Task Force

I

ICLARM	International Centre for Living Aquatic Resources Management

ICTSD	Information and Communication Technology for sustainable Development
ILO	International Labour Organization
ILS	Instrument Landing System
IPD	Information Preparation and Dissemination
IPM	Integrated Pest Management
ISEAS	Institute of Southeast Asian Studies
ISQAP	Industrial Standards and Quality Assurance Programme (ASEAN-EC Programme)

J

| JACPP | Japan-ASEAN Cooperation Promotion Programme |
| JAEP | Japan-ASEAN Exchange Projects |

K

| KIET | Korea Institute for Industrial Economics |

L

| LCR | Living Coastal Resources |

M

M-ATM	Meeting of ASEAN Tourism Ministers
MITI	Ministry of International Trade and Industry
MFRD	Marine Fisheries Research Department
MOU	Memorandum of Understanding
MRA	Mutual Recognition Arrangements
MT-NIT	Multimodal Transport and New Information Technology
MU	Ministerial Understanding

N

NBRUs	National Biodiversity Reference Units
NCSW	National Council on Social Welfare
NERIC	National Environment Resource Information Centres
NGOs	Non-Governmental Organizations
NGUT	Natural Gas Utilization in Transport Programme
NIEO	New International Economic Order
NIIT	National Institute of Information Technology
NRSE	New and Renewable Sources of Energy
NTB	Non-Tariff Barrier

NTO	National Tourism Organizations

O

ODS	Ozone Depleting Substances
OSHNET	ASEAN Occupational Safety and Health Network

P

PIDS	The Philippine Institute for Development Studies
PLANTI	Plant Quarantine and Training Institute
PMC	Post Ministerial Conference
POATAC	Program of Action in Transportation and Communications
PROSEA	Plant Resources in Southeast Asia

Q

QASAF	Quality Assurance Systems for ASEAN Fruits
QR	Quantitative Restriction

R

R & D	Research and Development
RETA	Regional Technical Assistance
RHAP	Regional Haze Action Plan
ROD	Regional Ocean Dynamics
ROK	Republic of Korea
RTP	Regional Training Programme

S

SAEI	Southeast Asian Environmental Initiative
SCF	Special Cooperation Fund (ASEAN-ROK)
SCIRD	Sub-Committee on Science and Technology Infrastructure and Resources Development
SCMG	Sub-Committee on Meteorology and Geophysics
SCMST	Sub-Committee on Materials Science and Technology
SCNER	Sub-Committee on Non-Conventional Energy Research
SDI	Selective Dissemination of Information
SEAFDEC	South East Asia Fisheries Development Centre
SEANWFZ	Southeast Asia Nuclear Weapon Free Zone
SEOM	Senior Economic Officials Meeting

SoER	State of the Environment Report
SFM	Sustainable Forest Management
SL	Sensitive List
SLOA	Supplementary Letters of Agreement
SLORC	State Law and Order Restoration Council
SME	Small and Medium Enterprises
SOM	Senior Officials Meeting
SOME	Senior Officials Meeting on Energy
SORDPE	Senior Officials on Rural Development and Poverty Eradication
SSN	Social Safety Nets
S & T	Science and Technology
STOM	Senior Transport Officials Meeting

T

TAC	Treaty of Amity and Cooperation in Southeast Asia
TCDC	Technical Cooperation Among Developing Countries
TEL	Temporary Exclusion List
TPAS	Technology Promotion and Assistance Services
TQM	Total Quality Management
TROPMED	Tropical Medicine and Public Health

U

UNIDCP	United Nations International Drug Control Programme
UNESCO	United Nations Educational, Scientific, and Cultural Organization
UNHCR	United Nations High Commission on Refugees

V

| VAY | Visit ASEAN Millennium Year |

W

WEC	West-East Corridor
WGASME	The Working Group on ASEAN Seas and Marine Environment
WGEE	The Working Group on Environmental Economics
WGEIPAE	The Working Group on Environmental Information, Public Awareness, and Education

WGIPC	The Working Group on Intellectual Property Cooperation
WGNC	The Working Group on Nature Conservation
WGTP	The Working Group on Transboundary Pollution
WGEM	The Working Group on Environment Management
WHO	World Health Organization
WIPO	World Intellectual Property Organization
WTO	World Trade Organization

Y

Y2K	Year Two Thousand

Z

ZOPFAN	Zone of Peace, Freedom, and Neutrality

---

*Selected from the List of Abbreviations in the Association of Southeast Asian Nations Annual Report 1998-1999, pp. 135-143.

Bibliography

DOCUMENTS

1. The ASEAN Declaration (Bangkok Declaration), 8 August 1967.
2. ASEAN/MM/11DKT, Djakarta 8 August 1968
3. Zone of Peace, Freedom, and Neutrality Declaration (Kuala Lumpur Declaration), 27 November 1971.
4. Ninth ASEAN Ministerial Meeting, Manila, 24-26 June 1976.
5. Declaration of ASEAN Concord, Bali, 24 June 1976.
6. Treaty of Amity and Cooperation in Southeast Asia, Bali, 24 June 1976.
7. Tenth ASEAN Ministerial Meeting, Singapore, 5-8 July 1977.
8. Eleventh ASEAN Ministerial Meeting, Bangkok, 14-16 June 1978.
9. Vision 2020, Kuala Lumpur, 15 December 1997.
10. Common ASEAN Position on the Reform of the International Financial Architecture as Adopted at the Special ASEAN Finance Ministers' Meeting in Manila, 30 April 1999.
11. Declaration on Terrorism by the Eighth ASEAN Summit, Phnom Penh, 3-5 November 2002.
12. Declaration on the Conduct of Parties in the South China Sea, Phnom Penh, 04 November 2002.
13. Press statement by the Chairman of the Eighth ASEAN Summit, the Sixth ASEAN + 3 Summit and the ASEAN + China Summit, Phnom Penh, 04 November 2002.
14. Joint Declaration of ASEAN and China on Cooperation in the Field of Non-Traditional Security Issues, Phnom Penh, 04 November 2002.
15. The Ninth Meeting of the ASEAN Regional Forum, Bandar Seri Begawan, 31 July 2002.

BOOKS

Almond, G.A. and J.S. Coleman (eds.). *Politics of Developing Areas*. Princeton: Princeton University Press, 1960.

Antolik, Michael. *ASEAN and the Diplomacy of Accommodation*. New York: M.E. Sharpe, Inc., 1990.

——. "ASEAN and the Utilities of Diplomatic Informality", in Sereno and Santiago (eds.) *The ASEAN: Thirty Years and Beyond*. Quezon City: University of the Philippines Press, 1977.

——. "The ASEAN Regional Forum: the Sprit of Constructive Engagement" in *Contemporary Southeast Asia*. Singapore: ISEAS, 1994.

Brinton, Crane. *From Many One*. Cambridge: Harvard University Press, 1948.

Dougherty, James E. and Robert C. Pfaltzgraff, Jr. *Contending Theories of International Relations*. New York: Harper and Row Publishers, 1981.

Etzioni, Amitai. *Political Unification*. New York: Holt, Rinehart and Winston, 1965.

Finklestein, Louis, Harold D. Lasswell, and R.M. MacIver (eds.). *Foundation of World Organization*. New York: Harper and Row, 1950.

From Strength to Strength, ASEAN Functional Cooperation: Retrospect and Prospect. Jakarta: The ASEAN Secretariat, 1993.

Haas, Ernst. *The Uniting of Europe*. Stanford: Stanford University Press, 1958.

Haas, Michael. *International Organization, An Interdisciplinary Bibliography*. Stanford: Stanford University Hoover Institution on War, Revolution and Peace, 1979.

Honigmann, John. *Understanding Culture*. New York: Harper and Row, 1963.

Kahin, George M. *et al*. (eds.). *Governments and Politics of Southeast Asia*. Ithaca: Cornell University Press, 1964.

Linton, Ralph. *The Tree of Culture*. New York: Alfred A. Knopf, 1957.

Mercado, Leonardo. *Elements of Filipino Philosophy*. Manila: Divine Word University, 1976.

Minshull, Roger. *Regional Geography*. Chicago: Aldine Publishing Co., 1967.

Mitrany, David. "Functional Approach to World Organization", *International Affairs*. XXIV (July 1948).

——. *A Working Peace System*. Chicago: Quadrangle Books, 1966.

Mungkandi, Wiwat and William Warren. *Thai-American Relations*. Bangkok: Chulalongkorn University Press, 1982.

Nye, Joseph (ed.). *International Regionalism: Readings*. Boston: Little, Brown, 1968.

Sandhu, K.S., Sharon Siddique, Chandran Jeshuran, Ananda Rajah, Joseph L.H. Tan and Pushpa Thambipillai, *The ASEAN Reader*. Singapore: ISEAS, 1992.

Selections from The ASEAN Reader

1. O.W. Wolters, "Early Southeast Asian Political Systems"
2. Donald G. McCloud, "Southeast Asia as a Regional Unit"
3. Russell H. Fifield, "the Southeast Asia Command"
4. Pushpa Thambipillai, "Negotiating Styles"
5. Chan Heng Chee, "Intra-ASEAN Political Security and Economic Cooperation"

6. Sharon Siddique, "Cultural Development: An ASEAN Overview"
7. Patya Saihoo, "Problems in Cultural Development"
8. Lau Teik Soon, "Cultural Cooperation Between the ASEAN States"
9. Trinidad S. Osteria, "Recent Trends in Urbanization"
10. Ungku A. Aziz, "Cooperation on Education in ASEAN"
11. John Wong, "The ASEAN Model of Regional Cooperation"
12. C.P.F. Luhulima, "Development Cooperation in Human Resources: the ASEAN Experience"
13. Tan Kong Yam, Toh Mun Heng, and Linda Low, "ASEAN and Pacific Economic Cooperation"
14. J.L.S. Girling, "Regional Security in Southeast Asia"
15. Michael Leifer, "Is ASEAN a Security Organization?"
16. Chan Heng Chee, "ASEAN and the Indo-China Conflict"
17. Noordin Sopiee, "ASEAN and Regional Security"
18. Sheldon N. Simon, "ASEAN and the Future of Regional Security"
19. Mochtar Kusuma-Atmadja, "Prospects of Trilateral Security Cooperation in ASEAN"
20. Jusuf Wanandi, "ASEAN Security Cooperation in the Post Cold War Era"
21. Ali Alatas, "ASEAN and the North-South Dialogue"

Sereno, Maria Lourdes A. and Joseph Sedfrey Santiago (eds.). *The ASEAN: Thirty Years and Beyond.* Quezon City: University of the Philippines Press, 1997.

Singh, Bilveer. *ZOPFAN and the New Security Order in the Asia-Pacific Region.* Malaysia: Palanduk Publication (CM) SDN Bhd., 1992.

Solidum., Estrella D. *ASEAN Engagements for Peace.* Manila: Yuchengco Center for East Asia, 1999.

Solidum, Estrella D., Teresita Saldivar-Sali and Roman Dubsky, *Security in a New Perspective.* Seoul, 1981. First printed in the *Asian Perspective* Vol. 5, 2 (Full-Winter 1981) of the Institute for Eastern Studies, Kyungnam University, Seoul.

Solidum, Estrella D. *Bilateral Summitry in ASEAN.* Manila: Foreign Service Institute, 1983. Also in *The ASEAN Reader.*

JOURNALS

1. *Asian Perspective*, Seoul: 1981.
2. *Association of Southeast Asian Nations Annual Report 1998-1999*, Jakarta: ASEAN Central Secretariat.
3. *Contemporary Southeast Asia*, Singapore: ISEAS, Vol. 16, no. 2, 1994.
4. *Current History*, New Series XXXIX. August, 1960.
5. *Foreign Relations Journal*, Manila, Vol. 1, no. 3, 1986.
6. *Foreign Relations Journal*, Manila, 1985.

7. *International Affairs* XXIV, July 1948.

8. *Kompas Daily*, July 23, 1984 and *Asia Research Bulletin*, Vol. 14, no. 3, August 1984.

9. Website Reports http://www.aseansec.org/history/ asn_his2.htm,str2.htm,ext3.htm,fnc2.htm,eco2.htm.

10. *World Affairs Quarterly*, XIII (October 1942).

Index